After Early Intervention, Then What?

Teaching Struggling Readers in Grades 3 and Beyond

Second Edition

EDITORS
Jeanne R. Paratore & Rachel L. McCormack

INTERNATIONAL
Reading Association
800 BARKSDALE ROAD, PO BOX 8139
NEWARK, DE 19714-8139, USA
www.reading.org

KH

The International Reading Association attempts, through its publications, to provide a forum for a wide spectrum of opinions on reading. This policy permits divergent viewpoints without implying the endorsement of the Association.

Executive Editor, Publications   Shannon Fortner
Managing Editor   Christina M. Terranova
Editorial Associate   Wendy Logan
Design and Composition Manager   Anette Schuetz
Design and Composition Associate   Lisa Kochel

Cover   Design: Alissa Jones; Photographs (clockwise from top right): Rachel L. McCormack, Jupiterimages/liquidlibrary/Thinkstock, Hemera/Thinkstock

The publisher would appreciate notification where errors occur so that they may be corrected in subsequent printings and/or editions.

Library of Congress Cataloging-in-Publication Data
After early intervention, then what? : teaching struggling readers in grades 3 and beyond / Jeanne R. Paratore and Rachel L. McCormack, editors. -- 2nd ed.
    p. cm.
 Includes bibliographical references and index.
 ISBN 978-0-87207-844-4
 1. Reading--Remedial teaching--United States. I. Paratore, Jeanne R. II. McCormack, Rachel L.
 LB1050.5.A36 2011
 372.43--dc22
                              2011014699

Suggested APA Reference
Paratore, J.R., & McCormack, R.L. (Eds.). (2011). *After early intervention, then what? Teaching struggling readers in grades 3 and beyond* (2nd ed.). Newark, DE: International Reading Association.

7/18/12

To teachers and children everywhere who inspire us every day to do our best to learn more about the effective teaching of reading and writing.

CONTENTS

SECTION I

Opening the Lens: Building Foundations in Literacy for Struggling Readers

Jeanne R. Paratore is a professor of literacy education and coordinator of the Reading Education and Literacy Education programs at Boston University in Boston, Massachusetts, USA. She directs the university-based reading and writing clinic that provides year-round academic support to school-age children who are experiencing learning difficulties, and she serves as advisor to the Intergenerational Literacy Program, a family literacy program she founded in 1989 to support the English literacy learning of immigrant parents and their children.

A former classroom teacher, reading specialist, and Title I director, Jeanne has conducted research and written widely on issues related to family literacy, classroom grouping practices, and interventions for struggling readers. She also served as cocurriculum director of the award-winning children's television series *Between the Lions*.

Jeanne is a recipient of the International Reading Association's (IRA) Celebrate Literacy Award and the New England Reading Association's Lifetime Achievement Award. She is a former member of IRA's Board of Directors. She is a frequent speaker on literacy instruction and has presented at local, national, and international conferences as well as in school districts throughout the United States.

Rachel L. McCormack is currently a professor of literacy education and the chair of the elementary education programs at Roger Williams University in Bristol, Rhode Island, USA. She also supervises student teachers in Rhode Island and Puerto Rico, where she conducts cross-site analyses of linguistic and cultural differences among Spanish-speaking students in both settings. She is a former classroom teacher and reading specialist.

Rachel has conducted research and written on issues related to peer talk in and out of the classroom, grouping practices, interventions for struggling readers, and reading interventions for deaf and hard of hearing students. She is a recipient of the International Reading Association's New Voices in Research Award. She is a frequent speaker at local, national, and international conferences on literacy as well as in school districts in New England and Puerto Rico.

Editor Information for Correspondence

Jeanne and Rachel welcome your questions and comments. Jeanne can be reached at jparator@bu.edu. Rachel can be reached at rmccormack@rwu.edu.

CONTRIBUTORS

Kathryn H. Au
Chief Executive Officer
SchoolRise, LLC
Honolulu, Hawaii, USA

Linda J. Dorn
Professor and Director of the
    Center for Literacy
University of Arkansas at Little
    Rock
Little Rock, Arkansas, USA

Douglas Fisher
Professor of Language and Literacy
    Education
San Diego State University
San Diego, California, USA

Susan Franks
Associate Professor of Education
Georgia Southern University
Statesboro, Georgia, USA

Nancy Frey
Professor of Literacy
San Diego State University
San Diego, California, USA

Robert W. Gaskins
Head of School
Benchmark School
Media, Pennsylvania, USA

Carolyn Groff
Assistant Professor of Literacy and
    Language
Monmouth University
West Long Branch, New Jersey,
    USA

Janis M. Harmon
Professor of Literacy
University of Texas at San Antonio
San Antonio, Texas, USA

Wanda B. Hedrick
Professor of Literacy
University of North Florida
Jacksonville, Florida, USA

Shannon C. Henderson
Assistant Professor of Reading and
    Literacy Education
The University of Alabama
Tuscaloosa, Alabama, USA

Brian Kissel
Assistant Professor of Reading
    Education
University of North Carolina at
    Charlotte
Charlotte, North Carolina, USA

Melanie R. Kuhn
Associate Professor of Reading
    Education
Boston University
Boston, Massachusetts, USA

Diane Lapp
Distinguished Professor of
    Education
San Diego State University
San Diego, California, USA

Gail E. Lovette
Doctoral Candidate in Reading
University of Virginia
Charlottesville, Virginia, USA

Jennifer Lubke
Doctoral Candidate in Reading
    Education
University of Tennessee
Knoxville, Tennessee, USA

Joyce E. Many
Associate Dean and Professor
    of Language and Literacy
    Education
Georgia State University
Atlanta, Georgia, USA

Rachel L. McCormack
Professor of Literacy Education
Roger Williams University
Bristol, Rhode Island, USA

Anne McGill-Franzen
Professor and Director of the
    Reading Center
University of Tennessee
Knoxville, Tennessee, USA

Michael C. McKenna
Thomas G. Jewell Professor of
    Reading
University of Virginia
Charlottesville, Virginia, USA

Lesley M. Morrow
Professor of Literacy and Chair of
    the Department of Learning and
    Teaching of the Graduate School
    of Education
Rutgers, The State University of
    New Jersey
New Brunswick, New Jersey, USA

Jeanne R. Paratore
Professor of Education and
    Coordinator of the Reading
    Education and Literacy
    Education Programs
Boston University
Boston, Massachusetts, USA

C. Patrick Proctor
Assistant Professor of Literacy and
    Bilingualism
Boston College
Boston, Massachusetts, USA

Taffy E. Raphael
Professor of Literacy Education
University of Illinois at Chicago
Chicago, Illinois, USA

Nancy Roser
Professor of Language and Literacy
    Studies
University of Texas at Austin
Austin, Texas, USA

Karen D. Wood
Professor and Graduate Reading
    Program Coordinator
University of North Carolina at
    Charlotte
Charlotte, North Carolina, USA

Angie Zapata
Doctoral Candidate in Language
    and Literacy Studies
University of Texas at Austin
Austin, Texas, USA

INTRODUCTION

Jeanne R. Paratore and Rachel L. McCormack

In the Introduction to the first edition of this book (McCormack & Paratore, 2003), we noted that despite significant emphasis on and funding support for early intervention in literacy, substantial numbers of students continued to experience reading difficulty in the intermediate grades and beyond. In the years since, we have seen an increase in attention to struggling learners in the middle elementary and later school years, and evidence suggests that such attention may be having at least a small effect. On the National Assessment of Educational Progress, students at 4th-, 8th-, and 12th-grade levels all showed small increases in literacy achievement in comparison with previous years. Even so, at each of these grade levels, large numbers of students continue to perform at the lowest levels of achievement; so although we acknowledge and celebrate the progress that has been made, there is yet much work to be done.

In this second edition, our purpose is to shine a light on some of the work that we think holds great promise for continuing the upward trend in literacy achievement of students who struggle during the upper elementary, middle, and secondary school years. As in the first edition, in each chapter, the authors—mostly teams of researchers and teacher researchers—share evidence of what works for struggling readers and writers in grades 3 through secondary school. New to this edition is a section at the end of each chapter, entitled Try It!, providing suggestions for readers to act on the ideas presented.

The book's chapters are organized into three major sections. Section I, "Opening the Lens: Building Foundations in Literacy for Struggling Readers," focuses on the development of foundational literacy skills. In Chapter 1, "Reading Fluency Beyond the Primary Grades: Helping Make Difficult Texts Accessible," Melanie Kuhn, Carolyn Groff, and Lesley Morrow remind us that like younger struggling readers, older students often experience difficulty with reading fluency, and when they do, the effects are especially problematic. Low rates of fluency affect not only comprehension but also the amount of text that students can read, setting them behind their peers both in the quality of their comprehension and in the amount of reading they complete. We think this chapter is notable not only for the detailed nature of the recommended strategies but also

After Early Intervention, Then What? Teaching Struggling Readers in Grades 3 and Beyond (2nd ed.) edited by Jeanne R. Paratore and Rachel L. McCormack. © 2011 by the International Reading Association.

for the emphasis the authors place on helping students read what they call "stretch" texts. Stretch texts are challenging texts that when appropriately mediated, have the potential to help students acquire higher level vocabulary and conceptual and content knowledge even as they improve their reading fluency.

In Chapter 2, "Enter Laughing: Poetry and Diverse Learners," Nancy Roser and Angie Zapata take us down a path that often is reserved for capable readers and writers: reading and writing poetry. The authors provide a compelling argument that poetry reading and writing "meshes triumphantly with the guiding principles for effective Response to Intervention…, providing for close observation and assessment, responsive teaching within a comprehensive view of literacy instruction, and collaboration among participants" (p. 23). The chapter comes alive in the context of Ms. Acosta's third-grade classroom, where bilingual students experience a "poetry flood" during which they read, discuss, write, and perform poetry. We are confident that you will come away convinced, as we did, that when struggling readers and writers are provided opportunities similar to those that Roser and Zapata describe, they will grow as readers and writers of every genre.

In Chapter 3, "'Getting Started in English: Teaching for Vocabulary Depth With Bilingual Learners," C. Patrick Proctor continues the focus on bilingual learners, this time with a description of a "depth of vocabulary" (p. 42) approach to instruction. He first draws on theory and research to support his underlying argument that deep vocabulary knowledge emerges from three domains: semantics, morphology, and syntax. He then provides detailed examples of two instructional approaches that build on this evidence, and he offers strong evidence of the positive effects of these approaches in trials with bilingual fourth- and fifth-grade students.

In Chapter 4, "Research-Based Vocabulary Instruction: Recommendations for Struggling Readers," Karen Wood, Janis Harmon, Brian Kissel, and Wanda Hedrick provide yet another look at vocabulary instruction. Like Proctor, they emphasize the importance of explicit and focused instruction, and they provide detailed descriptions of useful strategies. Within these descriptions, we think teachers will time and again see themselves and their students and, as a result, easily pick up the strategies for use in their own classrooms.

In Chapter 5, "Grouping Routines and Instructional Practices That Mediate Difficult Text," we, the editors of this volume, provide a reminder that in addition to providing fundamentally strong instruction in essential literacy domains (e.g., fluency, word study, vocabulary, comprehension, writing), accelerating the achievement of struggling readers also requires attention to instruction that brings difficult and complex text within the reading range of struggling readers. We visit three different classroom settings in which teachers implemented grouping routines and instructional mediations such that students were able to read initially difficult text with high levels of word reading accuracy and comprehension.

In Section II, "Focusing the Lens: Self-Monitoring and Comprehension for Struggling Readers," we shift our attention to research and theory related to self-monitoring and comprehension and the practical implications of the evidence. In Chapter 6, "Accessible Comprehension Instruction Through Question–Answer Relationships," Taffy Raphael and Kathryn Au argue that too often educators' response to disappointing assessment results fails to recognize the complexity of the reading process in general and the comprehension process in particular. The authors note that despite years of research in comprehension, in many classrooms, we still lack a "comprehensive comprehension curriculum" (p. 119) that provides students with systematic and strategic comprehension instruction that will lead to sustained ability to read and respond to texts with deep understanding. The authors suggest question–answer relationships (first introduced by Raphael in 1982) as a framework for implementing such a curriculum and provide detailed examples to support readers' implementation of their ideas.

In Chapter 7, "Supporting Students Who Struggle With Comprehension of Text: Using Literature Discussion Groups in Grades 3–6," Shannon Henderson and Linda Dorn take us into Ms. Leibig's fourth-grade classroom and let us eavesdrop on a brief part of a conversation as students discuss the themes of friendship and loss in response to their reading of *Old Yeller*. The authors remind us that even the most expertly planned, evidence-based lessons will serve struggling readers poorly if we fail to carefully observe and respond to students' needs in the context of each and every lesson. Henderson and Dorn present seven research-based principles for teaching comprehension and provide detailed examples to help us apply the principles in the classrooms in which we work.

In Chapter 8, "Helping Students Understand Expository Text About History by Applying the Action Cycle Approach," Robert Gaskins focuses the lens on the particular challenges that reading and understanding expository texts pose for struggling readers. His work, intended in particular to help struggling readers develop "organized knowledge" (p. 163), is especially timely, as evidence of general knowledge as a fundamental contributor to overall literacy achievement is becoming increasingly recognized. Through insightful, integrated summaries of related research and theory and detailed descriptions of how he and his colleagues applied the evidence to develop and implement the action cycle instructional approach, Gaskins's work will help other teachers realize the same positive literacy outcomes as those observed at the Benchmark School.

In Chapter 9, "Understanding and Scaffolding Students' Research Processes: Stories From the Classroom," Joyce Many speaks to us about a topic that every upper elementary, middle, and high school student will encounter as central to learning throughout schooling and across the lifetime: research processes. Many defines the process of conducting research as "constructing a personal understanding" (p. 187). She explains that viewed in this way, students must go beyond the common practice of merely collecting information and then expressing the collected information in their own words. Many takes us into two classrooms, a third grade and a sixth grade, and shows us how teachers use skillful instructional conversations to help students use the comprehension strategies described in previous chapters to help them locate, comprehend, interpret, and share information in ways that are likely to lead them to deeper, transformative understandings of their topics of study.

Michael McKenna, Susan Franks, and Gail Lovette open Chapter 10, "Using Reading Guides With Struggling Readers in Grades 3 and Above," with a description of a teacher many will recognize: Ms. Williams is hardworking and continually seeks ways to update and improve her teaching. She has used many practices and strategies that are typically recommended as effective in supporting comprehension, yet her students continue to struggle as they read the science text. McKenna, Franks, and Lovette note that one solution to the challenge that conceptually dense, linguistically complex content area texts present to students is a reading guide to focus their attention on particular ideas as they read. In contrast to earlier work on reading guides, these authors present evidence that students as young as third grade benefit from such guides and, moreover, that the guides have transfer effects; that is, students who used the guides on a selected text also had higher levels of performance on selections not covered by the guides. The authors emphasize the importance of developing guides in response to individual learning needs, rather than in accordance with a particular template or framework, and provide detailed guidelines, as well as examples, that will help teachers do so.

Section III, "Widening the Lens: School and District Policies, Initiatives, and Interventions for Struggling Readers," opens the scope beyond individual classrooms to schoolwide practices. In Chapter 11, "Under the Radar, Struggling to Be Noticed: Older At-Risk Students," Anne McGill-Franzen and Jennifer Lubke remind us that as the reading "goes silent" (p. 221) in the upper grades and evaluation is restricted to largely superficial measures (e.g., short-answer responses on worksheets, numbers of books or pages read), students with significant reading needs often go unnoticed and, as a consequence, fail to receive the type of instruction that will prepare them to read with the deep levels of understanding demanded for success in higher levels of education and in life. The authors make the needs of such students come alive through the stories of Jason and Lauren (pseudonyms), detailing both the types of assessments that will help teachers come to understand their students' needs and also the types of instruction that will lead to engaged and successful readers.

Finally, in Chapter 12, "It's Never Too Late to Learn: Implementing RTI² With Older Students," Douglas Fisher, Nancy Frey, and Diane Lapp take us into an urban secondary school where they have developed and implemented Response to Instruction and Intervention, an approach to intervention that extends the original Response to Intervention model from a focus on individuals to a schoolwide initiative in which resources are systematically matched with carefully assessed student needs. To help us contextualize and understand the ways that the model works, the authors introduce us to a few of their students, each with a long history of school failure; Fisher, Frey, and Lapp also provide detailed descriptions of the types of interventions they provide, beginning with their work in general education classrooms and extending to supplemental settings as necessary. They provide compelling evidence that when teachers maintain high standards for every learner, but differentiate the type and amount of help they provide students as they work toward the standards, students make notable progress.

As we made our way through all chapters and reflected on them both individually and as a collection, we were inspired by the work. As in the first edition, we again found that the chapters are unified by some common themes: the emphasis on explicit instruction, a challenging curriculum, responsive teaching, and respectful interactions, as well as a joyfulness about teaching and learning. We also found, as we did in the previous edition, clear differences in the approaches described in each chapter, again reminding us of the critically important principle that there is no one right way to meet the needs of students who find reading and writing difficult. We expect that when thoughtful, dedicated teachers draw on these ideas and tweak the described practices and approaches to fit more precisely the needs of the students in their classrooms and their own teaching styles, the teachers will see both accelerated growth in reading and writing and increased motivation and engagement to read in and out of school. The latter may be the most important outcome, as it is fundamental to our responsibility to teach in ways that allow students to learn both with and without us.

REFERENCE

McCormack, R.L., & Paratore, J.R. (Eds.). (2003). *After early intervention, then what? Teaching struggling readers in grades 3 and beyond*. Newark, DE: International Reading Association.

Opening the Lens: Building Foundations in Literacy for Struggling Readers

Reading Fluency Beyond the Primary Grades: Helping Make Difficult Texts Accessible

Melanie R. Kuhn, Carolyn Groff, and Lesley M. Morrow

I t may seem surprising that a book written for older students would include a chapter on fluency, a component of literacy development and instruction that is typically considered a focus for the primary grades. However, it is often the case that struggling readers experience difficulties with reading fluency that persist into late elementary school and beyond (e.g., Rasinski et al., 2005; Wexler, Vaughn, Edmonds, & Reutebuch, 2008). This can be problematic both because a lack of fluency interferes with text comprehension and because it affects the sheer volume of material that these readers are able to cover (Ash & Kuhn, 2010). Because the texts that students are required to read as they get older increase not only in terms of complexity but also in terms of quantity and length, disfluent readers often find themselves at a significant disadvantage in comparison to their more skilled peers. Fortunately, there are a number of highly effective instructional approaches that can assist these learners with their fluency development while simultaneously increasing their access to challenging, or "stretch," texts. In this chapter, we first address the role of fluency in the reading process, both broadly and as it relates to older, disfluent readers. We then present several approaches that support students' fluency development while simultaneously increasing their access to difficult texts.

Fluency in the Reading Process

For most learners, fluency develops between the second and third grade (Chall, 1995). Generally, we think about this stage as occurring after learners have established a basic level of word recognition and are beginning to make the transition to automaticity. According to Chall, this period allows learners to confirm what they are learning about print, enabling them to establish automatic word recognition. Regrettably, many struggling readers

After Early Intervention, Then What? Teaching Struggling Readers in Grades 3 and Beyond (2nd ed.) edited by Jeanne R. Paratore and Rachel L. McCormack. © 2011 by the International Reading Association.

fail to establish such automaticity. As a result, their word recognition continues to be halting, making reading a difficult and disagreeable activity. This can lead to avoidance, a process that contributes to the achievement gap and the negative spiral associated with the Matthew effects (Stanovich, 1986). According to Stanovich, readers who experience such difficulties avoid reading, which severely limits the amount of practice they receive. As a result, their rates of progress are less than those of their peers who enjoy reading. This, in turn, leads to an ever-expanding gap between those who have experienced success with their reading and those who have not.

However, while automatic and accurate word recognition—often measured as the number of correct words per minute—is critical to skilled reading and has recently come to be emphasized in many classrooms, there is a second aspect of fluency, that of prosody, that needs to be considered in conjunction with automaticity. According to Kuhn and Stahl (2003), as "reading becomes increasingly less halting, they [learners] develop the ability to represent what is read in ways that imitate natural or conversational tones" (p. 3). We argue that a focus on the development of automaticity without a corresponding focus on prosody is not only ill conceived, but also it can lead struggling readers to the misconception that reading quickly rather than for understanding should be their ultimate goal (e.g., Applegate, Applegate, & Modla, 2009). An emphasis on both aspects of fluency helps ensure that learners focus on intonation and proper pacing rather than just speed. Further, as we explain in the section that follows, emphasizing both aspects is important, because both prosody and automaticity contribute to learners' ability to construct meaning from text (Benjamin, Schwanenflugel, & Kuhn, 2009).

Contribution of Automatic Word Recognition to Fluency

Proficient readers not only identify words accurately but also recognize most of them instantly and effortlessly. This is important because, as with any cognitive task, individuals have a limited amount of attention available while reading (Adams, 1990; LaBerge & Samuels, 1974; Samuels, 2004; Stanovich, 1980). As a result, whatever attention readers expend on word recognition is, necessarily, attention that is unavailable for comprehension. As a result, students who experience difficulty with decoding also often experience difficulty with comprehension.

So what do older students need to do to move from the point where decoding is purposeful to the point where it becomes automatic? There is a general consensus that this transition best occurs through practice and that this practice should consist of supported reading of a wide variety of connected texts in conjunction with any word identification instruction that may occur (e.g., Kuhn & Stahl, 2003; Mostow & Beck, 2005). As learners repeatedly encounter words in print, they need to direct progressively less attention toward decoding them, until the words eventually become part of their sight-word vocabulary. However, for struggling readers, this transition can take far longer than it does for their peers (Torgesen, 2005). As a result, it is even more critical that struggling readers are provided with the types of scaffolded, or supported, reading experiences that help develop appropriate rate and pacing.

Contribution of Prosody to Fluency

The second component of fluency is prosody. As we mentioned earlier, fluent reading consists of more than simply reading words quickly and accurately; it also involves the prosodic reading of text. This includes the elements of language that, when taken together, constitute expressive reading, such as intonation, stress, tempo, and appropriate phrasing (Dowhower, 1991; Erekson, 2003; Schreiber, 1991). In contrast, readers who are disfluent often read either in a word-by-word manner or in awkward groupings that fail to preserve the meaning of the text. Prosody has also been shown to contribute to comprehension above and beyond that of word recognition (Benjamin et al., 2009). Further, the use of expression contributes to learners' engagement with text, helping bring text to life and adding nuance to their reading. This is especially critical for struggling readers who are far less likely to engage with a text that they find unappealing, and it points to another reason why instruction must focus on supporting the development of appropriate pacing, intonation, and phrasing rather than simply speedy word recognition.

Still Not Reading Much...

Studies have long indicated that struggling readers often are engaged in a range of literacy activities that relate to, but do not include, the actual reading of connected text (Allington, 1977; Brenner, Hiebert, & Tompkins, 2009; Gambrell, 1984; Swanson, Wexler, & Vaughn, 2009). As a result, many forms of instruction encountered by struggling readers contribute to the very disparity that these forms were meant to eliminate. For example, in 1984, Gambrell found that students were reading, on average, between one and three minutes per day during teacher-directed reading lessons. Over two decades later, it seems that little has changed: Brenner and colleagues (2009) noted that during a typical 90-minute period of reading instruction, students averaged around nine minutes of independent reading and another nine minutes of assisted reading of connected texts. Instead of reading, the researchers found that students spent most of their time engaged in activities that support reading development, such as grammar lessons or word work, but not in the actual reading of texts. In another example, Groff (2007) found that middle-grade students in special education classrooms spent less than 40% of a 90-minute language arts block engaged in reading connected texts, and much of their actual reading centered around round-robin reading or its variants, instruction that does little to improve students' reading (Ash, Kuhn, & Walpole, 2009).

This lack of engagement with connected texts, or "opportunity to read" (Hiebert & Martin, 2009), can be part of a negative cycle that perpetuates a gap in the amount of learning that occurs for struggling readers in comparison to their more skilled peers (Cunningham & Stanovich, 1998; Stanovich, 1986). As a result of the difficulties that struggling readers experience, it is often the case that they get stuck in simple texts that do little to expand the range of words they encounter or the breadth of concepts that are presented (Gambrell, 2009; Stanovich, 1986). Furthermore, since struggling readers have difficulty reading grade-level texts, especially content area materials, teachers often resort to presenting the information orally, frequently through a lecture format as students get older (Shanahan, 2007). So, rather than spending significant amounts of time in the scaffolded reading of connected text, these students often barely engage with texts at all. Such practices are in direct conflict with evidence that students who spend the greatest amount of time engaged in the scaffolded reading of connected text, regardless of instructional approach used, make the greatest reading gains (e.g., Kuhn & Schwanenflugel, 2008).

Instructional Approaches to Increase Fluency

The evidence relating the importance of fluency to word recognition and comprehension, together with the evidence of the types of reading experiences that typify instruction for struggling readers, leads us to pose two important questions: How might teachers increase the amount of reading that struggling readers do, and how might teachers increase struggling readers' access to more challenging stretch texts? We have seen positive results with older struggling readers using a range of approaches in both classrooms and reading clinics or reading labs (e.g., Kuhn, 2009; McKenna & Stahl, 2003). The specific approaches we suggest for a particular situation is determined by three factors:

1. The number of students in a given class who need fluency support
2. The reading levels of these students
3. The types of instructional texts (The more challenging the text, the more support students will need to read it, likely necessitating a smaller group size.)

We present a range of approaches, some of which can be used flexibly as part of the general literacy curriculum, and others that are designed for group work, dyads, or work with individual learners. Additionally, we present an argument for a reconsideration of independent reading time.

General Fluency Approaches

There are three approaches to fluency development that are flexible enough to be used with many types of texts in many situations and form the underpinnings of many of the strategies that follow: partner reading, echo reading, and choral reading.

Partner Reading. Partner reading is a simple yet effective method of developing reading fluency. It significantly increases the amount of reading that students can complete in a given period, especially when compared with traditional oral reading approaches such as round-robin or popcorn reading (e.g., Optiz & Rasinski, 1998). For example, rather than individuals reading for one or two minutes during a 30-minute period of popcorn reading, students engaged in partner reading read for about 15 minutes each. Although this approach has been shown to be highly effective (Meisinger & Bradley, 2008), one question often arises: How can partners best be selected? Interestingly, studies have indicated that the two most effective ways to create pairs of learners involve having students either self-select the person they want to read with or dividing the class so that the best reader is matched with one of the average readers and another of the average readers is matched with the most struggling reader (Meisinger & Bradley, 2008; Strickland, Ganske, & Monroe, 2002). During partner reading, teachers can circulate and listen to students as they read, troubleshoot as necessary, and work with pairs of students, or even individuals, on a random or rotating basis depending on students' needs.

It is also important to bear in mind that the amount of text that each student in a pair reads should increase as the learners become comfortable with the process. The procedure begins with the students taking turns reading alternating paragraphs. While one student reads aloud, the partner follows along. As students get used to the turn-taking aspect of partner reading, the amount of text should increase so that eventually each partner is reading approximately a page of text at a time. In addition, the partner who is listening should provide the reader with support and assistance. This support does not involve jumping in every time the reader hesitates over a word, but it can include asking the partner if a word makes sense in a sentence, providing positive feedback or encouragement, and helping the reader keep track of his or her place in the text. At the level of decoding, after appropriate wait time, support can also consist of helping sound out words, providing unknown words, and correcting misread words. You may want to help students internalize these forms of assistance by modeling them for your students both in your own instruction and in demonstrations that you conduct for your learners. Similarly, it is helpful to remind students of the ways that they can help their partners before the reading period begins. It is also important to remember that this strategy can be used with any text in the classroom, including language arts and content area materials. The texts used must be appropriate for the learners. As such, when using particularly challenging texts, it is helpful to precede partner reading with an initial reading that is scaffolded by the teacher.

Echo Reading. Also a simple procedure, echo reading provides both modeling and a significant amount of scaffolding for the reader. In this process, the teacher reads a section of text aloud while students follow along in their own copies. Upon completion of the section, the students read, or echo, the same text that has just been read aloud. This procedure provides students with a model of accurate word recognition, phrasing, pacing, and use of intonation and also allows teachers to adjust the amount of text read at any one time according to the difficulty of the material and the comfort level of the students. When introducing the procedure, teachers might use shorter passages, such as a sentence or two, until students get used to the process and then expand the length to a paragraph or more. Similarly, teachers can use longer sections of text when the selection is easier, and shorter sections when the passage is more challenging. As with partner reading, echo reading can be used with any material, including content area texts. However, given the amount of scaffolding provided, echo reading is particularly well suited to challenging (i.e., stretch) texts. Because this strategy is helpful not only in developing students' fluency but also in providing them with access to texts that would otherwise be too difficult for them to read independently, this approach can help begin to close the gap between struggling readers and their more academically successful peers. As such, it can be a valuable component of the literacy curriculum.

Choral Reading. Choral reading is also a teacher-assisted instructional practice, although one that offers less scaffolding than echo reading. Still, the modeling that occurs provides learners with the opportunity to develop both their automaticity and their prosody. In choral reading, teachers and learners simultaneously read a text, or a section of a text, aloud. However, while choral reading is a tool that is both appropriate and engaging for students in the primary grades, it may seem a less natural approach for students in the upper elementary grades and beyond. Although we agree that this approach is inappropriate for most classroom instruction with older struggling readers, we recommend that teachers consider this practice for texts designed to be read aloud, such as plays, poetry, speeches, and texts for multiple voices. At the same time, given the amount of text that these students need to read to begin to close the achievement gap, we suggest choral reading be used sparingly, because in our experience, plays and poetry rarely provide the amount of daily practice that we have found is necessary to ensure that students develop as skilled readers. This is not to say that students should not read poetry or plays as part of a well-rounded literacy curriculum, but rather to suggest that these texts rarely provide learners with enough connected text reading to increase their fluency.

While we feel partner, echo, and choral reading should each have different roles in your literacy instruction, they all provide students with support and varying opportunities to read connected text. As such, they can all be viewed as effective means of accessing text to a greater or lesser degree.

Fluency Approaches for Flexible Groups

There are also several approaches to fluency development that build on the general approaches described previously. These approaches are more structured in terms of design and have been shown to be effective at assisting students with their fluency development.

Fluency-Oriented Oral Reading and Wide Fluency-Oriented Oral Reading. Among the first approaches intentionally designed to compare a traditional approach to fluency development, that of repeated reading, with the equivalent amount of nonrepeated reading of text, were fluency-oriented oral reading (FOOR) and wide fluency-oriented oral reading (Wide FOOR; Kuhn, 2009; Schwebel, 2007). Both have been shown to increase students' reading fluency, and since these approaches are designed for small numbers of learners and incorporate significant amounts of scaffolding, both also can be used with stretch texts.

The first instructional method, FOOR, is a modified repeated-readings technique that engages students in echo or choral reading of a single text during three sessions. The second approach, Wide FOOR, engages students in an echo or choral reading of a different text during each of three sessions. The two methods require virtually no preparation and are easy to implement. In comparative studies of the two approaches, researchers found that both groups made gains in word recognition in isolation, prosody, and correct words per minute (Kuhn, 2009; Schwebel, 2007). Additionally, the Wide FOOR group made gains in comprehension.

It may be that the difference in comprehension outcomes between the two groups resulted from the differences in how the approaches were implemented. Although there was some naturally occurring discussion of the readings, there was no specific comprehension instruction during the sessions. As was the case in other studies (e.g., O'Shea, Sindelar, & O'Shea, 1985, 1987), the lack of focus on comprehension may have led students to develop their own sense of what the focus of the lessons should be. Because the FOOR lessons emphasized repetition, the students in that group may have perceived the primary purpose as improving word recognition and prosody. Conversely, every Wide FOOR lesson dealt with a new text, so the students may have understood construction of meaning as a central focus. Importantly, earlier research on repeated readings has indicated that simply asking students to focus on the meaning of the story leads to an increase in their comprehension (e.g., O'Shea et al., 1985, 1987). Given this, it may be important to add a meaning focus to the lessons, which may have allowed the students in the FOOR group to make gains in comprehension similar to those made by the students in the Wide FOOR group.

Because the initial work with FOOR and Wide FOOR took place with struggling second graders, it is important to note ways in which the approaches can be modified to meet the needs of older struggling readers. First, the texts used were very challenging for the learners, but because of the length of texts for learners at this age, it was often possible to read an entire book, such as *Whistle for Willie* (Keats, 1977), *The Fire Cat* (Averill, 1988), or *Aunt Eater Loves a Mystery* (Cushman, 1987), in one session. However, for older students, it makes sense to use either passages or chapters from longer texts and incorporate content texts as well as fiction as a way of exposing these students to important vocabulary and concepts (Hirsch, 2003). Second, because of time constraints, the original groups met three times a week for 15–20-minute sessions. Because the achievement gap is often greater for older struggling readers and their more successful peers, daily sessions would likely result in greater gains. Finally, although these methods were originally used with six students in each group, we recommend numbers ranging anywhere from two to six students, depending on their needs.

Simply Reading With Support. Several years ago, we were presenting at a reading conference when a teacher shared the work that she was doing with two struggling high school readers. Her students were adamant that they be given the opportunity to read the kind of books that the kids in the advanced classes read, so she decided to read *Don Quixote* with them. She got each of the students a copy of the book, and the three of them took turns reading sections of the text aloud. She considered this to be a successful interaction but also believed that her success might demonstrate that round-robin reading can be effective.

Although we also have had positive experiences in similar situations, we argue that calling this round-robin reading would be a misnomer. In fact, we argue that this has far more in common with partner reading. Overall, we consider there to be three critical differences between the two approaches. First, when reading with two (or, at the most, three) students, each person will read a substantial proportion of the text (between one third and one fourth) rather than just a small portion of the material (as little as one twentieth or less), as is often the case with round-robin reading. Second, because the number of readers is limited and each is responsible for supporting their peers, it is more likely that the readers will focus on the text even when it is not their turn to read, and it is easier to notice when they are not engaged and refocus them on the material. Third, students are not performing unrehearsed material in front of their entire class. Instead, they are reading with peers in an atmosphere that is supportive and conducive to practice. Despite its simplicity, the procedure can be a highly effective means of ensuring that students have access to challenging texts while simultaneously building their fluency.

Finally, it is important to note that this is mainly an opportunity to let the students work on their reading development. While teachers can and should discuss the material and assist their students when they run into difficulty with the mechanics of the text, the primary focus should not be on comprehension or word recognition strategies. That is, the time should not be used for minilessons on word recognition, and discussions of the content should come at naturally occurring breaks; although critical to overall reading development, instruction in these areas should be undertaken with other selections. Instead, this sharing of a text should be a time when teachers simply read with their students to ensure their access to and enjoyment of challenging material.

Approaches for Individuals

It may be that teachers only have one or two students who need fluency-oriented instruction. There are certain advantages and disadvantages to working with these students that are important to bear in mind. For example, we have found that older disfluent readers rarely have sufficient opportunities to read texts at any level (e.g., Shanahan, 2007), because most of the texts used in their classes are too difficult for them to read independently. Yet they often shun books at their independent reading level, because these are generally written for much younger students. However, it is far easier to choose appropriate strategies and texts for an individual student than it is for a whole class or even a small group of learners. Luckily, there are several fluency-oriented instructional approaches that were created specifically for individual learners. Of the two that we focus on here, the first allows students to work independently with stretch texts, and the second gives students a purpose for reading texts designed for younger readers.

Reading-While-Listening. The first of the approaches, reading-while-listening (Chomsky, 1976), is meant to assist students who are having difficulty transitioning from word recognition instruction to reading connected text. Originally used with struggling third-grade readers, this approach was designed to expose them to significant amounts of connected text, ranging in reading levels from second to fifth grade, in an accessible format. The process involves using recorded versions of books that are too challenging for the students to read on their own. Students listen repeatedly to the recordings as they read along with the text until they are able to read the material fluently; to ensure this, it is important that there be a range of recordings that are appropriate for the learners. Additionally within this approach, there are a number of choices that students can make. For example, they should be able to choose which of the available selections they want to read. Further, it is recommended that they determine their own pace for reading the material, although they may need help setting a time frame regarding how long they should read at one sitting and how many days or weeks it should take for them to practice reading a particular selection. The process may be slow at first, and students may have difficulty coordinating their eye movements with the narrator's voice. However, this procedure usually becomes easier with practice.

It is also critical that students recognize the need to practice reading along with a particular selection until they are able to provide a fluent rendition of it independently. Once they have achieved this goal, they should move on to another selection at approximately the same level. However, as students develop their fluency, it often takes less time to reach mastery for a new selection, which is an indicator that improvements in word recognition, pacing, and intonation not only occur on the material they are reading but also transfer to previously unpracticed passages. Since this procedure requires less direct monitoring on the part of the teacher than does a traditional repeated-readings method, there may be a concern that students can simply listen to the recording without reading along. To prevent this, students should be held accountable for their reading of these texts either through the use of a running record or simply by asking them to read the material aloud on a regular basis, such as once a week. Once students find that their initial reading of a text at a given reading level is fairly fluent, the degree of difficulty should increase so that they are constantly being challenged.

Because creating digital recordings of a range of texts can be time consuming, it is possible to buy unabridged versions of many books or to ask volunteers or other students to create recordings for you (one way to implement the latter alternative is presented below). Further, although this approach was designed for individual learners, it is possible to use an adaptor that would allow several students to work with a given text simultaneously (e.g., Hollingsworth, 1978). If your students are each reading along in their own copies of the material as they listen to the recording, and the text is at an appropriate challenge level, this modification could be effective with multiple learners. Finally, numerous studies have indicated that students not only enjoy this procedure but are also proud of their growing reading ability (see Kuhn & Stahl, 2003, or Rasinski, Reutzel, Chard, & Linan-Thompson, 2011, for a discussion of the reading-while-listening procedure). They can even chart their own progress in terms of correct words per minute so that they have a visual record of their accomplishments and gain needed self-regulation skills.

Cross-Age Reading. Our second strategy, cross-age reading (Labbo & Teale, 1990), provides a meaningful way to get older struggling readers to read texts that they would otherwise view as babyish; this is especially important given the fact that such practice would likely benefit these students. By having learners take on the role of guest reader for younger students, this procedure provides learners with a real purpose for reading such texts. To take on this role, the older students need to practice reading books that younger students will enjoy and are able to undertake this practice without looking as though they are simply trying to improve their own reading. There are three steps to preparing the readers for their performance. First, they must be taught to select texts that their audience will likely enjoy. Second, they need to have sufficient opportunities to practice reading their selection until they are able to read it smoothly and expressively. Third, they need to learn how to engage their audience in a discussion of the books they are planning to read.

The research conducted on this procedure has indicated that it not only helped participating students "break poor oral reading habits" (Labbo & Teale, 1990, p. 365) but also proved to be an enjoyable experience for both the older readers and their younger audience. However, given the increasing array of time constraints that many teachers are facing, it may be difficult to ensure regular cross-classroom visits. One effective alternative is to arrange for students to create digital recordings of texts to be either placed in listening centers or used as resources for the reading-while-listening approach for younger students.

In addition, teachers might take advantage of other forms of technology for use with this procedure. For example, there are many websites, such as Eyejot (www.eyejot.com), that allow students to make video messages and send them to other classrooms, friends, or family members. Students can read their practiced text into the video and send it to a primary-grade classroom so that those students can watch it on their computer. This would allow struggling readers to engage in the practice necessary to acquire fluency while also engaging with technology, something that is often extremely motivating for them.

What About Independent Reading Time?

One approach that both whole schools and individual classrooms have implemented in an attempt to increase the amount of reading that students undertake is sustained silent reading, also known as uninterrupted sustained silent reading and Drop Everything and Read (Hasbrouck, 2006), which involves having students independently read self-selected material for 10–30 minutes per day. Such reading can also be followed by an independent writing activity in response to the material read. This approach has a great deal of potential for students who readily engage with text; as avid readers, we embrace whatever opportunities we have to read, especially when there are no restrictions on our text choices. Unfortunately, struggling readers often experience sustained silent reading very differently from their peers who enjoy reading. For struggling readers, time set aside for independent reading is often spent flipping through a book, staring into space, or thinking of ways to avoid the task altogether (e.g., Kuhn, 2009).

While we applaud the motivation for independent reading time, we think that providing learners with a range of alternatives during a set reading period has the potential to ensure that the time be used to greater effect (e.g., Reutzel, Jones, Fawson, & Smith, 2008; Stahl, 2004). Further, we strongly believe that by offering these options to everyone rather than simply targeting struggling readers, certain students can be prevented from feeling as though they have been singled out. To begin with, we argue that there should be an element of accountability introduced into the reading time. In fact, rather than using this as an opportunity to model reading, a teacher could instead integrate some additional instruction into the classroom that would otherwise not fit into an already crammed schedule. For example, this time could be used to work with various groupings of students, from individuals to dyads to small groups. Again, by including the more skilled readers as well as those experiencing difficulties, teachers can avoid some of the stigma that may be attached to additional reading instruction.

In terms of actual options, we suggest that students should be allowed to partner read self-selected books. If students are reading independently, it would be useful to randomly select individuals to confer about their choices. Also, if they are rereading a selection or using a digital recording as a model to develop their fluency, they should occasionally be asked to read part or all of the selection aloud, which will allow for progress monitoring as well as reinforce the understanding that this activity is not designed simply as a listening time. Finally, we recommend the use of scaffolded silent reading (Reutzel et al., 2008), because it is important not only to develop students' oral reading fluency but also to help them transfer to independent silent reading (Hiebert & Martin, 2009). This approach is designed to do just that. It provides students with guidance in choosing books across a range of genres and at an appropriate challenge level, and encourages accountability by helping learners establish a time frame for reading, confer with their teacher, and complete book response projects. In this way, it provides "students with the necessary support, guidance, structure, accountability, and monitoring so they can transfer their successful oral reading skills to successful and effective silent reading practice" (Reutzel et al., 2008, p. 196).

Final Thoughts

Although we have presented a range of fluency-oriented instructional approaches, teachers should reevaluate their learners' abilities to read texts at a given level every few weeks (see Kuhn, 2007, for a discussion of effective oral reading fluency assessment). If students are reading at an appropriate pace with good phrasing and intonation, then they are ready to work with more challenging texts. Further, when students demonstrate that they are able to read grade-level material comfortably, with fluency *and* understanding, it is worth considering whether their fluency instruction should be reduced significantly or perhaps eliminated entirely. At this point, it may be more beneficial to work on the transition to silent reading, along with a corresponding increase in comprehension instruction. The answer to this will depend on the learners' varying needs and the amount of scaffolding they require to ensure their continued success within the classroom.

TRY IT!

Because many older struggling readers can benefit from fluency instruction, we have several suggestions for assisting with its development. While all of the approaches described above will help students become more skilled readers, the suggestions below are good ways to get started. It is important to remember that the strategies require challenging texts, but the amount of challenge depends on the amount of scaffolding provided. We believe that these, as well as the other options described throughout the chapter, can assist students as they make the transition to skilled reading.

1. Select several texts, both narrative and expository, and follow the procedure outlined for FOOR and Wide FOOR for several weeks. See which of the approaches students prefer as well as how easy it is to implement these strategies.

2. Assist learners in identifying books that are not only challenging for them but would also be enjoyable for younger students, for example, *Stellaluna* (Cannon, 1993). Allow the older students to practice reading the book until their reading is smooth and expressive. Once their rendition is fluent, ask them either to perform the selection in front of a primary classroom or to record the selection digitally for the younger students' listening center.

3. Select poems, monologues from plays, or speeches that run anywhere from one to several pages in length. Try to select passages that have a good sense of voice—that lend themselves well to oral expression and meaningful reading. Have students practice these pieces, emphasizing their own interpretation of the selections. Once they are able to read the material expressively, ask for volunteers to perform their interpretations in front of their classmates or others in the school.

REFERENCES

Adams, M.J. (1990). *Beginning to read: Thinking and learning about print.* Cambridge, MA: MIT Press.

Allington, R.L. (1977). If they don't read much, how they ever gonna get good? *Journal of Adolescent & Adult Literacy, 21*(1), 57–61. doi:10.1598/JAAL.21.1.10

Applegate, M.D., Applegate, A.J., & Modla, V.B. (2009). "She's my best reader; she just can't comprehend": Studying the relationship between fluency and comprehension. *The Reading Teacher, 62*(6), 512–521. doi:10.1598/RT.62.6.5

Ash, G.E., & Kuhn, M.R. (2010, April). *Wide reading: Effects of oral and silent reading.* Paper presented at the 55th annual meeting of the International Reading Association, Chicago.

Ash, G.E., Kuhn, M.R., & Walpole, S. (2009). Analyzing "inconsistencies" in practice: Teachers' continued use of round robin reading. *Reading & Writing Quarterly, 25*(1), 87–103. doi:10.1080/10573560802491257

Benjamin, R., Schwanenflugel, P.J., & Kuhn, M.R. (2009, May). *The predictive value of prosody: Differences between simple and difficult texts in the reading of 2nd graders.* Paper presented at the College of Education Research Conference, University of Georgia, Athens, GA.

Brenner, D., Hiebert, E.H., & Tompkins, R. (2009). How much and what are third graders reading? Reading in core programs. In E.H. Hiebert (Ed.), *Reading more, reading better* (pp. 118–140). New York: Guilford.

Chall, J.S. (1995). *Stages of reading development* (2nd ed.). Orlando, FL: Harcourt Brace.

Chomsky, C. (1976). After decoding: What? *Language Arts, 53*(3), 288–296, 314.

Cunningham, A.E., & Stanovich, K.E. (1998). What reading does for the mind. *American Educator, 22*(1/2), 8–15.

Dowhower, S.L. (1991). Speaking of prosody: Fluency's unattended bedfellow. *Theory Into Practice, 30*(3), 165–175. doi:10.1080/00405849109543497

Erekson, J. (2003, May). *Prosody: The problem of expression in fluency.* Paper presented at the 48th annual meeting of the International Reading Association, Orlando, FL.

Gambrell, L.B. (1984). How much time do children spend reading during teacher-directed reading instruction? In J.A. Niles & L.A. Harris (Eds.), *Changing perspectives on research in reading/language processing and instruction: Thirty-third yearbook of the National Reading Conference* (pp. 193–198). Rochester, NY: National Reading Conference.

Gambrell, L.B. (2009). Creating opportunities to read more so that students read better. In E.H. Hiebert (Ed.), *Reading more, reading better* (pp. 251–266). New York: Guilford.

Groff, C.A. (2007). *Going straight to the source: Students with reading difficulties talk about reading, self-efficacy and reading instruction.* Unpublished doctoral dissertation, Rutgers, The State University of New Jersey, New Brunswick, NJ.

Hasbrouck, J. (2006). Drop everything and read—but how? For students who are not yet fluent, silent reading is not the best use of classroom time. *American Educator, 30*(2), 22–31.

Hiebert, E.H., & Martin, L.A. (2009). Opportunity to read: A critical but neglected construct in reading instruction. In E.H. Hiebert (Ed.), *Reading more, reading better* (pp. 3–29). New York: Guilford.

Hirsch, E.D., Jr. (2003). Reading comprehension requires knowledge—of words and the world: Scientific insights into the fourth-grade slump and the nation's stagnant comprehension scores. *American Educator, 27*(1), 10, 12–13, 16–22, 28–29, 44, 48. Retrieved February 15, 2011, from www.aft.org/newspubs/periodicals/ae/spring2003/index.cfm

Hollingsworth, P.M. (1978). An experimental approach to the impress method of teaching reading. *The Reading Teacher, 31*(6), 624–626.

Kuhn, M.R. (2007). Effective oral reading assessment (or why round robin reading doesn't cut it). In J.R. Paratore & R.L. McCormack (Eds.), *Classroom literacy assessment: Making sense of what students know and do* (pp. 101–112). New York: Guilford.

Kuhn, M.R. (2009). *The hows and whys of fluency instruction.* Boston: Allyn & Bacon.

Kuhn, M.R., & Schwanenflugel, P.J. (Eds.). (2008). *Fluency in the classroom.* New York: Guilford.

Kuhn, M.R., & Stahl, S.A. (2003). Fluency: A review of developmental and remedial practices. *Journal of Educational Psychology, 95*(1), 3–21. doi:10.1037/0022-0663.95.1.3

Labbo, L.D., & Teale, W.H. (1990). Cross-age reading: A strategy for helping poor readers. *The Reading Teacher, 43*(6), 362–369.

LaBerge, D., & Samuels, S.J. (1974). Toward a theory of automatic information processing in reading. *Cognitive Psychology, 6*(2), 293–323. doi:10.1016/0010-0285(74)90015-2

McKenna, M.C., & Stahl, S.A. (2003). *Assessment for reading instruction.* New York: Guilford.

Meisinger, E.B., & Bradley, B.A. (2008). Classroom practices for supporting fluency development. In M.R. Kuhn & P.J. Schwanenflugel (Eds.), *Fluency in the classroom* (pp. 36–54). New York: Guilford.

Mostow, J., & Beck, J. (2005, June). *Micro-analysis of fluency gains in a reading tutor that listens.* Paper presented at the 12th annual meeting of the Society for the Scientific Study of Reading, Toronto, ON, Canada.

Optiz, M.F., & Rasinski, T.V. (1998). *Good-bye round robin: 25 effective oral reading strategies.* Portsmouth, NH: Heinemann.

O'Shea, L.J., Sindelar, P.T., & O'Shea, D.J. (1985). The effects of repeated readings and attentional cues on reading fluency and comprehension. *Journal of Reading Behavior, 17*(2), 129–142.

O'Shea, L.J., Sindelar, P.T., & O'Shea, D.J. (1987). The effects of repeated readings and attentional cues on the reading fluency and comprehension of learning disabled readers. *Learning Disabilities Research, 2*(2), 103–109.

Rasinski, T.V., Padak, N.D., McKeon, C.A., Wilfong, L.G., Friedauer, J.A., & Heim, P. (2005). Is reading fluency a key for successful high school reading? *Journal of Adolescent & Adult Literacy, 49*(1), 22–27. doi:10.1598/JAAL.49.1.3

Rasinski, T.V., Reutzel, D.R., Chard, D., & Linan-Thompson, S. (2011). Reading fluency. In M.L. Kamil, P.D. Pearson, E.B. Moje, & P.P. Afflerbach (Eds.), *Handbook of reading research* (Vol. 4, pp. 286–319). New York: Routledge.

Reutzel, D.R., Jones, C.D., Fawson, P.C., & Smith, J.A. (2008). Scaffolded silent reading: A complement to guided repeated oral reading that works! *The Reading Teacher, 62*(3), 194–207. doi:10.1598/RT.62.3.2

Samuels, S.J. (2004). Toward a theory of automatic information processing in reading, revisited. In R.B. Ruddell & N.J. Unrau (Eds.), *Theoretical models and processes of reading* (5th ed., pp. 1127–1148). Newark, DE: International Reading Association.

Schreiber, P.A. (1991). Understanding prosody's role in reading acquisition. *Theory Into Practice, 30*(3), 158–164. doi:10.1080/00405849109543496

Schwebel, E.A. (2007). *A comparative study of small group fluency instruction—a replication and extension of Kuhn's (2005) study*. Unpublished master's thesis, Kean University, Union, NJ.

Shanahan, T. (2007, April). *Differentiating instruction when embedding literacy*. Presentation at the 39th annual Conference on Reading and Writing, Rutgers, The State University of New Jersey, Somerset, NJ.

Stahl, S.A. (2004). What do we know about fluency? Findings of the National Reading Panel. In P. McCardle & V. Chhabra (Eds.), *The voice of evidence in reading research* (pp. 187–211). Baltimore: Paul H. Brookes.

Stanovich, K.E. (1980). Toward an interactive-compensatory model of individual differences in the development of reading fluency. *Reading Research Quarterly, 16*(1), 32–71.

Stanovich, K.E. (1986). Matthew effects in reading: Some consequences of individual differences in the acquisition of literacy. *Reading Research Quarterly, 21*(4), 360–407. doi:10.1598/RRQ.21.4.1

Strickland, D.S., Ganske, K., & Monroe, J.K. (2002). *Supporting struggling readers and writers: Strategies for classroom intervention 3–6*. Portland, ME: Stenhouse.

Swanson, E.A., Wexler, J., & Vaughn, S. (2009). Text reading and students with learning difficulties. In E.H. Hiebert (Ed.), *Reading more, reading better* (pp. 210–230). New York: Guilford.

Torgesen, J.K. (2005, September). *Teaching every child to read: What every teacher needs to know*. Paper presented at the Georgia Reading First Pre-Service Conference, Atlanta.

Wexler, J., Vaughn, S., Edmonds, M., & Reutebuch, C.K. (2008). A synthesis of fluency interventions for secondary struggling readers. *Reading and Writing, 21*(4), 317–347. doi:10.1007/s11145-007-9085-7

LITERATURE CITED

Averill, E. (1988). *The fire cat*. New York: HarperCollins.

Cannon, J. (1993). *Stellaluna*. Orlando, FL: Harcourt.

Cushman, D. (1987). *Aunt Eater loves a mystery*. New York: HarperCollins.

Keats, E.J. (1977). *Whistle for Willie*. New York: Puffin.

CHAPTER 2

Enter Laughing: Poetry and Diverse Learners

Nancy Roser and Angie Zapata

> **Jack: Room 105—Miss Stretchberry**
>
> SEPTEMBER 13
>
> I don't want to
> because boys
> don't write poetry.
> Girls do.
>
> SEPTEMBER 21
>
> I tried.
> Can't do it.
>
> Brain's empty.
>
> © 1998 by Sharon Creech. Used by permission of HarperCollins Publishers.

I n Sharon Creech's (1998) remarkable novel in verse *Love That Dog*, a reluctant child poet, Jack, questions poetry's purposes, meanings, and even how it takes shape on the page. He grouses in his journal, "then any words / can be a poem. / You've just got to / make / short / lines" (p. 3). However, Jack's teacher, Miss Stretchberry, has a plan to win him over: read and reread poetry, read from a variety of poets, talk about poetry, and try writing your own. Even so, Jack is not an easy sell. He resists Robert Frost ("I think Mr. Robert Frost / has a little / too / much / time / on his / hands," p. 21) and does not understand the "wheelbarrow guy" (p. 5), William Carlos Williams. Walter Dean Myers and his poem "Love That Boy" finally open Jack to poetry and show him a way to write through his grief over the death of his beloved dog.

Teachers resonate with Creech's book: Jack's resistance to poetry feels real to them—the way lots of students react to poetry. Why, then, in this volume on effective strategies for our most disenfranchised learners, do we select a genre that can give even avid readers pause? Our experience in bringing poetry to students has taught us that if we are willing to be a bit

After Early Intervention, Then What? Teaching Struggling Readers in Grades 3 and Beyond (2nd ed.) edited by Jeanne R. Paratore and Rachel L. McCormack. © 2011 by the International Reading Association.

iconoclastic about what counts as poetry, it will be as easy to reclaim poetry fans as it was to get them to respond to rhymes, finger plays, songs, and chants when they were babies or toddlers. Poet and teacher David Harmer (2000) claims that most kids "burst through our doors each day with a head full of it...jingles, adverts, raps, songs, and very often—poems" (p. 15).

Jack's teacher, Miss Stretchberry, offered her students the poems of Frost and Williams from the very start. In contrast, the third-grade teacher with whom we worked, Ms. Acosta (all names are pseudonyms), began with jump-rope jingles, hip-hop, and rhymes about food fights, dead squirrels, smelly feet, and sports. In this chapter, we describe her classroom of diverse third graders who came to poetry through laughter and stayed long enough to try Frost ("I like *Love That Dog,*" one student told Ms. Acosta, "but this poem by Robert Frost *could* use some work").

When students' introduction to poetry is through nonsense rhymes, lyrics, jingles, and spoken poetry, each student can read fluently and, in so doing, learn to read better. Poetry, perhaps more than any other genre, can ensure reader fit through its bounty of accessible texts. Poetry's demands for energetic performance claim some turned-off readers, and its invitations for quiet reflection and pondering claim others. Yet poetry does not stop there. It offers support on the page, especially when poems follow patterns; it reaches and represents cultures; and its reassuring length, white space, and line lengths signal, "You can read this," and, "You can write it, too."

Myra Cohn Livingston (1975), a prolific and award-winning poet, warns against the ready acceptance of children's poetic attempts as true poetry:

> Among my files are hundreds of...booklets, newsletters, pamphlets, magazines...containing the so-called poetry of children. Most of it is shoddy, presented with pride by conscientious teachers, librarians, parents...who, unfortunately, know little of the tools, the voice, or the craft of poetry. We do our children a striking disservice when we accept for publication this work in the name of poetry....At an age when children should be striving to improve by profiting from error, their work is accepted as complete, finished, perfect. (p. 571)

Livingston argues that the moniker of "poet" is won at too high a cost to be offered lightly to students who have scribbled doggerel or attempted verse. Her works rest on deep understanding of the voices of poetry, its sounds, rhythms, metrics, and forms (Sloan, 2001). Others such as Meek have disagreed, arguing that children's fresh uses of language attest to their "natural" bent toward poetry (as cited by Livingston, 1984, p. 4). With a deep bow to Livingston's eminent status and high standards for poetry (see Helbig, 1986), we duck into the alley to give kids this subliminal message: Start here with this ooey, gooey, pleasing mass of sounds and words. Let's consider it poetry for now, and let's call you a poet—not because it or you have met outsiders' critical standards, but because you are new to poetry and have intended to write poetry.

This chapter offers a close look at introducing readers and writers to poetry as a way to nurture literacy for those who have experienced less success than they should have or have not yet selected poetry as their reading/writing choice. Indeed, instruction around accessible poetry meshes triumphantly with the guiding principles for effective Response to Intervention produced by the International Reading Association's Commission on Response to Intervention, providing for close observation and assessment, responsive teaching within a comprehensive view of literacy instruction, and collaboration among participants (see www.reading.org/resources/resourcesbytopic/responsetointervention/overview.aspx).

We tell the story of the exploration of reading and writing poetry in Ms. Acosta's classroom as evidence of the way one teacher nurtured readers and writers of poetry. We begin with a brief review of the contemporary research literature on sharing poetry in classrooms, followed by a description of a whole-class literacy intervention focused on poetry study and its effects. Although poetry is meant to blend across the day and throughout the year (Bauer, 1995; Denman, 1988), we treat it as a planned genre study designed to build an affinity for words and well-chosen language, as well as to support students' reading, writing, and literary meaning making.

Poetry Study in Today's Classrooms

As a prelude to their investigation of how kindergarten through fourth-grade teachers shared poetry with their students, Elster and Hanauer (2002) argue that there have been few empirical studies examining how poetry is read and shared in classrooms, or how poetry contributes to literacy learning. These researchers position their study within literacy as a culturally situated practice rather than a set of skills, and they contend that as students learn to read and write different text genres, they are learning the social and psycholinguistic processes associated with the genre.

Although poetry may have less cachet than do stories in contemporary classrooms (Kamberelis, 1999), professional journals and texts are filled with recommendations for its inclusion. In the last decade, teachers and researchers have offered a host of teaching practices that engage students with poetry (Wolf, 2006), including using it as a starting place for critical literacy discussions (Ciardiello, 2010; McCall, 2004), relying on rhyming poetry for building fluency and rapid word recognition (Rasinski, Rupley, & Nichols, 2008), and installing poetry across the curriculum (Frye, Trathen, & Schlagal, 2010; Von Drasek, 2007).

When researchers ask middle graders what they like to read (e.g., Worthy, 1996), the students are more likely to say comics, magazines, and series books than poems. Even so, poetry advocates like Harmer (2000) maintain that "children love poems...love to learn them, read them, write them, and perform them" (p. 15). In their study of poetry preferences, Kutiper and Wilson (1993) found that 14 of children's 30 favorite choices were the works of Shel Silverstein and Jack Prelutsky, and that humorous poetry was preferred over all other kinds. It is easy to argue that students find Prelutsky and Silverstein on their own, so these poets should make way in classrooms for their poet peers; it is also easy to observe that when students find the works of these beloved poets in classrooms, there are sighs of pleasure, shouted requests, and other evidence of deep satisfaction.

Poetry Study in Ms. Acosta's Class

There is still much to learn about classroom poetry study, much to investigate about how students come to read and write poetry, and much to understand about how preferences in poetry take shape. Further, poetry continues to be the neglected genre (Duthie & Zimet, 1992). For Ms. Acosta, however, poetry is not just another genre to study. She subscribes fully to poetry's power to make students active participants in their literacy learning. She believes that poetry, more than other literary genres, readily exposes its structures and features for inspection, offers opportunities for rereadings and deeper readings, develops awareness of fresh uses of language, and lends itself to visual thinking. Because poetry comes in such an abundance of topics, styles, and treatments, it can reach into every classroom to speak to every literate life. Best of all, perhaps, Ms. Acosta finds evidence that poetry convinces reluctant readers and writers to try reading and writing in this genre. The features of poetry, she reasons, play an important part in her goals to reach all students, traditional and underserved, with good books; teach purposefully; ensure that students find reasons to read and write; observe closely; and teach into her observations (Wixson, Lipson, & Johnston, 2010).

The Context

The urban school in which Ms. Acosta teaches third grade enrolls children of graduate students at the nearby university as well as children of poverty; more than half of the school's students qualify for free and reduced-cost lunch, although the demographic makeup includes both middle-income children and temporary residents of public shelters. Her 21 third graders spoke four different home languages and represented diverse cultural heritages. Ms. Acosta is a fluently bilingual Latina, with nearly a decade of teaching experience at the time we worked in her classroom. An acclaimed teacher, she is accustomed to visitors in her classroom. We were able to observe and videotape, as well as participate, in the classroom throughout a four-week poetry study during her language arts blocks (a total of approximately 90 minutes daily). As participant-observers, we (university-based teacher educators) were invited to help plan the unit, add books to the poetry library, confer with students, and debrief with Ms. Acosta. We also took notes, ran the recorders, photographed the evidence of poetry study, and interviewed the students.

The four-week poetry immersion followed this sequence:

- A poetry flood that included reading, sampling, and sharing poems
- Talking over poetry and producing open-ended charts to collect students' discoveries about poetry
- Growing the stack of revisited poems and favorite poets in order to explore poets' choices (e.g., found poetry, concrete poems, rhyming and nonrhyming poems), while continuing to read poetry aloud
- Providing each student with a poetry journal to hold favorite poems and his or her own writing
- Publishing and performing original poetry

Poetry Immersion

Enter Laughing (a Flood of Silly Verse). Denman (1988) speaks powerfully against teachers choosing the popular poetry/verse that incites laugh riots in classrooms; he believes that students' long-term impressions of poetry are tied to the quality of the initial selections that teachers offer. Similarly, in her compelling account of discovering the "'great' poetry" within her students, Certo (2004) chides herself for being a teacher who once overrelied on Silverstein while admitting that "Silverstein was instrumental in focusing my own interest in poetry as a child" (p. 266). Just *begin* with laughter, Ms. Acosta might argue back, and trust the kids.

For the first day of poetry study, Ms. Acosta had filled bins in her classroom with poetry to laugh about. The students sat in a circle to be initiated into the book bounty. There were Robin Hirsch's (2002) *FEG: Ridiculous (Stupid) Poems for Intelligent Children*, with the fun poem "Counting to Infinity," Douglas Florian's *Mammalabilia: Poems and*

Figure 2.1. A Poetry Flood of Third Graders

Paintings (2000) as well as Florian's *Insectlopedia: Poems and Paintings* (1988). There were Maya Angelou's (1993) *Life Doesn't Frighten Me*, Jack Prelutsky's (2007) *Good Sports: Rhymes About Running, Jumping, Throwing, and More*, Bruce Lansky's (1991) *Kids Pick the Funniest Poems: Poems That Make Kids Laugh*, and X.J. Kennedy's (2002) *Exploding Gravy: Poems to Make You Laugh*. There were Michael Rosen's (1996) *Food Fight: Poets Join the Fight Against Hunger With Poems to Favorite Foods*, Nadine Westcott's (1994) *Never Take a Pig to Lunch: And Other Poems About the Fun of Eating*, Dennis Lee's (1978) *Garbage Delight*, and a full helping of Shel Silverstein. There were also themed compilations of poets of renown, anthologies of a single poet, single poems in picture book formats, and much more (about 75 books in all).

Even the most tantalizing of poems and the most intriguing of titles, Ms. Acosta believes, require introduction. As Hickman (1983) argues, books and readers are like guests at a party, and hosts (teachers) must work to ensure that the guests find their common ground through skillful introductions. Prepared with those introductions, Ms. Acosta dipped into poems that she had marked for sharing; she read and recited with merriment, told particular students that she had thought of them when she selected a specific poem, and reread on request. It was too soon to notice metrical schemes or savor internal rhymes. The third graders just crowed, "Read it again!" "Read with me?" she countered. Then, onto the document camera went the poem, and voices chimed in, echoing the way she had read. Ms. Acosta, the poetry Siren, sampled and dappled and invited for the next 30 minutes. Finally, the students spread out the volumes on the rug, and after a reminder that the books would be companions over days and days in the classroom, readers alone or in pairs set to choosing volumes, discovering poems, pointing them out to others, trying them aloud, and marking choices for whole-class reading (see Figure 2.1). Poetry study had begun. What would set it apart from the study of other literary genres would be its ready accessibility to the range of readers in the class, its transparent structures, its shorter length as an opportunity to reread and look closely, and its readiness for performance art (think *singing*), with fully participating learners.

Producing Open-Ended Charts to Collect Students' Observations About Poetry. Poetry instructional time slid into the direct teaching portion of the literacy block, what Ms. Acosta called the "focus lessons" of the reading/writing workshop. Like others who teach genre studies (e.g., Ray, 2006), Ms. Acosta pulled chart paper and markers for her first focus lesson, asking her students to share what they had noticed about poetry during the poetry flood (see Figures 2.2 and 2.3). Ms. Acosta opened the discussion of poetry by asking, "What does poetry seem to be?" and explaining, "Let's write what we're seeing." This lesson served as the first invitation to think of poetry as a form, a set of decisions that a poet makes, and a genre with particular force. Students offered their responses readily, because there had been time not only to inspect a number of collections, but also to participate with poetry.

Our notes and the charts record what the students said, such as the following:

- "Short lines"
- "Repeats"
- "Makes music with words"
- "Makes us feel"
- "Put spaces between"
- "The way you say the words"
- "Doesn't have to make sense"

Over the ensuing days, equipped with sticky notes, students continued to identify (and change their minds about) ways they "know it's poetry." As their experiences with poems expanded, the chart grew to include responses such as the following:

- "A special shape on the page, sort of like a paragraph, but not"
- "Can see it in your head"
- "Lots of repeating"
- "Can go up and down."
- "Mixes the words up"

Figure 2.2. Charting Poetry Features

Figure 2.3. Growing and Organizing the Poetry Features Chart

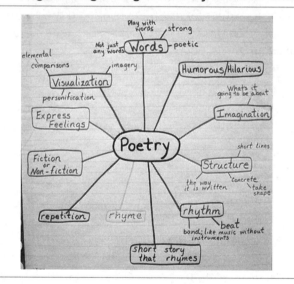

They also came to understand, as poet Eve Merriam (1964) reminds us, "It doesn't always have to rhyme." Before the unit was over, the chart included the following:

- "Strong words"
- "Powerful"
- "Says a lot without using many words"
- "Some people don't do poetic: They just make a sentence to rhyme"

In addition to building their "What Is Poetry?" chart, Ms. Acosta and the third graders developed other collaborative charts across the days of poetry study, each chart reflecting the content and collected efforts of the focus lessons, including "Poets Write About...," "Words We Like," "Different Kinds of Poetry," "Don't Miss This One" (poem recommendations), and "Poets' Choices." The latter chart was designed to collect the specialized lexicon of poetry study as it relates to the creation and appreciation of poetry, such as attention to the sounds of language (e.g., the repeating sounds of alliteration, the mimicking sounds of onomatopoeia). As noted, poetry's special terms were seeded by focus lessons, which served to increase awareness of poets being choosy about words to achieve fresh and surprising uses of language. What seemed critical to the time each day set aside for sharing poetry was noticing a poet at work, as well as naming and tracking this accruing set of insights.

Besides whole-group focus lessons, poetry study also included self-selected poetry reading (cf. Sekeres & Gregg, 2007). Each student was provided a poetry binder, serving as a place to copy favorite poetry and collect reprints of verses that Ms. Acosta and the class chose to read and reread. The binders' holdings became a favorite source of selections during independent reading time. Thus, poems nobly served literacy growth. For example, as students read in pairs or alone, Ms. Acosta listened in on poetry readings, attending to and supporting students' developing fluency and word recognition strategies. Poetry became an additional text for serving word recognition and meaning making.

Growing the Stack of Familiar Poetic Forms: Found, Concrete, Culturally Relevant, and Topical. Besides charts, poetry itself went onto the walls, and Ms. Acosta asked students to post their thinking on sticky notes next to the poems (see Figure 2.4). She also introduced concrete poems, which take the page in shapes that underscore the poems' meanings, such as a lightning bolt, the long tail of a mouse, or lines that bounce across the page like a tennis ball or toggle like a windshield wiper. As John Grandits (2004) explains on the bookflap of his collection of concrete poems, *Technically, It's Not My Fault*, "words, ideas, type, and art combine to make pictures and patterns. You may have to turn the book— or your mind—sideways and upside town to *read them*, but laughter is 100% guaranteed." "Wow," said Ms. Acosta's students as they viewed the projected concrete forms of J. Patrick Lewis's (1998) *Doodle Dandies: Poems That Take Shape* and Joan Graham's (1999) *Flicker Flash*. The students

Figure 2.4. A Wall of Poetry

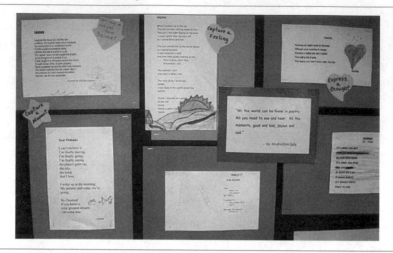

wanted more examples, so "concrete poetry" went onto the chart and concrete poems went onto the classroom walls.

Next, Ms. Acosta asked the students to dedicate a section of their binders to "found poems" for words they discovered or heard that seemed so fresh and right they deserved remembering—and possibly borrowing for their own poems someday. Next came accessible haiku (e.g., Matthew Gollub's [1998] *Cool Melons—Turn to Frogs! The Life and Poems of Issa*) and sijo (e.g., Linda Sue Park's [2007] *Tap Dancing on the Roof: Sijo [Poems]*), the students' first introduction to more rule-governed forms. The ancient Korean poetry of sijo typically has three lines (sometimes broken on narrower pages into six)—the first serving as an introduction, the second to respond to or develop the first, and the third offering a surprising turn—all in 14–16 syllables per line. However, guidelines for sijo were not the essential understanding for these readers (and soon-to-be writers) of poetry, but rather the recognition that poets have choices in topic and form, and that audiences resonate with different poems.

Poetry Performance. The poems and rhymes of home were invited onto the walls and into the poetry binders from the very beginning, and students began to share aloud. However, before there were many solo performances, there were group and paired readings. During poetry share, the third graders began to suggest ways to add meanings to poetry read-alouds by varying the pace, rhythm, and stress. Ms. Acosta was ready. She projected a copy of a favorite poem onto the screen and entertained suggestions as to how the poem could be interpreted (i.e., whether and where a chorus of voices should blend, solo, echo, take turns, overlap, stress, fade) to alter meanings. "Let's try it this way," said Antanasia, "clapping the beat like this," and they did. "Uh-uh," disagreed Mara, "Can't hear the words. Gotta bump/swish our hands like this," and she demonstrated a shuffle slide of the poem's rhythm. They tried again. Marked with highlighter, other poems were broken into parts, words were stressed, and ways to echo and chorus the refrains tried out. Elizabeth Swados's (2002) *Hey You! C'mere: A Poetry Slam* appealed to the students' sense of performance, as did poems already prepared for multiple voices (e.g., Sara Holbrook's [2002] *Wham! It's a Poetry Jam: Discovering Performance Poetry*).

Besides blending voices and changing rhythms and stress, performing poetry can mean deciding on appropriate movements and actions. Swaying, conga lines, and developing hand movements bring poetry to life. Antanasia read Shel Silverstein's (1974) "The Loser" from *Where the Sidewalk Ends* as hip-hop, moving to its rhythms, whereas Riley reinterpreted it as a near dirge. Rather than decide which was better, students discussed how each performance made them feel.

Because Ms. Acosta realizes that poems can mirror students' lives, she planned for performances and discussion of poems written in the voices of children. Andrea Cheng's (2008) poems in *Where the Steps Were* are offered from the perspectives of five third graders in the year before their school's closing. In this poetry novel written for five voices, the children recount a social injustice that they experienced on a field trip and plan how to respond to it. Jane Medina's (1999) *My Name Is Jorge on Both Sides of the River: Poems in English and Spanish* allowed Ms. Acosta's students to voice the perception, confusions, and slights to an immigrant child. Together, Ms. Acosta and the students marked the lines into parts and planned ways to orchestrate their voices to surface their connections with Jorge's need to be addressed by name, as in the following reading with two voices in groups using lines from the poem "T-Shirt":

Boys: Teacher?

Girls: George, please call me "Mrs. Roberts."

Boys: Yes, Teacher.

Girls: George, please don't call me "teacher."

Boys: Yes, T—I mean, Mrs. Roberts.

Girls: You see, George, it's a sign of respect to call me by my last name.

Boys: Yes...Mrs. Roberts.

Girls: Besides, when you say it, it sounds like "t-shirt." I don't want to turn into a t-shirt!

Boys: Mrs. Roberts?

Girls: Yes, George?

Boys: Please, call me Jorge.

In *DeShawn Days* by Tony Medina (2001) with R. Gregory Christie's bold illustrations, the contrasting images of a danger-filled neighborhood and a warm, loving home helped the students decide how to voice the verses. Even so, looking back at the classroom footage showed us that using the collective term "the students" makes too sweeping a claim. Not all students sought solo parts or offered ways to interpret poetry in performance. Some mumble read and resisted movement. Performance was not everyone's thing, but writing poetry would be.

Putting Poetry on Paper. Wooldridge (1996) contends, "It's impossible to *teach* anyone to write a poem. But we can set up circumstances in which poems are likely to happen" (p. xii). Ms. Acosta, the new owner of a puppy, demonstrated her own way through a poem. She boldly placed paper on the document camera, explaining how the puppy had crowded into her heart and that she had surprised herself with the hours she spent just watching him. "I want to put some of my feelings and thoughts into a poem," she told the class. She thought aloud to write some words that came to mind, talking as she wrote: "snuggles / nestles in for rest / gives in to sleep / whirl! twirl! catch that tail! / running in circles." She paused to cross out "running in" and substituted the word "dizzy," explaining that "dizzy circles" might be a way that a poet could describe the puppy's movement using very few words while contributing to an image in the reader's mind. "You know how pugs are," she told the students, "all that loose skin...a mound of it." She wrote, "He ends up peaceful / a mound of loose skin." Rereading aloud, she crossed out "He ends up" and inserted "Satisfied" so that her stanza read, "Satisfied / Peaceful / A mound of loose skin." By working on her poem, but not finishing it, Ms. Acosta demonstrated how poems can transmit feeling and help readers see in a new way. Together, they looked again at her cross-outs, her false starts, and her reaches for just-right words to reflect those feelings.

"I just wanna write one," came one voice, then lots more: "Can *we* write some poems?" As though it had never occurred to her, Ms. Acosta paused and then, pretending to ponder the question, slowly answered, "I guess so." Later, outside the classroom, her fists pumped the air: "Yes!" She told us she believed that previously she had asked for poetry to be written too soon. "In the past, it was almost as though kids were to read a poem, write a poem," she explained. "I've come to believe it takes more steeping, enjoying, sharing, and experiencing poetry's choices before the Muse should be invited in." Postponing invitations to write poetry seemed to work to whet appetites for taking up the poet's plume (Duthie & Zimet, 1992). In addition, the humorous poems that opened the unit often rhymed, but students' first poems can be constrained by adherence to a rhyming scheme. Experience with more poems provided students with alternative ways to take up poetry.

When original poems began to appear in the poetry binders, Ms. Acosta opened more time for writing and sharing poetry during workshop time. Volunteers began to offer to read their poems aloud, revise them when they seemed worthy, and give consent for their poems to be typed and added to the walls. At the outset, writers leaned on the writers they loved. Alicia leaned on Silverstein's (1974) "Ickle Me, Pickle Me, Tickle Me Too" from *Where the Sidewalk Ends*; Silverstein had, in turn, leaned on Eugene Field's 1889 Dutch lullaby "Wynken, Blynken, and Nod." Alicia's poem began, "Giggle, Pickle, and Natel me / Went for a ride in a flying sea. / 'So what?' / 'Who cares?' / Said Giggle, Pickle, and Natel me." The words had taken the page, and Alicia found them pleasing and hysterical. She went to work on further verses.

Greg drew from concrete poems and wrote in careful print on a pencil-outlined computer screen:

Computer

You type.
You play.
There are games and all.
And it does my homework
Best of all.

Learning English, Patrice wrote the following:

A Few Words

I'm a girl of few words
I barely talk in sentences.
I almost only say
"Yes" or "No."

But just listen
And I'll tell you
I'm a girl of few words.

Riley, a sportsman but not a fancier of poetry at first, was drawn to concrete poetry, inspired by *Doodle Dandies*, *Flicker Flash*, and others. His first unprodded writing for the year was a poem with words that circled a big, orange basketball, so the words ran together endlessly:

I heard some say
we're playing basketball
at the casketball
tournament as... [now you're back to the beginning].

Aurelia wrote of her sister, leaving home:

Ana

I'll miss her so
She's stuck inside of me
She'll never leave
I don't want her to go.
I'll remember
Her smiles
Her laughs
Her face.
I don't want her to go.

There was really no end to the unit. Poetry stayed in the classroom and continued to contribute to insights and learning. At the formal end of the unit of study, there was a poetry performance party at which students read their original works to an audience of parents, the school principal, staff members, and invited guests from the university (us). Each poetry binder lay open on the students' presentation desk next to a copy of the published classroom anthology containing a poem from each student. Readers filled in and left response sheets for the poets, with notes such as, "I REALLY liked how you wrote about your sister!" (see Figure 2.5). The walls were full of poetry, poetry charts, and sticky note addenda. The environment spoke, "Poetry written and read here." Buddy took the microphone to introduce each poet, but the students were used to audiences for their poems, had read and shaped them repeatedly, and there seemed to be little nervousness (see Figure 2.6). In every case, the reading was fluid, well paced, and audience aware.

Figure 2.5. Leaving Notes for Third-Grade Poets on Poetry Performance Day

Figure 2.6. A Third Grader Performing Poetry

Conclusions

Miss Stretchberry trusted that poetry would eventually collect the students and believed that "dailyness" was required, as well as a belief in students to make meanings and keep going. Poetry in her fictional classroom and in Ms. Acosta's real-life one gave students time to look closely, hear joyfully and thoughtfully, and write when their hearts were full. Both teachers made sure that the right poetry book reached the right hands. Both made room for a scholar's stance: What makes for poetry? How will we know it when we see it? To become a lifetime reader of poetry (the kind who reads poetry on trains and subways), students must have access to its bounty of possibilities, and time to revel in the images elicited by words.

Poet Lee Bennett Hopkins (2004) notes that we must give students the finest poetry: "They deserve that....Bring on poets. Let them write poetry. Let us read it, share it, embrace it" (p. 699). Heard (1999) recommends a classroom environment that sends messages that each student matters and that adults are deeply listening. Yet, in Ms. Acosta's classroom, it all began with laughter. Something can be said about opening an inquiry into poetry with students responding to silliness while taking pleasure in rhythms, rhymes, and word choices. Beginning with the songs and rhymes of home, rollicking jingles, nonsensical clap-snaps, song lyrics, slams, and more, students gain the momentum—the stamina, the strategies—to take on the poems that will rock their socks. Most central, it seemed, was that Ms. Acosta stuck by her literacy learners to make sure that each one found poetry that fit and wrote poetry that satisfied.

We interviewed third grader Nat at year's end:

Interviewer: Have you ever written any poetry?

Nat: Yeah.

Interviewer: Talk about that.

Nat:
Well, when I write poetry,
I try to think
about my life...
the times that
I have lost something that I wanted
The times that
I have found something
that I lost
and didn't know I had
until I found it again.
Times that make me

happy
sad
angry
glad....
Feelings.

Interviewer: You just made a poem with your words.

Nat: Yeah, I know.

TRY IT!

1. *Fresh perspectives with digital photography*—It is one thing to talk to young poets about observing closely and choosing the right words. It is quite another challenge to help them learn to see through and around, think symbolically, and find emotional connections. Wolf (2006) advocates taking up the digital camera and encouraging students to see the world differently, then using those new understandings to create poetry. By encouraging young writers to change perspectives (e.g., tightening the camera's lens on the tracks left in dirt, examining the crisscross of the playground fence), students are recomposing their world just by "looking closely and wondering about the possibilities" (p. 19). Next will come the invitation to use words that are equally fresh and surprising to represent the deep meanings in these new vistas and close-ups. "Serious seeing," as Wolf calls it, is part of the work that young poets must engage in to focus on the art of crafting poetry (p. 10).

2. *Verse for two voices and in two languages*—Our classrooms are full of ways with words (Heath, 1983). When students who speak different home languages work together to compose silly rhymes for two voices, they are bound to learn something about language and its speakers and have fun. Imagining and composing conversational turns between English and Spanish speakers opens up possibilities for comedic miscommunications. Ultimately, though, each "poet" is totally understandable to the other, but their audiences don't have to know! Poems might take shape as follows:

Hello
Adiós.
¿Donde está biblioteca?
Thank you very much. How are you?
No comprendo. Lo siento.
It's nice to see you, too.

Then, English can come first:

> Hi, I'm new here. I'm lost.
> Muy bien, gracias. ¿Y tú?
> Would you kindly point my way home?
> Veo la luz. Veo la luz.

Only when one's first language takes the second and fourth lines do the poets have to produce rhyme. Working on lines 1 and 3 only demands adherence to a rhythmic scheme.

REFERENCES

Bauer, C.F. (1995). *The poetry break: An annotated anthology with ideas for introducing children to poetry.* New York: H.W. Wilson.

Certo, J.L. (2004). Cold plums and the old men in the water: Let children read and write "great" poetry. *The Reading Teacher, 58*(3), 266–271. doi:10.1598/RT.58.3.4

Ciardiello, A.V. (2010). "Talking walls": Presenting a case for social justice poetry in literacy education. *The Reading Teacher, 63*(6), 464–473. doi:10.1598/RT.63.6.3

Denman, G.A. (1988). *When you've made it your own: Teaching poetry to young people.* Portsmouth, NH: Heinemann.

Duthie, C., & Zimet, E.K. (1992). "Poetry is like directions for your imagination!" *The Reading Teacher, 46*(1), 14–24.

Elster, C.A., & Hanauer, D.I. (2002). Voicing texts, voices around texts: Reading poems in elementary school classrooms. *Research in the Teaching of English, 37*(1), 89–134.

Frye, E.M., Trathen, W., & Schlagal, B. (2010). Extending acrostic poetry into content learning: A scaffolding framework. *The Reading Teacher, 63*(7), 591–595. doi:10.1598/RT.63.7.6

Harmer, D. (2000). Poetry in the primary school. *Education 3–13, 28*(2), 15–18.

Heard, G. (1999). *Awakening the heart: Exploring poetry in elementary and middle school.* Portsmouth, NH: Heinemann.

Heath, S.B. (1983). *Ways with words: Language, life, and work in communities and classrooms.* New York: Cambridge University Press.

Helbig, A.K. (1986). Myra Cohn Livingston offers a "new mythology" in *The child as poet. Children's Literature Association Quarterly, 11*(3), 150–152.

Hickman, J. (1983). Classrooms that help children like books. In N. Roser & M. Frith (Eds.), *Children's choices: Teaching with books children like* (pp. 1–11). Newark, DE: International Reading Association.

Hopkins, L.B. (2004). "Ah, poetry!" *The Reading Teacher, 57*(7), 699.

Kamberelis, G. (1999). Genre development and learning: Children writing stories, science reports, and poems. *Research in the Teaching of English, 33*(4), 403–460.

Kutiper, K., & Wilson, P. (1993). Updating poetry preferences: A look at the poetry children really like. *The Reading Teacher, 47*(1), 28–35.

Livingston, M.C. (1975). But is it poetry? *The Horn Book Magazine, 51*(6), 571–580.

Livingston, M.C. (1984). *The child as poet: Myth or reality?* Boston: Horn Book.

McCall, A.L. (2004). Using poetry in social studies classes to teach about cultural diversity and social justice. *The Social Studies, 95*(4), 172–176. doi·10.3200/TSSS.95.4.172-176

Rasinski, T.V., Rupley, W.H., & Nichols, W.D. (2008). Two essential ingredients: Phonics and fluency getting to know each other. *The Reading Teacher, 62*(3), 257–260. doi:10.1598/RT.62.3.7

Ray, K.W. (2006). *Study driven: A framework for planning units of study in the writing workshop.* Portsmouth, NH: Heinemann.

Sekeres, D.C., & Gregg, M. (2007). Poetry in third grade: Getting started. *The Reading Teacher, 60*(5), 466–475. doi:10.1598/RT.60.5.6

Sloan, G. (2001). But is it poetry? *Children's Literature in Education, 32*(1), 45–56. doi:10.1023/A:1005266021601

Von Drasek, L. (2007). Animal poetry. *Teaching Pre K–8, 37*(7), 56–57.

Wixson, K.K., Lipson, M.Y., & Johnston, P.H. (2010). Making the most of RTI. In M.Y. Lipson & K.K. Wixson (Eds.), *Successful approaches to RTI: Collaborative practices for improving K–12 literacy* (pp. 1–19). Newark, DE: International Reading Association.

Wolf, S.A. (2006). The mermaid's purse: Looking closely at young children's art and poetry. *Language Arts, 84*(1), 10–20.

Wooldridge, S.G. (1996). *Poemcrazy: Freeing your life with words.* New York: Three Rivers.

Worthy, J. (1996). A matter of interest: Literature that hooks reluctant readers and keeps them reading. *The Reading Teacher, 50*(3), 204–212.

LITERATURE CITED

Angelou, M. (1993). *Life doesn't frighten me.* New York: Stewart, Tabori & Chang.

Cheng, A. (2008). *Where the steps were.* Honesdale, PA: Wordsong.

Creech, S. (1998). *Love that dog.* New York: HarperCollins.

Florian, D. (1988). *Insectlopedia: Poems and paintings.* Orlando, FL: Harcourt.

Florian, D. (2000). *Mammalabilia: Poems and paintings.* Orlando, FL: Harcourt.

Gollub, M. (1998). *Cool melons—turn to frogs! The life and poems of Issa.* New York: Lee & Low.

Graham, J.B. (1999). *Flicker flash.* New York: Houghton Mifflin.

Grandits, J. (2004). *Technically, it's not my fault: Concrete poems.* New York: Clarion.

Hirsch, R. (2002). *FEG: Ridiculous (stupid) poems for intelligent children.* New York: Little, Brown.

Holbrook, S. (2002). *Wham! It's a poetry jam: Discovering performance poetry.* Honesdale, PA: Boyds Mills.

Kennedy, X.J. (2002). *Exploding gravy: Poems to make you laugh.* Boston: Little, Brown.

Lansky, B. (Ed.). (1991). *Kids pick the funniest poems: Poems that make kids laugh.* Deephaven, MN: Meadowbrook.

Lee, D. (1978). *Garbage delight.* Boston: Houghton Mifflin.

Lewis, J.P. (1998). *Doodle dandies: Poems that take shape.* New York: Atheneum.

Medina, J. (1999). *My name is Jorge on both sides of the river: Poems in English and Spanish.* Honesdale, PA: Wordsong.

Medina, T. (2001). *DeShawn days*. New York: Lee & Low.

Park, L.S. (2007). *Tap dancing on the roof: Sijo (poems)*. New York: Clarion.

Prelutsky, J. (2007). *Good sports: Rhymes about running, jumping, throwing, and more*. New York: Alfred A. Knopf.

Rosen, M.J. (Ed.). (1996). *Food fight: Poets join the fight against hunger with poems to favorite foods*. San Diego, CA: Harcourt Brace.

Silverstein, S. (1974). *Where the sidewalk ends*. New York: HarperCollins.

Swados, E. (2002). *Hey you! C'mere: A poetry slam*. New York: Arthur A. Levine.

Westcott, N.B. (Ed.). (1994). *Never take a pig to lunch: And other poems about the fun of eating*. New York: Orchard.

ADDITIONAL POETRY FOR NOVICES (AND SOME FOR NUDGES) IN MIDDLE GRADES

Barnwell, Y.M. (1998). *No mirrors in my Nana's house*. Orlando, FL: Harcourt Brace.

Brown, C. (2006). *Flamingos on the roof*. New York: Houghton Mifflin.

Bryan, A. (1997). *Ashley Bryan's ABC of African American poetry*. New York: Atheneum.

Crew, G. (2003). *Troy Thompson's excellent peotry book*. La Jolla, CA: Kane/Miller.

Cullinan, B.E., & Wooten, D. (Eds.). (2009). *Another jar of tiny stars: Poems by more NCTE award-winning poets* (Expanded ed.). Honesdale, PA: Wordsong.

Dakos, K. (1990). *If you're not here, please raise your hand: Poems about school*. New York: Four Winds.

Esbensen, B. (1992). *Who shrank my grandmother's house? Poems of discovery*. New York: HarperCollins.

Field, E. (2008). *Wynken, Blynken, and Nod*. New York: Schwartz & Wade.

Fleischman, P. (2000). *Big talk: Poems for four voices*. Cambridge, MA: Candlewick.

Fletcher, R. (2005). *A writing kind of day: Poems for young poets*. Honesdale, PA: Wordsong.

Florian, D. (2010). *Poetrees*. New York: Beach Lane.

Frost, H. (2004). *Spinning through the universe: A novel in poems from room 214*. New York: Farrar, Straus & Giroux.

George, K.O. (2005). *Fold me a poem*. Orlando, FL: Harcourt.

Giovanni, N. (Ed.). (2008). *Hip hop speaks to children: A celebration of poetry with a beat*. Naperville, IL: Sourcebooks Jabberwocky.

Greenfield, E. (2003). *Honey, I love*. New York: HarperCollins.

Grimes, N. (1994). *Meet Danitra Brown*. New York: Lothrop, Lee & Shepard.

Grimes, N. (2004). *What is goodbye?* New York: Hyperion.

Grimes, N. (2005). *It's raining laughter*. Honesdale, PA: Boyds Mills.

Heard, G. (Ed.). (2009). *Falling down the page: A book of list poems*. New York: Roaring Book.

Herrick, S. (2008). *Naked bunyip dancing*. Asheville, NC: Front Street.

Hopkins, L.B. (Ed.). (1999). *Spectacular science: A book of poems*. New York: Simon & Schuster.

Hopkins, L.B. (Ed.). (2010). *Sharing the seasons: A book of poems*. New York: Margaret K. McElderry.

Hudson, W. (Ed.). (1993). *Pass it on: African-American poetry for children*. New York: Scholastic.

Hughes, L. (2006). *Poetry for young people* (D. Roessel & A. Rampersad, Eds.). New York: Sterling.

Janeczko, P.B. (Ed.). (2001a). *A poke in the I: A collection of concrete poems*. Cambridge, MA: Candlewick.

Janeczko, P.B. (Ed.). (2001b). *Dirty laundry pile: Poems in different voices*. New York: HarperCollins.

Janeczko, P.B. (Ed.). (2005). *A kick in the head: An everyday guide to poetic forms*. Cambridge, MA: Candlewick.

Janeczko, P.B., & Lewis, J.P. (2006). *Wing nuts: Screwy haiku*. New York: Little, Brown.

Lansky, B. (Ed.). (1997). *No more homework! No more tests! Kids' favorite funny school poems*. New York: Meadowbrook.

MacLachlan, P., & Charest, E.M. (2006). *Once I ate a pie*. New York: HarperCollins.

Merriam, E. (1964). *It doesn't always have to rhyme*. New York: Atheneum.

Merriam, E. (1973). *Out loud*. New York: Atheneum.

Mitton, T. (2003). *Plum*. New York: Arthur A. Levine.

Mora, P. (1996). *Confetti: Poems for children*. New York: Lee & Low.

Myers, W.D. (2009). *Looking like me*. New York: Egmont.

Paschen, E. (Ed.). (2005). *Poetry speaks to children*. Naperville, IL: Sourcebooks.

Prelutsky, J. (2010). *Camille Saint-Saëns's* The carnival of the animals. New York: Alfred A. Knopf.

Raschka, C. (2010). *Hip hop dog*. New York: Harper.

Sidman, J. (2010). *Ubiquitous: Celebrating nature's survivors*. Boston: Houghton Mifflin.

Silverstein, S. (1981). *A light in the attic*. New York: Harper & Row.

Silverstein, S. (1996). *Falling up*. New York: HarperCollins.

Singer, M. (2010). *Mirror, mirror: A book of reversible verse*. New York: Dutton.

Weatherford, C.B. (2001). *Sidewalk chalk: Poems of the city*. Honesdale, PA: Wordsong.

Weatherford, C.B. (2006). *Dear Mr. Rosenwald*. New York: Scholastic.

CHAPTER 3

"Getting Started in English": Teaching for Vocabulary Depth With Bilingual Learners

C. Patrick Proctor

Too often, across too many settings in the United States, Latino/a students, particularly those from Spanish-speaking and immigrant households, lack the same access to curriculum and literacy development as their monolingual standard English–speaking peers. Recent statistics reveal that Latinos account for approximately three fourths of all students matriculated in U.S. schools today who speak home languages other than English (Kominski, Shin, & Marotz, 2008). What is disturbing is that Latinos also have the highest high school dropout rate in the United States (22.5%) relative to their African American (10.8%), white (6.0%), and Asian American (2.8%) counterparts (Child Trends DataBank, 2005). In an age when states are increasingly adopting laws that preclude native-language instruction and hasten mainstreaming of students acquiring English as a second language, many teachers struggle to teach to the broadening range of linguistic backgrounds of their students. This issue is further exacerbated by mainstream curricula that are not typically designed from the outset with a broad range of students in mind (Rose & Meyer, 2002). Indeed, the language and content of published curricula tend to be fixed, with appended suggestions for modifying or supplanting assignments and activities for English learners (ELs).

In contrast, my colleagues and I believe that focusing on depth of vocabulary instruction that meets the expectations of state-level curricular frameworks while providing flexibility of content and language (Dalton & Proctor, 2008; Rose & Meyer, 2002) has a strong potential for improving language and literacy outcomes for bilingual students. Quality depth of vocabulary instruction does more than simply teach students more words. It is content-specific, language-based teaching in which students are engaged in relevant, appealing topics that allow them to make connections between words and concepts as well as between languages (in the case

After Early Intervention, Then What? Teaching Struggling Readers in Grades 3 and Beyond (2nd ed.) edited by Jeanne R. Paratore and Rachel L. McCormack. © 2011 by the International Reading Association.

of the research reported within this chapter, Spanish and English). Alternative means of engaging with language, learning, and assessment are key to quality depth instruction.

The following section details three important and interrelated domains of vocabulary depth and the crucial role of the linguistic context of linguistically diverse classrooms. Subsequent sections provide descriptions of these instructional and assessment approaches in the form of overviews of two recently completed projects: Improving Comprehension Online (ICON) and a biliteracy pilot intervention. I conclude with some parting thoughts about depth of vocabulary instruction.

Depth of Vocabulary

In close collaboration with my colleague Silverman (see Proctor & Silverman, 2011), we have identified three domains of vocabulary knowledge that are instructionally robust and applicable in cross-linguistic settings: semantics, morphology, and syntax. Figure 3.1 displays these domains of depth of vocabulary knowledge that have guided the development of the instructional materials and curricula described later in this chapter. Double arrows are placed between each construct to show that aptitude in one domain is often required with another. The linguistic contexts for the work to be described were semiurban classrooms with large percentages of Latino/a students who spoke Spanish in the home and sometimes alongside their monolingual English-speaking peers. Thus, the units and activities that comprised the curricula frequently focused on the similarities and differences between Spanish and English within a depth of vocabulary approach. The three domains and the linguistic context of instruction are discussed in this section.

Semantics

Semantics refers to the conceptual relationships that exist between words. A student with good semantic depth of word knowledge for *table*, for example, understands that this word means something completely different when sitting down for dinner as compared with studying the atomic numbers of the elements in science class. Semantic awareness is characterized by the ability to identify how words are conceptually linked to one another. Developing semantic awareness in students allows for conceptual connections across related words, and for understanding the nuanced ways in which words convey meaning in language and texts. Teachers who adhere to semantically based instruction typically work

Figure 3.1. Depth of Vocabulary Instructional Model

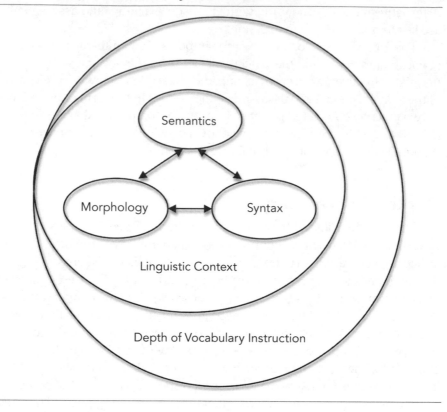

with their students to "identify the relationship between words, respond to words affectively as well as cognitively, and apply words to various contexts" (McKeown, Beck, Omanson, & Pople, 1985, p. 526). Stahl and Nagy (2006) further argue that allowing students to create scenarios from the discussion of single words is a powerful means by which to stimulate deep processing of word meanings, particularly with respect to the multiple contexts in which words occur.

Semantic understandings appear to have a developmental component such that younger students are less likely to have developed strong conceptual associations among more abstract words and ideas, and accordingly, general vocabulary size is sufficient to understand semantic range (Tannenbaum, Torgesen, & Wagner, 2006; Vermeer, 2001). However, research with older elementary school students in grades 3–6 has shown that students' abilities to make conceptual connections among words is associated with reading comprehension above and beyond the role of general vocabulary size (Nation & Snowling, 2004; Oullette, 2006; Proctor, Uccelli, Dalton, & Snow, 2009). Deliberate semantic relations instruction with ELs, then, may serve to provide important conceptual links between different words that students may not have made on their own through reading.

Morphology

Knowledge of the morphology of words enables students to generalize the meaning of root words to their morphological derivations (Kieffer & Lesaux, 2007). Thus, the semantically and morphologically aware student who encounters the word *table* is able to understand its relationship with *tabulate* in a science context. Further, a student who is aware of the meanings of the suffixes *–ness* and *–less*, as well as the prefix *em–*, is able to create and understand a series of new derivations, for example, from the root word *power*, such as *powerless* (an adjective), *powerlessness* (a noun), and *empower* (a verb). Indeed, research that has compared students with strong versus weak morphological awareness has revealed stronger reading profiles for morphologically aware students even when both groups were comparable on general vocabulary knowledge (Carlisle, 2000, 2007; Kieffer & Lesaux, 2008; Nagy, Berninger, & Abbott, 2006). This phenomenon has been observed most keenly among upper elementary–age students, because older students are more likely to have developed stronger language proficiency and thus can make deeper linguistic insights than their younger peers.

Kuo and Anderson (2006) trace this morphological trajectory as moving from inflectional in very young students (e.g., *dog* + *s* = *dogs*), to compound (e.g., *tooth* + *brush* = *toothbrush*), and finally to derivational (e.g., *electric* + *ity* = *electricity*), with the importance of morphological awareness in relation to reading increasing over time. Oral development of morphological awareness proceeds in advance of morphological awareness in print. Children as young as 3 and 4 experiment with derivational morphology in speech, but it is not until students can fluently access the language of written text (i.e., once decoding skills become automatic) that the full potential of morphological awareness on literacy outcomes can be assessed. Upper elementary–age students are thus at a ripe age for introducing morphological awareness into literacy instruction. Morphological awareness instruction may be particularly important with some ELs, because expecting

> morphological analysis to be discovered by students on their own means that those who are in some way challenged by language learning are

likely to be left behind their peers in the development of vocabulary, word reading, and reading comprehension. (Carlisle, 2007, p. 90)

Syntax

The hypothetical student with a deep understanding of the word *table* would be able to parlay his or her semantic and morphological understandings in a syntactic context. Specifically, understanding that *table* is a noun at which one sits during dinner differs from how the word would be used as a scientific noun or verb. At dinner, the student is aware that we sit at the table, but in reading a science text or conducting an experiment, he or she also understands that a table is something to be read or created. Morphologically, the student further comprehends that while *table* is a noun, its derivation, *tabulate,* is a verb. Thus, to create a table, one must tabulate relevant data, perhaps while seated at the dinner table.

Such knowledge of the structure of language is essential for students to appropriately develop and apply their expanding semantic and morphological word knowledge. As students broaden their understandings of particular words, they learn the syntactic constructions in which these words typically and appropriately appear, as well as the words from which other semantic classes commonly co-occur. Syntactic knowledge can be particularly challenging for ELs. Students who are developing syntactic awareness in English may experience interference from syntactic knowledge of their first language (Nation, Clarke, Marshall, & Durand, 2004; Wolter, 2006). For example, a Spanish-speaking student might say "The boy intelligent" in English, which emanates from the correct Spanish syntactic construction "El niño inteligente." While the benefit of direct grammar and syntax instruction is a subject of ongoing debate, direct instruction of semantics and morphology in the context of content learning allows teachers to present syntax and grammar to advance text comprehension, rather than for the sole purpose of improving decontextualized grammatical or syntactic knowledge.

Linguistic Context

The fact that ELs at the very least speak or understand (or both—and, in many cases, read and write) a language in addition to English is important in designing instruction. Recent models of English reading tested with Spanish–English bilingual students suggest that although the reading process can be substantively explained with English reading variables, including Spanish literacy skills tends to improve the fit of these models

(Nakamoto, Lindsey, & Manis, 2008; Proctor, August, Carlo, & Snow, 2006; Uccelli & Páez, 2007).

This cross-linguistic perspective has been most thoroughly researched with respect to the importance of cognate awareness among Spanish–English bilingual learners. A cognate is a word that looks similar and shares meaning across two languages. For example, *tranquil* and *tranquilo* are English–Spanish cognates. Cognate recognition may be especially useful for Spanish–English bilinguals, because conversational words in Spanish (e.g., *tranquilo*) are often less common academic terms in English (e.g., *tranquil*).

One means of recognizing cognates is by simply noting an identical spelling relationship between the two words in question (e.g., *honor* in Spanish and English). However, cognates are also semantically and morphologically bound, and with instruction, bilingual and biliterate students can link affixes and root words across languages. For example, the suffix *–mente* in Spanish always translates to the English suffix *–ly*. Thus, a Spanish–English bilingual who is aware of the cognate relationship between *rapid* and *rápido* and also aware of those consistent cross-linguistic suffix relations would be able to encounter the word *rapidly* and make a link to *rápidamente*. Some research has shown that Spanish–English bilinguals may draw on cognate awareness to make sense of vocabulary and texts, particularly when instruction is targeted toward cognate recognition (Nagy, García, Durgunoğlu, & Hancin-Bhatt, 1993; Proctor & Mo, 2009). Vocabulary instruction that privileges nondominant languages as a means for creating instruction results in bilingual learners receiving linguistically relevant information that is useful for leveraging understanding in English. Their English monolingual counterparts receive exposure to foreign-language learning, which is often a requirement for high school graduation.

Of course, it is not reasonable to expect that all teachers possess adequate proficiency in the native languages of their students. Amazingly, in some U.S. states (specifically, Arizona and Massachusetts, and to a less severe degree, California), it is even illegal to provide literacy instruction in a non-English language! However, depth of vocabulary instruction in linguistically diverse classrooms only requires that teachers know something about the languages their students speak, which can be facilitative when it comes to instruction (and perfectly legal in Arizona, California, and Massachusetts). Swan and Smith (2001) provide detailed descriptions of how English and a variety of languages interact with one another, from orthographic comparisons to rhetorical traditions, providing educators with the means by which to learn about multiple languages while not having to actually acquire them. This type of knowledge is invaluable for classroom teachers of linguistically diverse students.

Having established the instructional components for depth of vocabulary teaching, the subsequent sections are devoted to describing in detail how these were applied in two instructional interventions in linguistically diverse classrooms.

Instructional Approaches and Artifacts: ICON

The first intervention, ICON, was funded by the Institute of Education Sciences. The ICON intervention consisted of an Internet-based series of eight fiction and nonfiction short texts (averaging 1,350 words per text; see Proctor, Dalton, & Grisham, 2007, for details) that were embedded with a number of vocabulary supports designed to leverage comprehension of challenging text. Using the tenets of Universal Design for Learning (see Rose & Meyer, 2002) and in collaboration with Dalton, Uccelli, Snow, and pioneering colleagues at the Center for Applied Special Technology (www .cast.org), we developed the ICON prototype, which can be freely accessed online (psi.cast.org/icon3/demo). The prototype is cross-platform but may perform differently given ever-changing browser configurations. To access, simply type the URL into a browser, choose a class (Teacher 1, 2, or 3 or Test), and select a username (student1, student2, etc.). The password will be the same as the username. Finally, select a level and a text to begin.

Over the course of three years, we iteratively developed, tested, and finalized these supports in response to student learning outcomes and feedback from teachers and students (Dalton, Proctor, Uccelli, Mo, & Snow, 2011), and culminated with a 16-week quasi-experimental intervention with 240 fifth-grade students in 12 classrooms across four schools (Proctor et al., 2011). Students worked two times per week for 50-minute periods individually at computers for the duration of the intervention. The goal was to provide deep vocabulary instruction that formed the foundation of a larger literacy intervention, with comprehension as the ultimate outcome. We infused depth approaches into prereading and within-reading activities, which are described in the next sections.

Prereading Activities

Vocabulary instruction for each text was systematic and occurred both prior to reading and during reading activities. For each text, five "power" words were chosen for a total of 40 words across all eight texts. Selection of the power words was based on four categories:

1. Tier 2 academic register (Beck, McKeown, & Kucan, 2002)
2. Degrees of morphological or semantic richness or both
3. Relatedness with the Spanish translation of the word (i.e., cognates such as *anxiously/ansiosamente*)
4. Centrality of the word's meaning to comprehension of the target text

More than half of the 40 words chosen were Spanish–English cognates and represented a variety of parts of speech, with the additional goal of attending to the role of syntax and grammar. Semantically, a central premise of all activities was not just to teach a word's meaning but also to broaden the students' lexical range. So, when students worked with the word *anxiously*, semantically related terms such as *nervous, agitated, calm*, and *peaceful* were part of the instructional language, as were morphologically related terms such as *anxious* and *anxiety*.

Table 3.1 provides an overview of the instructional activities for the prereading vocabulary work that students completed for each word in the

Table 3.1. Activities That Promote Semantics, Morphology, and Syntax

Activity Group	Activity Name	Description
Wade in	Hear It!	Students click to hear the power word pronounced by a native English speaker.
	Say It!	Students record their own pronunciation of the word.
	Connect It!	Students write or record a personal connection to the power word that uses lived experiences, knowledge, and feelings.
	Language Alert	Students hear a brief message that calls their attention to semantic, morphological, and cross-linguistic relations for the power words.
Dive in	Web It!	Students fill in a word web with the target word at the center. Each target word is surrounded by three related words that represent example/nonexample, synonym/antonym, or situational/nonsituational.
	Caption It!	Students are given an image that relates to the target word and are prompted to write or record a caption for the image that both uses the word and demonstrates understanding of it. Students are encouraged to experiment with statements, dialogues, and questions.

prototype. For every 50-minute intervention session, the students worked for approximately 20 minutes on the prereading activities, after which they spent the remainder of the time reading and responding to the text. During prereading activities, students had consistent access to each word's definition, its Spanish translation, an example sentence, and a relevant image. The digital architecture of ICON aligned with a Universal Design for Learning instructional philosophy (see Dalton & Proctor, 2008; Rose & Meyer, 2002) that embraces technology as a vehicle capable of providing students with multiple means by which to access text. For example, ICON provided students with (a) Spanish and English versions of each text, (b) read-alouds of each text in both languages, and (c) the option of written (typed) and oral (audiotaped) response modalities. Using a Universal Design for Learning approach, we were able to include a much broader array of learners in our study, including students who spoke very little English and native English-speaking students who possessed more limited decoding and fluency skills.

Prereading vocabulary was divided into two groups of activities: Wade In and Dive In. Wade In activities were designed to establish initial familiarity with the words, share existing knowledge that students already possessed about each word, and provide an informational sound bite about each word. Dive In activities were designed for students to work more intensively with the power words in a variety of reading and writing contexts that privileged the semantic, morphological, syntactic, and cross-linguistic characteristics of the words.

In Wade In, students first listened to a recording of a native English speaker pronouncing the power word (the Hear It! activity), after which they recorded themselves pronouncing the word (Say It!). These two activities were designed to provide a phonological anchor for each word (Silverman, 2007), which is good for many monolinguals but essential for English-learning bilinguals. Next, students were prompted by the system to either write or record a personal connection to a given word (Connect It!). This approach of simply asking students, "What do you think about when you hear this word?" resulted in a wealth of information that gave participating teachers input as to where word knowledge was breaking down for students and how their understandings of words and concepts could open up offline instructional avenues. Consider, for example, a student's response to *hospitality*: "I showed hospitality when my grate granfother was in the hospital and he hade kidney problems now he died now i'm really sad and my life has changed without him." Her teacher gained two important insights: First, the student's use of the word showed a misapplication of morphological awareness, as the student extracted the base *hospital*; second, and more important, this particular student's distracted demeanor over the previous two weeks was likely associated with the loss of her grandfather.

In the final segment of Wade In, students listened to a Language Alert that highlighted novel cross-linguistic, morphological, or semantic information about the power word. For example, the alert for the word *anxiously* was, "Think about a Spanish word that looks or sounds like the English word. If they have similar meanings, they are cognates. *Anxiously* and *ansiosamente* are cognates. Is all this talk of cognates making you anxious?"

Dive In activities required students to apply their growing word knowledge more directly in multiple-choice and writing environments that were designed to simultaneously teach and assess students' word knowledge. The first Dive In activity (Web It!) required students to work with a programmed word web (see Figure 3.2 for an example) in which

Figure 3.2. Screenshot of a Web It! Activity for Fifth Graders

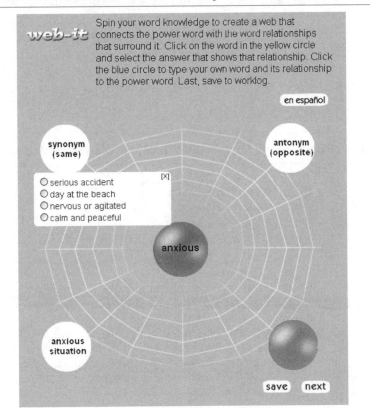

the power word was situated at the center of an illustrated web. Students chose items from a drop-down menu that included examples/nonexamples, synonyms/antonyms, or situations/nonsituations. The point of this activity, however, was not to assess the students' word knowledge directly but to promote it. Thus, when students selected an incorrect response, they were notified by a digital "coach" who appeared on the screen and provided a hint meant to steer the student toward the correct response. Thus, the goal of the activity was 100% correctness, although the system kept track of how many attempts were necessary to arrive at that level of performance. Also important to lexical development, students filled in their own bubble to show a relationship with the power word, which provided another window into their developing word knowledge.

Finally, in the culminating Dive In activity (Caption It!), students viewed a representative image (photograph or clip art) of a target word and were prompted, "Make this image come alive by adding an interesting caption that includes the power word and shows your understanding of the word. Try using statements, dialogues and questions." This final activity was designed to provide a window into the degree of depth of word knowledge that students had developed over the course of the vocabulary activities (see Proctor et al., 2009, for details). We were particularly interested in degrees of semantic depth for this activity and thus developed a semantic scoring inventory that we used to determine degrees of depth of word knowledge. The inventory items and scoring ranges are presented in Table 3.2.

Table 3.2. Writing Rubric for Semantic Depth of Word Knowledge

Item	Scale
Syntactic accuracy	0 = Syntactically inaccurate 1 = Syntactically accurate
Use of target word	0 = Absence of target word 1 = Presence of target word
Semantic depth	1 = Response displays no semantic relation to either the picture or the target word. 2 = Response relates to the picture but is semantically unrelated to the target word. 3 = Response conveys the meaning of the target word in an appropriate but isolated or minimal context. 4 = Response conveys the meaning of the target word in an appropriate and elaborate context, including coherently connected details that serve as evidence of deep understanding of the target meaning.

Note. Scores range from 1 to 6.

Within-Reading Word Work

While the students were reading the texts in the ICON intervention, they were able to access the meanings of many of the texts' words via hyperlink. If a student encountered a word that he or she did not know while reading, a single mouse click would provide the student with a student-friendly definition, the part of speech, an example sentence, the Spanish translation, and a representative image (if appropriate). Further, students were required to maintain a personalized digital word wall (called My Glossary) for each text. To completely finish a given text, a student had to add at least three words to My Glossary and provide an explanation as to why the particular word was chosen. Of course, one reason that students provided for choosing words was the fact that it was required. However, previous work with this prototype indicated that students were posting, on average, 4.3 words per text and that the majority of posts were accompanied by thoughtful reasons, including recalling word meanings and personal connections to words (Proctor et al., 2007).

Results from the final study showed that students who completed the ICON program in its entirety significantly outperformed their control group counterparts on standardized and researcher-developed measures of vocabulary. Further, the Latino/a students in the ICON condition significantly outperformed their monolingual English-speaking counterparts in the control condition on semantic scoring inventory performance, which we assessed using a definition and captioning measure (see Proctor et al., 2011).

Instructional Approaches and Artifacts: Biliteracy Pilot

In the second study, my colleague Vargas and I worked with eight Spanish-speaking EL fourth graders who were enrolled in one school's structured English immersion program, in which they received substantially separate, sheltered instruction in English only, per Massachusetts state law. Vargas and I worked with the students once per week for 90 minutes with most of our instruction conducted in Spanish, applying the tenets of depth of vocabulary instruction derived from the primarily English-language research base described previously. These sessions were held each Monday for 12 weeks during the students' literacy instructional block, taking the place of English literacy instruction for that day. Each weekly session varied in its content, depending on where in a given text the class had left off. However, like the ICON intervention, each class was anchored by vocabulary instruction that set the stage for subsequent activities. The general format for each session was:

- Vocabulary instruction (20 minutes)
- Spanish phonics/phonemic awareness (15 minutes)
- Read aloud with discussion (30 minutes)
- Group project work (25 minutes)

Before beginning the intervention, we conducted an individual structured interview with each of the students, in the student's language of choice, to gain a sense of immigration context, time in the United States, and literacy experiences and attitudes as they related to Spanish and English, the school, and the home. We used an interview protocol that drew on the work of Brisk and Harrington (2007), the components of which are displayed in Table 3.3. Although we directly interviewed the students

Table 3.3. Topics for Fifth-Grade Students' Interviews Before the Biliteracy Pilot Intervention

Family and Immigration	Language and Literacy	Attitudes Toward Language, Literacy, and Culture
Age	Parents' language and literacy skills (in Spanish and English)	Family attitudes toward language and literacy (Spanish and English)
Country of origin	Language(s) used at home	Conceptions of literacy
Date of arrival	Language(s) used for reading and writing in the home	Motivation to read and write in school and at home
Previous school experiences	Home literacy exposure (in Spanish and English)	Preferred topics for reading and writing
Reasons for coming to the United States	First language of literacy development	
Intended length of stay in the United States	English literacy level	
Parents' occupations	Spanish literacy level	
Parents' education levels	Strategies used for reading and writing	

Note. Interviews were conducted in the student's choice of either English or Spanish.

for the purposes of this particular project, other teachers have adapted this protocol by having students interview each other at the beginning of the school year as a means of gleaning important information and allowing students to get to know one another.

We selected texts that were directly related to the backgrounds and histories of the students. We chose the first text, *"Quetzal No Muere Nunca"* ("Quetzal Never Dies"; Barlow, 1995), because it relates directly to Mayan culture and was thus familiar to the Central American and Mexican students who comprised more than half the class. The second text was a descriptive poem of Cuban origin, entitled "Sensemayá" (Guillén, 1937), that very simply describes a snake and relays its treacherous and deadly nature. The poem was also set to music (Guillén & Salinas, 1990) and thus provided another means by which students could access the poem beyond its text base. This poem also served as the impetus for a class project in which all eight students collaborated to create a bilingual poster presentation about "Sensemayá," snakes, and poetry. Finally, *Papelucho* is one of a series of 12 books by a Chilean author (Paz, 1947/1997) about a young boy who makes daily, humorous, and descriptive journal entries that describe the events of his life. This book was particularly robust as a read-aloud, as the colloquial language employed was highly accessible to the students, engaging them in the ruminations of a young child's life experiences. By contrast, when texts were read aloud in English in the structured English immersion classroom, this depth of engagement was noticeably absent, as the students' levels of English proficiency impeded their comprehension of idioms and nuances that make many texts come alive. Because of its length, this text received the bulk of the instructional time, and the majority of the instructed words were selected from this text.

Vocabulary Instruction

All vocabulary instruction was contextual. Words pulled from the three texts were introduced and discussed at the beginning of each weekly session. As with ICON, selecting words for instruction was a complicated endeavor. Recent admonitions among vocabulary researchers indicate that most words selected for instruction "should be very high utility in nature; specifically, the words taught should be general-purpose academic words" (Lesaux, Kieffer, Faller, & Kelley, 2010, p. 198). Hiebert (2005) also cautions against selecting interesting words that have little utility across a variety of academic domains. However, we targeted both high- and low-frequency words with the goal of deriving a semantically rich array of related words and ideas that would bolster comprehension of the text and the target word, as well as promote acquisition of a broader conceptual array. The words, their translations, their cognate status, and the area of instructional focus (semantics, morphology, or both) are displayed in Table 3.4.

The centerpiece of direct vocabulary instruction was the coconstruction of vocabulary maps, in which students generated a student-friendly definition of a word; discussed related words, concepts, and background knowledge; made connections across languages; and considered differing morphological forms of the words. Discussions revolved around personal connections to the words, their English translations, and whether they looked similar or different in their written format (i.e., whether the words were cognates).

One such map targeted the Spanish words *veranear, viaje,* and *costa.* Vargas, a native Spanish speaker, led the group discussion while I took notes on chart paper for the class to reference. All students reported having experienced summer trips, yet they had not encountered the term *veranear* (to go on summer vacation), which provided an opportunity to link with its very familiar derivation *verano* (summer). A definition was determined (*Cuando uno va de vacaciones a otros sitios durante el verano*/When you go on vacation to other places during the summer), and students offered examples from their personal experiences. The term *viaje* (trip), a word with which the students were quite familiar, provided a stable context within which to make a morphological link to its derivation (the verb *viajar*/to travel). A definition for *viaje* was created by the class (*Cuando una persona va a otros sitios*/When a person goes to other places), and the different means by which one might take a trip were discussed. Finally, the word *costa* was discussed, and while the term was quite familiar to the students in Spanish, none knew its English translation (coast), which provided the opportunity to present the English word, discuss the cognate relationship, and generate a variety of semantically related terms along with a third, rather poetic, student-generated definition (*Un lugar que queda al lado del mar*/A place found at the edge of the sea). Table 3.5 displays the nature of the discussion for these three target words and the array of responses generated by area of instructional focus.

Phonics/Phonemic Awareness

Given the wide variability in the students' Spanish literacy skills, it was determined that some attention to sound–symbol relationships and word

Table 3.4. Texts and Vocabulary for the Fifth-Grade Biliteracy Pilot Intervention

Text	Targeted Spanish Word	English Translation	Cognate Status	Depth Characteristics
"Quetzal No Muere Nunca"[a]	Quetzal	Quetzal	Not applicable (name)	Semantic
	Destino	Destiny	Cognate	Semantic
	Predestinación	Predestination	Cognate	Morphological
	Amuleto	Amulet	Cognate	Semantic
"Sensemayá"[b]	Patas	Paws	Noncognate	Semantic
	Pies	Human feet	Noncognate	Semantic
	Culebra	Snake	Noncognate	Semantic
	Serpiente	Serpent	Cognate	Semantic
Papelucho[c]	Diario	Diary	Cognate	Morphological
	Invento	I invent	Cognate	Semantic
	Inventor	Inventor	Cognate	Morphological
	Promesa	Promise	Cognate	Semantic
	Prometer	To promise	Cognate	Semantic
	Veranear	To go on summer vacation	Noncognate	Semantic and morphological
	Viaje	Trip	Noncognate	Semantic and morphological
	Costa	Coast (noun)	Cognate	Semantic awareness
	Mecánico	Mechanic	Cognate	Semantic awareness
	Naufragar	To sink (boat), to shipwreck (person)	Noncognate	Semantic and morphological
	Castigar	To punish or ground, to castigate	Cognate	Semantic awareness

[a]*Quetzal No Muere Nunca* [Quetzal Never Dies], in G. Barlow (Ed.), *Stories From Latin America/Historias de Latinoamérica* (pp. 16–24), Lincolnwood, IL: Passport.
[b]*Sensemayá* [poem], by N. Guillén, 1937, retrieved February 16, 2011, from home.wlu.edu/~barnettj/lit295/guillen.htm.
[c]*Papelucho*, by M. Paz, 1997, Santiago, Chile: Editorial Universitaria, original work published 1947.

Table 3.5. Breakdown of Vocabulary Map for *Veranear*, *Viaje*, and *Costa*

Discussion Category	Veranear	Viaje	Costa
Student-derived definition	*Cuando uno va de vacaciones a otros sitios durante el verano*/When you go on vacation to other places during the summer	*Cuando una persona va a otros sitios*/When a person goes to other places	*Un lugar que queda al lado del mar*/A place found at the edge of the sea
Semantic derivations	*Campo*/country	*Avión*/jet	*Playa*/beach
	Descanso/rest	*Bote*/boat	*Mar*/sea
	Países/countries	*Barco*/ship	*Sol*/sun
	Piscina/swimming pool	*Carro*/car	
	Playa/beach	*Auto*/car, automobile	
	Vacaciones/vacation	*Lambourghini*/ lamborghini	
		Moto/motorcycle	
		Bicicleta/bicycle	
		Tren/train	
		Andar/to walk	
		Camioneta/van	
		Autobús/bus	
		Guagua/bus (caribbean origin)	
Morphological derivations	*Verano*/summer	*Viajar*/to travel	Not applicable
Cross-linguistic connections	A single word in Spanish has no direct translation in English (i.e., to go on summer vacation).	Not applicable	Cognate relationship: *costa* and *coast*

recognition was necessary. However, as there was limited instructional time in any given week, we wanted to steer clear of typical seatwork practices in the decoding arena that many students find tedious and uninteresting. We also sought to take advantage of the facilitative links that have been found between spelling and phonemic awareness (Byrne & Fielding-Barnsley, 1991). In response, we developed a game we called

Creapalabras (a loose translation is Word Creation), in which students formed heterogeneous groups with high and low levels of Spanish reading and writing proficiency. Each group was then provided a single worksheet that allowed students to work with two or more consonants and all five vowels. Using only the allowed consonants and any vowel, the groups created and wrote down as many words as possible in a 10-minute session. If two or more groups came up with the same word, that word was eliminated. Invented words were disqualified if the students could not define it and use it appropriately in a sentence. Students found this to be an engaging activity that served to promote spelling, phonemic, and phonological awareness, but the most striking aspect of this activity was the students' discussion about the words they created and whether they were genuine or invented. Ultimately, *Creapalabras* merged vocabulary learning with text-level skills development.

Read-Alouds

Drawing on the work of Santoro, Chard, Howard, and Baker (2008), we took advantage of the oral language context of read-alouds to create rich dialogic spaces in which the focus of instruction was on text comprehension, vocabulary development, and language structure. Having introduced the relevant vocabulary words earlier in the class, we began with the read-aloud, stopping repeatedly for students to share insights about their countries (e.g., *"Quetzal No Muere Nunca"* takes place in Guatemala), provide knowledge they possessed about the biology or nature of snakes (*Sensemayá* is a frightening snake described in great detail in the poem), or relate to Papelucho's inability to understand how adults speak to one another.

As the read-alouds progressed and target vocabulary was encountered, time was taken to recognize the word and also discuss the syntactic structure in which the word occurred. For instance, the word *naufragar* generated a discussion focused on the syntactic uses of the term. In Spanish, *naufragar* has two meanings depending on the context in which the word occurs. The word can be used to give action to a sinking boat (i.e., to sink) but can also be used to give action to the person on the boat who survives on a desert island (i.e., to be shipwrecked). Discussions often centered around the ways in which language was used to convey meaning, particularly with respect to the vocabulary words targeted by a given read-aloud.

Group Project Work

In the interest of promoting student–student dialogic interactions, we devoted considerable instructional time for the students to work in small groups to create a poster that was presented to their class as well as in the weekly whole-school assembly. The students were quite interested in the poem and song "*Sensemayá*" and elected to expand on this text for their group presentation. As a whole group, we discussed the students' interests in snakes and poetry, and students were placed together in their interest groups. Nicolas, Ingrid, and Antonio (all student names are pseudonyms) focused on poetry and Spanish–English translation. Nicolas translated the original poem from Spanish into English, Ingrid decided to write a poem in Spanish that expressed her abiding revulsion toward snakes, and Antonio translated Ingrid's poem into English.

Veronica and Karen, who showed relatively strong Spanish literacy profiles, were interested in learning more about snakes and asked research questions about the nature of snakes and reproduction, which they independently researched. Fernando and Carlos, both of whom possessed more limited literacy skills in Spanish, discussed what they knew about snakes and decided to follow up with more detailed, supported research that allowed them to elaborate on their knowledge. Finally, Leandro and Antonio worked together to create illustrations of Veronica and Karen's investigations. The students paid particular attention to the cognates *serpent* and *serpiente* in their framing of the poster, while also making sure that their organization was clear to an uninformed audience. An image of the final poster is presented in Figure 3.3.

The biliteracy pilot was nonexperimental. However, students showed statistically significant growth in three areas: Spanish decoding skill, English vocabulary, and English reading comprehension. Students also took a researcher-developed English vocabulary posttest that included equal numbers of cognate and noncognate items (August et al., 2001); 5% of the students' correct responses on this test were the Spanish–English cognate items (e.g., *rapid, tranquil*).

Equally important to the research was the students' voices as an evaluation measure. Students were interviewed postintervention to gain an understanding of response to intervention that privileged their opinions alongside the standardized and researcher-developed assessment measures. In responding to questions targeting the pilot and their attitudes toward language, students focused more intently on how Spanish remains a part of their everyday lives and how its maintenance provides a structure for community and identity. Students also discussed cross-linguistic awareness, providing instructional direction when considering

Figure 3.3. Fifth-Grade Group Poster Presentation After the Biliteracy Pilot Intervention

native language use in linguistically diverse classrooms. These findings are summed up nicely in this exchange between a teacher and her students following a presentation of the group poster:

Teacher: What was the fun part of learning in Spanish and English?

Antonio: It's because we got to learn more English words, and in Spanish if you knew a word, you could get starting in English.

Nicolas: And too also, that, like, the Spanish class helps you to learn not to forget your language.

Karen: And the fun, I think, it was to work together hard and make the project. And for learning more new words.

In response to the teacher's very simple question, Karen offered the notion of a classroom community where the goal "was to work together hard and make the project." Nicolas provided insight into identity, suggesting that Spanish maintenance "helps you to learn not to forget your language." Finally, Antonio made the cross-linguistic connection, noting that "in Spanish if you knew a word, you could get starting in English."

Conclusion

In this chapter, I describe a linguistically driven approach to deep vocabulary instruction that can be designed to meet the needs of monolingual and bilingual learners in mainstream or substantially separate settings. Although the linguistic contexts of classrooms vary tremendously, there is increasing evidence that depth of vocabulary instruction can help bridge linguistic differences between students in linguistically diverse classrooms. Linguistic diversity and awareness among teachers is of importance in a 21st-century educational landscape where instructional differentiation is key to ensuring that all students have comparable curricular access.

TRY IT!

1. Recall the Wade In and Dive In activities described in this chapter. Choose a few words related to a text that students are about to read and consider how you would apply the recommended guidelines for engaging students in word study. In particular, consider which words you will showcase as power words. What tasks will you use to help students think about semantic, morphological, syntactic, and cross-linguistic characteristics of the words? Ask your students to make the power words come alive by adding interesting captions that include the power words and shows understanding of the words by using statements, dialogues, and questions.

2. Based on the description in this chapter, what types of activities would you use to prompt productive group work? Which of the instructional activities and tasks in this chapter would you use to prepare your students for successful work within their small groups? What type of task will you use to have students display the work they accomplished together? What framework or task will you use to draw students together and share the work they completed in small groups?

NOTES

The ICON project was funded by a grant (R305G050029) from the Institute of Education Sciences within the U.S. Department of Education to CAST, Inc. The opinions expressed are those of the author and do not represent views of the Institute or the U.S. Department of Education. The work reported in this chapter would not have been possible without the participating students and teachers, who continue to inspire.

REFERENCES

August, D., Kenyon, D., Malabonga, V., Louguit, M., Caglarcan, S., & Carlo, M. (2001). *Cognate Awareness Test*. Washington, DC: Center for Applied Linguistics.

Beck, I.L., McKeown, M.G., & Kucan, L. (2002). *Bringing words to life: Robust vocabulary instruction*. New York: Guilford.

Brisk, M.E., & Harrington, M.M. (2007). *Literacy and bilingualism: A handbook for all teachers* (2nd ed.). Mahwah, NJ: Erlbaum.

Byrne, B., & Fielding-Barnsley, R. (1991). Evaluation of a program to teach phonemic awareness to young children. *Journal of Educational Psychology, 83*(4), 451–455. doi:10.1037/0022-0663.83.4.451

Carlisle, J.F. (2000). Awareness of the structure and meaning of morphologically complex words: Impact on reading. *Reading and Writing, 12*(3/4), 169–190.

Carlisle, J.F. (2007). Fostering morphological processing, vocabulary development, and reading comprehension. In R.K. Wagner, A.E. Muse, & K.R. Tannenbaum (Eds.), *Vocabulary acquisition: Implications for reading comprehension* (pp. 78–103). New York: Guilford.

Child Trends DataBank. (2005). *Dropout rates*. Washington, DC: Author. Retrieved March 18, 2009, from www.childtrendsdatabank.org/pdf/1_PDF.pdf

Dalton, B., & Proctor, C.P. (2008). The changing landscape of text and comprehension in the age of new literacies. In J. Coiro, M. Knobel, C. Lankshear, & D.J. Leu (Eds.), *Handbook of research on new literacies* (pp. 297–324). New York: Erlbaum.

Dalton, B., Proctor, C.P., Uccelli, P., Mo, E., & Snow, C.E. (2011). Designing for diversity: The role of reading strategies and interactive vocabulary in a digital reading environment for fifth-grade monolingual English and bilingual students. *Journal of Literacy Research, 43*(1), 68–100.

Guillén, N. (Writer), & Salinas, H. (Composer). (1990). Sensemayá [Recorded by Inti-Illimani]. On *Leyenda* [CD]. New York: Sony.

Hiebert, E.H. (2005). In pursuit of an effective, efficient vocabulary curriculum for elementary students. In E.H. Hiebert & M.L. Kamil (Eds.), *Teaching and learning vocabulary: Bringing research to practice* (pp. 249–269). Mahwah, NJ: Erlbaum.

Kieffer, M.J., & Lesaux, N.K. (2007). Breaking down words to build meaning: Morphology, vocabulary, and reading comprehension in the urban classroom. *The Reading Teacher, 61*(2), 134–144. doi:10.1598/RT.61.2.3

Kieffer, M.J., & Lesaux, N.K. (2008). The role of derivational morphology in the reading comprehension of Spanish-speaking English language learners. *Reading and Writing, 21*(8), 783–804. doi:10.1007/s11145-007-9092-8

Kominski, R.A., Shin, H.B., & Marotz, K. (2008, April). *Language needs of school-age children.* Paper presented at the annual meeting of the Population Association of America, New Orleans, LA.

Kuo, L., & Anderson, R.C. (2006). Morphological awareness and learning to read: A cross-language perspective. *Educational Psychologist, 41*(3), 161–180. doi:10.1207/s15326985ep4103_3

Lesaux, N.K., Kieffer, M.J., Faller, S.E., & Kelley, J.G. (2010). The effectiveness and ease of implementation of an academic vocabulary intervention for linguistically diverse students in urban middle schools. *Reading Research Quarterly, 45*(2), 196–228. doi:10.1598/RRQ.45.2.3

McKeown, M.G., Beck, I.L., Omanson, R.C., & Pople, M.T. (1985). Some effects of the nature and frequency of vocabulary instruction on the knowledge and use of words. *Reading Research Quarterly, 20*(5), 522–535.

Nagy, W.E., Berninger, V.W., & Abbott, R.D. (2006). Contributions of morphology beyond phonology to literacy outcomes of upper elementary and middle-school students. *Journal of Educational Psychology, 98*(1), 134–147.

Nagy, W.E., García, G.E., Durgunoğlu, A., & Hancin-Bhatt, B. (1993). Spanish–English bilingual children's use and recognition of cognates in English reading. *Journal of Reading Behavior, 25*(3), 241–259.

Nakamoto, J., Lindsey, K.A., & Manis, F.R. (2008). A cross-linguistic investigation of English language learners' reading comprehension in English and Spanish. *Scientific Studies of Reading, 12*(4), 351–371. doi:10.1080/10888430802378526

Nation, K., Clarke, P., Marshall, C.M., & Durand, M. (2004). Hidden language impairments in children: Parallels between poor reading comprehension and specific language impairment? *Journal of Speech, Language, and Hearing Research, 47*(1), 199–211. doi:10.1044/1092-4388(2004/017)

Nation, K., & Snowling, M.J. (2004). Beyond phonological skills: Broader language skills contribute to the development of reading. *Journal of Research in Reading, 27*(4), 342–356. doi:10.1111/j.1467-9817.2004.00238.x

Oullette, G.P. (2006). What's meaning got to do with it: The role of vocabulary in word reading and reading comprehension. *Journal of Educational Psychology, 98*(3), 554–566.

Proctor, C.P., August, D., Carlo, M.S., & Snow, C.E. (2006). The intriguing role of Spanish language vocabulary knowledge in predicting English reading comprehension. *Journal of Educational Psychology, 98*(1), 159–169.

Proctor, C.P., Dalton, B., & Grisham, D. (2007). Scaffolding English language learners and struggling readers in a multimedia hypertext environment with embedded strategy instruction and vocabulary support. *Journal of Literacy Research, 39*(1), 71–93.

Proctor, C.P., Dalton, B., Uccelli, P., Biancarosa, G., Mo, E., Snow, C., et al. (2011). Improving comprehension online (ICON): Effects of deep vocabulary instruction with bilingual and monolingual fifth graders. *Reading and Writing: An Interdisciplinary Journal, 24*(5), 517–544.

Proctor, C.P., & Mo, E. (2009). The relationship between cognate awareness and English comprehension among Spanish–English bilingual fourth grade students. *TESOL Quarterly, 13*(1), 126–136.

Proctor, C.P., & Silverman, R.D. (2011). Confounds in assessing biliteracy and English language proficiency. *Educational Researcher, 40*(2), 62–64.

Proctor, C.P., Uccelli, P., Dalton, B., & Snow, C.E. (2009). Understanding depth of vocabulary online with bilingual and monolingual children. *Reading & Writing Quarterly, 25*(4), 311–333. doi:10.1080/10573560903123502

Rose, D.H., & Meyer, A. (with Strangman, N., & Rappolt, G.). (2002). *Teaching every student in the digital age: Universal design for learning.* Alexandria, VA: Association for Supervision and Curriculum Development.

Santoro, L.E., Chard, D.J., Howard, L., & Baker, S.K. (2008). Making the *very* most of classroom read-alouds to promote comprehension and vocabulary. *The Reading Teacher, 61*(5), 396–408. doi:10.1598/RT.61.5.4

Silverman, R.D. (2007). Vocabulary development of English-language and English-only learners in kindergarten. *The Elementary School Journal, 107*(4), 365–383.

Stahl, S.A., & Nagy, W.E. (2006). *Teaching word meanings.* Mahwah, NJ: Erlbaum.

Swan, M., & Smith, B. (Eds). (2001). *Learner English: A teacher's guide to interference and other problems* (2nd ed.). New York: Cambridge University Press. doi:10.1017/CBO9780511667121

Tannenbaum, K.R., Torgesen, J.K., & Wagner, R.K. (2006). Relationships between word knowledge and reading comprehension in third-grade children. *Scientific Studies of Reading, 10*(4), 381–398. doi:10.1207/s1532799xssr1004_3

Uccelli, P., & Páez, M.M. (2007). Narrative and vocabulary development of bilingual children from kindergarten to first grade: Developmental changes and associations among English and Spanish skills. *Language, Speech, and Hearing Services in Schools, 38*(3), 225–236. doi:10.1044/0161-1461(2007/024)

Vermeer, A. (2001). Breadth and depth of vocabulary in relation to L1/L2 acquisition and frequency of input. *Applied Psycholinguistics, 22*(2), 217–234. doi:10.1017/S0142716401002041

Wolter, B. (2006). Lexical network structures and L2 vocabulary acquisition: The role of L1 lexical/conceptual knowledge. *Applied Linguistics, 27*(4), 741–747. doi:10.1093/applin/aml036

LITERATURE CITED

Barlow, G. (Ed.). (1995). *Quetzal No Muere Nunca* [Quetzal Never Dies]. In *Stories from Latin America/Historias de Latinoamérica* (pp. 16–24). Lincolnwood, IL: Passport.

Guillén, N. (1937). *Sensemayá* [Poem]. Retrieved February 16, 2011, from home .wlu.edu/~barnettj/lit295/guillen.htm

Paz, M. (1997). *Papelucho.* Santiago, Chile: Editorial Universitaria. (Original work published 1947)

CHAPTER 4

Research-Based Vocabulary Instruction: Recommendations for Struggling Readers

Karen D. Wood, Janis M. Harmon, Brian Kissel, and Wanda B. Hedrick

"Mrs. Jackson, what is *rag out*? I'm reading an online article about France for our social studies project, and it says something about a vegetable ragout and something about ratatouille. I think it's a food they eat in France because of the word *vegetable* in front of it. I saw a movie about a mouse, and I know *ratatouille* is French for soup or something like that. At least, that's what I think."

"You're really using the context and your own experiences to help you figure out what that word means, Jason. It's a French word like *ratatouille*, which you remembered from the movie. It's actually pronounced 'ra-goo',' which is different from how it looks by the spelling."

This vignette illustrates how a teacher provides prior instruction to help a student develop word awareness and word knowledge by using a combination of context and prior experiences. It also illustrates how important strategic vocabulary knowledge is in the reading and understanding of all types of text. Yet, growth in vocabulary is neither constant nor consistent across students (Chall, Jacobs, & Baldwin, 1990; White, Graves, & Slater, 1990). Struggling readers have more difficulties with vocabulary knowledge with each successive grade level, as more technical vocabulary is introduced, and more sophisticated words (e.g., *ragout, ratatouille*) are encountered.

From their study of the effects of prior knowledge and vocabulary in science, Rupley and Slough (2010) have identified four levels of learners found in almost every intermediate- and middle-level classroom:

After Early Intervention, Then What? Teaching Struggling Readers in Grades 3 and Beyond (2nd ed.) edited by Jeanne R. Paratore and Rachel L. McCormack. © 2011 by the International Reading Association.

1. *Struggling readers*—These students have difficulty reading and comprehending informational text, and their problems are compounded from grade to grade.

2. *English learners*—Generalizing from the Valencia and Buly study of 2004, which identified types of struggling readers, Rupley and Slough estimate that 60–70% of students struggling in intermediate-level classrooms are students for whom English is a second language.

3. *Breakthrough learners*—These students readily accumulate facts but need strategic instruction to help them make inferences and engage in deeper processing.

4. *Conceptual learners*—These learners are able to integrate their personal experiences and prior knowledge with content from multiple sources to engage in more complex thinking.

This classification system illustrates the broad range of ability levels prevalent in our classrooms today and suggests the many challenges that teachers face in planning and implementing effective instruction.

The suggestions provided in this chapter for developing the vocabulary and conceptual knowledge of struggling readers have been updated from previous reviews of the research on this topic (Harmon, Hedrick, & Wood, 2005; Wood, Harmon, & Hedrick, 2004). Teachers help students develop their vocabulary and conceptual knowledge by doing the following:

- Providing opportunities to engage in independent reading with texts that students can read (Allington, 2001; Harmon & Wood, 2001; Krashen, 2009; Nagy, 1988; Nagy & Anderson, 1984)

- Using contextual-based approaches (Chall & Snow, 1988; Graves, 1987)

- Allowing students to self-select terms to be studied (Carr, 1985; Harmon, Wood, Hedrick, & Gress, 2008; Ruddell & Shearer, 2002)

- Teaching key vocabulary explicitly (Merkley & Jefferies, 2000; D. Taylor, Mraz, Nichols, Rickelman, & Wood, 2009)

- Providing opportunities for multiple exposures to key terms (Manzo, Manzo, & Thomas, 2006; McKeown, Beck, Omanson, & Pople, 1985; Nagy, 1988; Stahl & Fairbanks, 1986)

- Avoiding drill and practice activities (Beck & McKeown, 1991; Ciborowski, 1992; Nagy, 1988)

- Introducing morphemic analysis strategies (Milligan & Ruff, 1990; Vacca, Vacca, & Mraz, 2011)

- Providing staff development training in effective vocabulary instruction (Blachowicz, Fisher, Ogle, & Watts-Taffe, 2006; Carr, 1985; Chall & Snow, 1988; Harmon, Katims, & Whittington, 1999; Walpole & McKenna, 2004)

For this chapter, we have taken these research findings, updated them, and divided them into three major recommendations for effective instruction for struggling readers: (1) promoting active engagement and interest in vocabulary development where we discuss the need to provide opportunities for practice in and exposure to reading all types of text, (2) using scaffolded instruction to teach vocabulary, which presents explicit models for teaching context clues and morphemic analysis, and (3) integrating technology with vocabulary instruction where we explore how new literacies can be used to motivate struggling readers as they build their vocabulary knowledge.

Promoting Active Engagement and Interest in Vocabulary Development

The need to engage learners of all ability levels in the learning of new vocabulary is a well-established fact. Simply memorizing a list of words, relying on glossary definitions, or using word puzzles are insufficient ways for ensuring a deep and lasting level of learning. As we see in the following sections, engaged learning activities for enhancing vocabulary knowledge are meaningful and thought-provoking, often involving peer interaction along with opportunities to read and self-select appealing and appropriate literature.

Provide Opportunities to Read

Common sense dictates that the more students read, the better and stronger they will be as readers. Just as athletes spend hours practicing their chosen sport and musicians devote large chunks of time playing their instruments to excel, we cannot expect struggling readers to become proficient readers without spending ample time engaged in silent, independent reading both at home and at school. Abundant evidence exists for the need to focus on independent reading alongside the remedial program to help students reading below grade level develop the habit of reading on their own (Spear-Swerling, 2005). Furthermore, there is an extensive body of research, both nationally and internationally, that indicates a strong relationship between the amount of time students engage in reading and their achievement in reading (Anderson, Hiebert, Scott, & Wilkinson, 1985; Anderson, Wilson , & Fielding, 1988; Elley, 1992; B. Taylor, Frye, & Maruyama, 1990). Research tells us that exposure to books in the form of independent reading and reading aloud to students is a viable and valuable means of developing the vocabularies of all ability levels of learners (Cunningham, 2005; Elley, 1989). In fact, there is research on vocabulary development to support the benefits of reading books over direct instruction (Anderson, 1996; Nagy & Herman, 1987).

The most important goal of any type of reading instruction is the extent to which it leads to lifelong reading habits (Irvin, 1998; Krashen, 2009). Engagement in silent, independent reading helps meet this goal by offering numerous benefits to students, including the following:

- Increases motivation to read
- Allows students the time they need to practice their reading skill silently
- Increases reading comprehension, vocabulary, fluency, and overall reading achievement
- Gives students ownership in what they are doing
- Allows choice, as students self-select the books they want to read
- Enables students to read books they can handle
- Fosters positive attitudes toward reading
- Provides opportunities for students to acquire new knowledge about vocabulary, concepts, and ideas
- Exposes students to a variety of writing styles and formats

Achieving such outcomes through independent reading, however, is jeopardized by at least two circumstances. First, an oft-cited study by Ivey and Broaddus (2001) reveals that although students enjoy the opportunity to engage in independent reading and look forward to that time, the books they are asked to read are often irrelevant and uninteresting, which diminishes the readers' engagement and the likelihood of positive effects. Second, in many classrooms, time spent focusing on high-stakes testing has replaced previously allocated time for independent reading.

The fact that as students get older, they tend to spend less time reading out of school because of an increase in extracurricular activities, electronic games, and other sources of entertainment that catch the attention of adolescents heightens the need to create classroom environments that support independent reading. Ideally, students are provided opportunities to read silently either daily or at least two or three times a week for

15–20 minutes; regardless of the frequency, it is important to maintain a consistent schedule so that students come to class expecting time to engage in reading independently. By allotting an elevated status to independent reading, students learn that engagement in voluntary reading is a highly valued and critical aspect of their reading development.

To develop and maintain an effective independent reading program, students need access to books from well-stocked school and classroom libraries containing a variety of books, articles, and magazines on different topics and at different reading levels. In high-poverty communities, school access to reading materials and a print-rich environment is a critical factor, since it is well established that students living in low-income neighborhoods often have less access to books (Neuman & Celano, 2001), fewer books at home (Feitelson & Goldstein, 1986), and in the case of students for whom English is a second language, insufficient access to books in English (Kim & Krashen, 1997).

Students also need specific guidelines to follow from the beginning of the school year. First and foremost, students need opportunities to choose their independent reading books. Self-selection builds a sense of ownership and often determines the success of independent reading programs. Second, students need to understand that it is acceptable to discontinue reading a book if it is not interesting to them. A good rule of thumb is to encourage students not to abandon the book until they have read at least 10 pages. Schoenbach, Greenleaf, Cziko, and Hurwitz (1999) claim that when it comes to pleasure reading, "abandoning a book...isn't the sign of a poor reader but of an intelligent, discriminating reader who knows what he or she wants from reading" (p. 65). Third, students need to know that it is acceptable to read "easy" books below their reading level and "hard" books above their level (Krashen, 2005).

An issue for teachers of struggling readers, and other students as well, is the challenge of helping students stay attuned to their self-selected texts during independent reading time and making that time instructionally meaningful. One suggestion is focused serial retellings, adapted from serial retellings (Wood, 2002) by Ms. Scott, one of our classroom teaching colleagues. Ms. Scott has observed that focused serial retellings help especially reluctant or struggling readers stay interested and engaged during independent reading time. These retellings are based on the premise that the first thing you want to do when you read a good book is share it.

In serial retellings, the teacher allows students to read their books silently for about 10 minutes (not the usual, uninterrupted 20 or 30 minutes previously advocated). After this time, students are instructed to share, with a partner, something from the book that is interesting, such as a character, event, or word. The dyads share their "news" for a few minutes, and then the teacher tells them to return to their silent reading time for 10 minutes more. Their sharing session is repeated, but this time with a little more information than before. Ms. Scott's adaptation involves focusing students' attention on specific words that they find interesting and want to share or on particular skills and strategies (e.g., inferencing, connecting with prior experiences, predicting story outcomes).

The dialogue that follows shows how focused serial retellings helps readers in Ms. Scott's class become more word conscious. Logan is reading *Water Sky* by Jean Craighead George (1987), and his partner, Haya, an English learner, has just begun *Dogsong* by Gary Paulsen (1987).

Logan: Remember how I told you that Lincoln was there to find his Uncle Jack? He wanted to help the Eskimos find other resources besides killing whales, and now he disappeared.

Haya: What happened to him?

Logan: I don't know yet, but Lincoln is going out on a whaling expedition. He has to wear white like his new Eskimo friends, because the whales perceive people in dark clothes and swim away.

Haya: Yeah, so they have to match the snow and ice, huh? That makes sense.

Logan: So, in this chapter, Lincoln is at a whaling camp with people who knew his Uncle Jack, but nobody can tell him where he is. They are on the lookout for types of whales: the baleen, the bowhead, the humpback. They are saying that the Taniks, the white people, don't think they should hunt the whale, and Uncle Jack was one of them. The word I want to learn and start using is *quota*. See on page 41, it says, "When we get our quota, we stop whaling." That's like a set amount.

Haya: My dad has a quota he has to reach each month in his sales job.

Logan: Yeah, or our teacher could say we have to increase our quota of homework assignments, but let's hope she doesn't say that!

Haya: Well, hearing about your book got me interested in Eskimos, so I started reading *Dogsong* by Gary Paulsen. It starts off with Russel and his father who hunt caribou. They have a food cache, which is an elevated wooden hut filled with caribou, fish, and seal meat. So, my word is *cache*. It is like a storage place for important things. I have a cache of pencils and other valuables in my desk.

Logan: Me, too, but I'm not telling you where my cache is or what's in it.

Haya: They also talk about the *umiak*, the skin boat, just like your book does, but your book spells it *umiaq*. I am finding out about Oogruk, who is old and tells stories and songs. I think he is going to be important for this story. I'll tell you what I find out about him after we finish the next reading.

Provide Opportunities for Choice

Research has shown that readers of all ability levels are motivated to read when teachers encourage students to choose their own books and reading materials, and ask students to conduct a thorough study of self-selected words from those readings (Dunston & Gambrell, 2009; Guthrie & Davis, 2003; Ruddell & Shearer, 2002). With the value of student choice and input as our rationale, we conducted a study of our "pick a word—not just any word" strategy with middle school students (Harmon et al., 2008). Ninety-four eighth-grade students participated, half of whom were reading at or above grade level and the other half reading below grade level. Students read passages on the Holocaust and were asked to identify five or six words that they felt were important for understanding the passage. We also asked adult educators to select words, then we made comparisons with their choices to the students' choices. Among our findings was the realization that students of varied ability levels are able to self-select terms critical to understanding. Although some students selected words that were not considered important by the adult educators, the students were able to provide reasons that actually pertained to the main points of the passage. Of further interest was the variability of word selections across the adult readers, a finding of which may be the result of the complex relationship between reading and comprehension as well as individual text interpretations.

The pick-a-word strategy consists of four phases and includes different learning contexts using whole-class, small-group, and individual contributions. In the first phase, the teacher models by thinking aloud the how, why, and what of the self-selection process using a passage with familiar content to transfer to actual material used in the content classroom. Then, with the teacher as guide, students are divided into two large groups, with each large group reading a different text about the same topic. Each large group is divided into two subgroups, and each subgroup selects important words to learn based on the passage they are reading. In the second phase, once both subgroups of each large group have their lists of words, students share within their large groups why they think their selected words are important. These subgroups then work collaboratively to determine the most important terms to be learned by all group members. They combine information from the content sources, both online and traditional text, which leads to a definition and deeper understanding of the target terms. Having students fill out a chart with three headings (i.e., words we need to know, why we should learn them, additional information) helps facilitate this process.

In the third phase, the two large groups meet separately and decide on a spokesperson. After the discussion and comparison of words, the group members decide which words to include in the teaching presentation, again giving reasons why the chosen words are important. Last, the participants in each large group decide on a format (e.g., PowerPoint, game, poster, performance) for presenting their words. Then, in the fourth and final phase, the students share their work with the whole class.

During each of these phases, the teacher is actively involved in the work of the large groups and the subgroups, monitoring their progress and prompting them to reconsider their decisions when chosen words are not important to the unit under study. Teachers can also develop checklists for the final presentation and rubrics to help assess and evaluate the content.

Provide Multiple Exposures in Multiple Contexts

Students, particularly those who struggle with print, need multiple exposures to significant vocabulary and in multiple contexts (McKeown et al., 1985). Multiple exposures can take many forms, including repeated readings, games, discussions, and writing activities. All of these forms have the potential to assist in deeper processing and broader conceptual knowledge (Baumann, Edwards, Boland, Olejnik, & Kame'enui, 2003; Baumann & Kame'enui, 2004; Beck, McKeown, & Kucan, 2002). Of particular importance is the need to focus on vocabulary within the before, during, and after framework (Vacca et al., 2011); that is, preteach significant terms in the before-reading stage of a lesson, highlight the terms in context while reading in the during stage, and then review, reinforce, and apply the new learning after the reading.

Manzo and colleagues (2006) advocate what they call a "community of language" (p. 616), which is based on an understanding that school is not "merely preparation for life; it is a part of life" (p. 617). Thus, in this approach, much like the sustained silent reading approach, the entire school participates in reading, and the school personnel, including the teachers, principal, and administrative and cafeteria staff, collectively focus on the language and vocabulary that they encountered when reading the shared book. In the school that Manzo et al. describe, a predetermined list of words is selected from a unit of instruction, various interdisciplinary lessons, the Scholastic Aptitude Test, or other test preparation sources. Then, everyone on the school staff is asked to use these words as often as possible throughout the school day. The words appear in varied settings (target words are **bold**):

- *The morning announcements*—"Our football team will be headed to more **bucolic** surroundings as they take on our neighbors in the valley. Yes, they will leave the city for the countryside to play Sun Valley Middle School."
- *The cafeteria*—"In case you have a **gargantuan** appetite today, I can put two helpings on your plate."
- *A computer screen in a classroom*—"**Abstain** from **adversity** and always be **amicable** to one another."

In this way, students' awareness of words is elevated while their learning and exposure occurs in a daily, meaningful context, deliberate yet not didactic. Nonetheless, we cannot expect that students will learn and retain their knowledge of key terms through incidental learning or multiple exposures alone; sometimes it is necessary to provide more direct instruction in the form of scaffolded teaching and learning with modeling, explanation, group, and individual practice. In the next section, we describe various scaffolded approaches to teaching vocabulary to struggling readers and students of all ability levels.

Using Scaffolded Instructional Approaches to Teach Vocabulary

Instructional approaches to teaching vocabulary are multifaceted and varied. For example, we generally have a specific focus or purpose for the type of vocabulary instruction we implement. In teaching a short story, the focus may be the words the author uses to describe the setting. In a science lesson, the vocabulary focus may be conceptually loaded words or the procedural terms for helping students navigate through the conceptual ideas presented. Some lessons may highlight the multiple meanings of some words, whereas other lessons may address synonyms, antonyms, idioms, and other categories of word meanings. Regardless of focus or purpose, appropriate, explicit instruction is especially needed for students who struggle with reading and language issues.

One particular type of vocabulary instruction involves helping students develop independent word learning strategies that will enable them to become lifelong word learners. These strategies include using context clues to decipher word meanings, recognizing word parts such as prefixes and roots to unlock meanings, and even resorting to outside references. This type of instruction, however, is more demanding than instruction involving predetermined words. Strategy teaching involves preparing students to strategically approach unfamiliar words in naturally occurring contexts while reading independently. Although difficult to teach, this type of instruction is critical for helping struggling adolescent readers, who often are not strategic in approaching unfamiliar words and, as a result, are unable to infer word meanings in connected texts (Jenkins, Stein, & Wysocki, 1984). Furthermore, struggling readers are impeded by their lack of metacognitive awareness of what they do when they approach unfamiliar words in reading (Lubliner & Smetana, 2005). Given the exponential increase in vocabulary acquisition needed to handle the reading demands of middle and high school academics (Miller & Gildea, 1987; Nagy & Herman, 1987), it is imperative that vocabulary instructional practices include time for teaching independent word learning strategies.

In the following sections, we provide examples of both explicit instruction for teaching targeted words and instruction for teaching independent word learning strategies.

Provide Explicit Instruction of Specific Words

One of the most effective instructional formats for teaching vocabulary comes from the work of Beck and her colleagues (2002). Their direct approach highlights several important features, including (a) clear, understandable definitions, (b) use of instructional contexts that offer students helpful clues to word meanings, (c) multiple opportunities for applying words in meaningful ways, and (d) a focus on how word meanings are connected to the text being read. In our example in the next subsection, we applied the tenets of Beck et al.'s work to an instructional framework comprising two major components: understanding word meanings and remembering word meanings. The category of understanding includes introducing words, using and applying word meanings, and connecting to the text. The category of remembering includes specific activities to help students remember and internalize newly learned words all related to using an interactive word wall.

The following example is an application of the framework to teaching vocabulary from "The Necklace" by Guy de Maupassant (1907), a short story of a woman who pays a high price for borrowing a necklace from a friend.

Understanding Word Meanings. Because of the heavy vocabulary load in this short story, we focused on 10 words that describe the main character, Mme. Loisel, and her husband: *lofty, humiliating, disconsolate, overwhelmed, anxiety, anguish, deprivation, odious, superb,* and *frugal.* For each word, we developed easily understandable definitions and instructional contexts. By presenting the instructional contexts first, students can form their own understanding of the words and then coconstruct understandable definitions with the teacher and classmates. For example, for the word *lofty,* the instructional context was, "Sandy always acted like she was better than the girls in the club. Her **lofty** attitude was so irritating to Janey that she would not invite Sandy to her Halloween party." The understandable definition for the word *lofty* can be "describes actions when people think they are better than someone else; proud; snobbish; conceited."

To help students connect the word meanings to different contexts, we followed Beck et al.'s (2002) suggestions for using word associations and sentence completions. Sample questions and prompts included the following:

- Which word goes with a conceited person?
- Which word goes with a sewage leak in the neighborhood?
- Describe a time when you might feel **overwhelmed**.
- Barbara could not believe the **anxiety** she felt before reading the coach's listing on the door, because _____.
- Would a **frugal** person likely be **overwhelmed** by the high cost of some things?
- Could an **odious** task cause you great **anguish**?

In this section, the goal is to relate the targeted words back to the text and discuss the primary focus—in this case, characters. Therefore, we developed questions that focused on how the author used the words, such as the following:

- How did Mme. Loisel feel about **lofty** women who were wealthy? How did she feel about not being rich? If she were rich, do you think she would have a **lofty** attitude about people who were not as well off as she?

- The author describes the husband as a **frugal** clerk. What evidence is there to support this description of him?

Remembering Word Meanings. To help struggling readers hold on to newly learned word meanings, we advocate the use of an interactive word wall (Harmon, Wood, Hedrick, Vintinner, & Willeford, 2009). Students work in groups to develop visual elements that aid in remembering word meanings. These visual elements are the mainstay of the interactive word wall, as students actively create clues that trigger word meanings. Some of the visual elements include the following:

- Students decide on a color to help them remember a word along with a reason for choosing the color. Then, they color the flashcard containing the word to place on the wall. For the word *superb,* for example, they may select the color gold, because gold can be associated with excellent picture frames or exquisite jewelry.

- Using an index card, students can draw a symbol that will trigger the targeted word's meaning. The card is then placed on the side of the flashcard on the word wall. For example, for the word *lofty,* students may draw a simple stick figure of a person with his or her nose up in the air.

- Students can also think of situations that describe the word, make simple sketches of the situation, and then post on the word wall. For example, a sketch of someone with a worried look on his face as he holds a pile of books may illustrate the feeling of the term *overwhelmed.*

- With comic websites available for free use, students can create a comic strip in which characters use the word or the situation presents hints of the word's meaning. Even these visuals can be posted on the word wall.

What Should Instruction of Independent Word Learning Strategies Look Like?

Teaching strategy instruction to those who need it the most is especially a challenge. To help struggling readers develop lifelong word learning strategies, it is important to focus on two primary sources used in problem solving about word meanings: context clues and word analysis.

Context Clues. In this section, we describe one way to address context clues using the well-known gradual release of responsibility model for strategy instruction: verbal explanation, modeling, guided practice, and independent practice (Duke & Pearson, 2002).

Verbal explanation—One way to introduce context clues is to use word riddles, for which students rely on what they know to figure out the riddle (Buikema & Graves, 1993). The following is an example:

> I am a two-digit number. If you are using me to talk about extra spending money you have, then I would probably be a lot of money. If you are using me to talk about the age of some people, then you could say that they are octogenarians. I am at least what you get when you double the number 40. I am also an even number. What number could I be?

The explanation about the use of context clues must connect to the word riddles and also indicate what students actually do as they try to figure out the word's meaning. The explanation can be the following:

> You used text clues and what you know about these clues to figure out the word being described in the riddle. You do the same thing when you come to an unfamiliar word in your reading. Sometimes the author gives you really obvious clues to the meaning of a word, and other times you have to figure out the word's meaning yourself, because the clues are not that clear. Let's look at some examples.

At this point, share examples of the type of context clues that authors use, such as appositives, synonyms, contrasts, and descriptions. Several texts contain examples to use (see Blachowicz & Fisher, 2006; Vacca et al., 2011).

Modeling—The teacher can model the process in the following manner:

> When I figure out the meanings of unfamiliar words as I read, I use what the author says and what I know to make a reasonable guess about the word's meaning. What I know involves making connections:
>
> **Things I Know in My Life**
> • The whole story
> • The immediate events
> • How the author uses the word
> • Why the author would use that word
>
> I am going to think aloud as I try to figure out the meaning of the **boldfaced** word in this sentence: "Because Darryl jokingly hid all the footballs at the school's football jamboree, the principal gave him the **odious** task of cleaning all the toilets in the school's restrooms."
>
> First, it looks like this word is describing the task of cleaning toilets. Now I am looking carefully at the word, but I don't see any part that really

helps me with the meaning. So, let me look at the text. What is the author telling me about what's happening here? The author says that a football game is going on, Darryl hid all the footballs, and the principal made him clean all the toilets for doing that. What do I know about that? Well, I know that it's not a good thing to hide footballs during a jamboree, because the teams cannot play without footballs. People are probably angry. I also know that toilets in school restrooms are used by many people, and the toilets can get really dirty and disgusting. The word *odious* described this task of cleaning toilets, so it might mean that it's a disgusting, gross, dirty task to do.

Guided practice—For guided practice, students can work in either pairs or small groups to problem-solve word meanings as the teacher provides needed support. At this point, the teacher can show a passage containing a highlighted, unfamiliar word and have the students figure out the word's meaning. Students can highlight or underline the cues they used to determine the meaning and talk about what they know about the clues. During subsequent discussions about what ideas students develop about the word meanings, it is important to emphasize that context clues may not provide enough clues, so finding at least a reasonable meaning for a word is acceptable.

Independent practice—Once students understand how to use context clues, it is important for them to use the strategy in authentic reading. One suggestion is to have the students find unfamiliar words in their personal reading and try out the strategy.

Word Analysis. Helping students analyze word parts—that is, looking for familiar prefixes, suffixes, and roots—is a powerful independent word learning strategy that works together with context clues. In fact, 60% of words that students encounter in reading across various content areas contain recognizable word parts (Nagy & Anderson, 1984). Strategic use of structural analysis is especially important for English learners, who need not only semantic knowledge of words to infer word meanings but also morphological word knowledge and word usage.

There are multiple suggestions for providing morphemic analysis support (Bear, Invernizzi, Templeton, & Johnston, 2004; Blachowicz & Fisher, 2006; Graves, 2006), many of which recommend explicit instruction that focuses on specific affixes and roots. One instructional plan can be the following:

- Target an affix or root, such as *audi* (to hear).
- Show students the definition of two or three words containing the same affix or root.

audible—describes a sound that you can hear

auditorium—a large room where you go to hear someone speak

- Ask students what spelling features in each word look similar and what the word meanings have in common. Then, tell them that the root *audi* means to hear.

- Ask students to construct sentences with you that contain the words.

    The song on the MP3 player was barely **audible**, so the students could not understand the lyrics.

    All of the students in the school went to the **auditorium** to listen to a guest speaker talk about global warming.

- Have students find other words that contain the root *audi*, such as *inaudible, audiometer,* and *audience.*

- Add the words to an interactive word wall that is categorized by affixes, roots, or both.

- Revisit the word wall list whenever students encounter words that contain the affixes, roots, or both.

- Remind students to examine the parts of an unknown word as they look for context clues to unlock the meaning.

Integrate Technology With Vocabulary Instruction

The introduction of multiliteracies ushers in a new era for readers and writers. Our students' literacies are now dominated by personal computer devices and the Internet, which continuously change and shift the way we read, write, and learn words (Bomer, Zoch, David, & Ok, 2010). We already know that students who struggle as readers have a significantly smaller vocabulary than their peers with a higher level of reading achievement (Stahl, 1999; Stanovich, 1986). This gap becomes compounded when students lack access to technology in which multiple exposures to words can provide students with opportunities to learn unfamiliar terms. In the process, students may experience a technological Matthew effect (Stanovich, 1986), in which the users of such technologies become richer with their word knowledge, whereas those denied access become poorer. Our task as teachers must be to bring these technologies forward into our classrooms to help expand the vocabularies of our struggling readers and writers. This can become a difficult task for teachers of school-age children who are technologically savvy and comfortable with different types of digital media but feel that their teachers may be out of touch with the current technology (Alvermann, 2004; Kinzer, 2010). In fact, two thirds of teachers feel unprepared to use such technologies within their classrooms (Kajder, 2005).

We know that readers and writers grow most of their knowledge of words through incidental exposure; that is, they read and view the word multiple times to build their understanding of what the words actually mean (Nagy, Herman, & Anderson, 1985). Knowing this, teachers can help students experience multiple exposures to words using digital tools to enhance students' vocabulary knowledge (Kamil, 2004). This provides an opportunity for students who are more likely to engage in reading and writing when a technological component is added to these acts. Multiliteracies, therefore, offer promise and possibilities for the classroom.

In this section, we discuss the different types of technology that students use in their everyday lives, and examine how teachers may use these technologies to build vocabulary knowledge within struggling readers.

Podcasts

Podcasts are a relatively new form of information and communication technology, in which an audio broadcast is digitally recorded and uploaded to the Internet. Users can download the broadcast and listen to the recordings on their computers or personal, portable listening devices. Essentially, podcasts work like radio broadcasts, providing entertainment, information, and instruction to listeners.

Recently, teachers have started to harness the power of podcasts in their own classrooms to help students broaden their vocabulary knowledge. In one such classroom, Kingsley created weekly podcasts for her fifth-grade students to deepen their knowledge of unfamiliar science terms (Putman & Kingsley, 2009). The podcasts included songs set to familiar tunes in which the original words were substituted with the scientific words. The songs were followed by a review of the words learned in the previous week's podcast, in which specific scientific words were integrated into familiar songs. This was followed by an examination of new words for the week. After students listened to the podcast, they were asked to respond in various spoken and written ways to increase the number of exposures that students would receive for each word. In posttests, students scored slightly higher on vocabulary. Perhaps more important, surveys indicated an increased level of enthusiasm for learning because of the podcasts used in the classroom.

Researchers have found that students who have continued exposure to vocabulary terms, within multiple contexts, tend to retain such words

(Baumann et al., 2003). Interactive podcasts, in which students have opportunities to listen to words repeatedly and then use the words within a variety of written and spoken contexts, can help those who struggle as readers.

Digital Storytelling

Digital storytelling is fast becoming a popular medium among young readers and writers. Digital stories are movies that students create by mixing their writing with images, music, and voice. Student writers often upload their movies to online movie portals such as YouTube to reach a larger, worldwide audience.

Because digital stories blend voice, image, and music, they can be powerful tools to help build vocabulary knowledge within struggling readers and writers. "Creating digital stories invites students to employ old and new literacies, and through the process of creating a movie, they erect, explore, and exhibit other literacies" (Sylvester & Greenidge, 2009, p. 284). This medium requires writers to construct texts that thoughtfully combine spoken words with images related to the words. When background music is added, writers read the words again to make sure that the music conveys the proper tone. Students who create, share, and view their videos have opportunities to engage with words in multiple contexts. Thus, a word learning cycle is formed: Words are written, spoken, read repeatedly to find appropriately matched music, and finally, heard as the movie is viewed.

Digital movies can also support vocabulary development across content areas. Students can listen and record movies in science to explore concepts and model experiments. In social studies, students can use movies to reenact historical events or role-play the actions, thoughts, and feelings of historical figures. In math, students record themselves solving complicated problems and share these videos with peers. In art, students can upload digital photos of their art pieces and combine words and music to build appreciation for the viewer. Within all of these curricular areas, students experience words via multiple modalities, using reading, writing, speaking, listening, viewing, and visually representing to learn new information. Using this medium gives students opportunities to be self-representative as they incorporate their aesthetic inclinations in multimodal ways (Vasudevan, 2010). Because students have the opportunities to use these multiple modalities repeatedly, digital storytelling becomes a potentially influential medium for struggling readers.

Blogs and Social Networking

Conversations are important acts that learners use to acquire word knowledge. As we speak and listen with one another, we acquire language. Our discourse shifts and expands depending on the setting in which we converse (Gee, 1992). In many ways, personal computing devices and the Internet have constricted some of these conversations. The isolated act of human with machine has, in some ways, distanced ourselves from conversations that we might otherwise engage in with others.

In this digital age, however, teachers have discovered ways to keep these conversations going. J.T. Kuzior, a third-grade teacher in Ohio, found a way to engage students in response using ThinkQuest, a digital blogging site (www.thinkquest.org/en/; Kist, Doyle, Hayes, Horwitz, & Kuzior, 2010). ThinkQuest allows students to create homepages, ask questions, post responses, make suggestions, and digitally interact with one another. It also contains a messaging service that allows students to "speak" with one another via instant messaging. Used as a classroom tool, students view, read, write, and respond to words they see through multiple exposures.

Kristen Cielocha, a fourth-grade teacher of bilingual and special education students, replaced reading binders with blogs when she discovered that her binder system did not fully support her students as reading responders (Handsfield, Dean, & Cielocha, 2009). Using Blogger (www.blogger.com), Kristen and her students created individual blogs that allowed them to respond to one another's musings about books. This positioned Kristen as a participant, along with her students, in ongoing conversations. With blogs, students diversified their audience to include those who could read posts and offer response—something that did not happen when Kristen was the only audience member in her now-defunct binder system. Because of this activity, students read and wrote more frequently, expanding their possibility of learning new words.

Jody Hayes, a fourth- and fifth-grade teacher in New Zealand, also saw the possibilities of using social networking sites within her classroom (Kist et al., 2010). Jody wrote a class blog, which enabled her to incorporate the language of the classroom into the wider learning community. Her students created their own blogs to reflect what they learned in class. They used this medium to read, write, respond, and question, and they had the ability to do this inside and outside the classroom, wherever such media was accessible. This digital connection formed connections among Judy, her students, and their parents as they used computers to make school and home worlds collide. For sure, the more active families are in their children's language development, the more successful students will be in acquiring language. Also, once again, the more exposure students have to the words they must learn, the more their vocabulary knowledge expands.

When literacy instruction, particularly vocabulary instruction, is embedded within digital and media technologies, students have the opportunity to learn new words within authentic and meaningful contexts. Technology provides promise for struggling readers who seem motivated and engaged by this medium. This is particularly important for our students as 21st-century learners who must be engaged in using, and producing, digital texts that enable them to be critically literate citizens (Leu, Kinzer, Coiro, & Cammack, 2004).

Summary

As mentioned in the introduction, students in any given classroom vary greatly in their ability to process our language in its many forms, from oral to traditional to digital text. It is often a lack of sufficient vocabulary knowledge that causes them to fall further behind with each successive grade level, as the concepts encountered become more specialized and sophisticated. Consequently, the task for teachers is critical and daunting. No longer are the drill-and-kill practices of the past sufficient for ensuring deeper understanding and retention. Students need robust, engaging, comprehension-based experiences with the new vocabulary, presented within a meaningful, appealing context. As reviews of the research have indicated (Blachowicz et al., 2006; Carr, 1985; Chall & Snow, 1988; Harmon et al., 1999; Walpole & McKenna, 2004), we need to "get the word out," to provide teachers, both preservice and inservice, with the most effective ways of developing vocabulary knowledge across the disciplines that meets the diverse needs of our nation's students.

TRY IT!

1. Talk to your principal, literacy coach, and instructional leaders about developing a community of language (Manzo et al., 2006) in your school by selecting some words that the students need to know, perhaps from novels, common core lists, or end-of-grade, system, or state assessments. Then, think of ways to expose these words to the students that would capture their attention. Encourage the students to use these new terms in their own language as they text one another, engage in classroom or social discussions, or collaborate on a written assignment.

2. Create your own blog using Edublogs (edublogs.org) or Weebly (www.weebly.com) and incorporate different vocabulary words throughout your daily or weekly posts. Create a podcast using a digital podcasting site like Audacity (audacity.sourceforge.net/) and upload the podcast to your class blog as well. Students can do the same on their own individual blogs.

REFERENCES

Allington, R.L. (2001). *What really matters for struggling readers: Designing research-based programs.* New York: Longman.

Alvermann, D.E. (Ed.). (2004). *Adolescents and literacies in a digital world.* New York: Peter Lang.

Anderson, R.C. (1996). Research foundations to support wide reading. In V. Greaney (Ed.), *Promoting reading in developing countries: Views on making reading materials accessible to increase literacy levels* (pp. 55–77). Newark, DE: International Reading Association.

Anderson, R.C., Hiebert, E.H., Scott, J.A., & Wilkinson, I.A.G. (1985). *Becoming a nation of readers: The report of the Commission on Reading.* Washington, DC: National Institute of Education, U.S. Department of Education.

Anderson, R.C., Wilson, P.T., & Fielding, L.G. (1988). Growth in reading and how children spend their time outside of school. *Reading Research Quarterly, 23*(3), 285–303. doi:10.1598/RRQ.23.3.2

Baumann, J.F., Edwards, E.C., Boland, E.M., Olejnik, S., & Kame'enui, E.J. (2003). Vocabulary tricks: Effects of instruction in morphology and context on fifth-grade students' ability to derive and infer word meanings. *American Educational Research Journal, 40*(2), 447–494. doi:10.3102/00028312040002447

Baumann, J.F., & Kame'enui, E.J. (Eds.). (2004). *Vocabulary instruction: Research to practice.* New York: Guilford.

Bear, D.R., Invernizzi, M., Templeton, S., & Johnston, F. (2004). *Words their way: Word study for phonics, vocabulary, and spelling instruction* (3rd ed.). Upper Saddle River, NJ: Pearson.

Beck, I.L., & McKeown, M.G. (1991). Social studies texts are hard to understand: Mediating some of the difficulties. *Language Arts, 68*(6), 482–490.

Beck, I.L., McKeown, M.G., & Kucan, L. (2002). *Bringing words to life: Robust vocabulary instruction.* New York: Guilford.

Blachowicz, C.L.Z., & Fisher, P.J.L. (2006). *Teaching vocabulary in all classrooms* (3rd ed.). Upper Saddle River, NJ: Pearson.

Blachowicz, C.L.Z., Fisher, P.J.L., Ogle, D., & Watts-Taffe, S. (2006). Vocabulary: Questions from the classroom. *Reading Research Quarterly, 41*(4), 524–539. doi:10.1598/RRQ.41.4.5.

Bomer, R., Zoch, M.P., David, A.D., & Ok, H. (2010). New literacies in the material world. *Language Arts, 88*(1), 9–20.

Buikema, J.L., & Graves, M.F. (1993). Teaching students to use context cues to infer word meanings. *Journal of Reading, 36*(6), 450–457.

Carr, E.M. (1985). The vocabulary overview guide: A metacognitive strategy to improve vocabulary comprehension and retention. *Journal of Reading, 28*(8), 684–689.

Chall, J.S., Jacobs, V.A., & Baldwin, L.E. (1990). *The reading crisis: Why poor children fall behind*. Cambridge, MA: Harvard University Press.

Chall, J.S., & Snow, C.E. (1988). Influences on reading in low-income students. *Education Digest, 54*(1), 53–56.

Ciborowski, J. (1992). *Textbooks and the students who can't read them: A guide to teaching content*. Cambridge, MA: Brookline.

Cunningham, A.E. (2005). Vocabulary growth through independent reading and reading aloud to children. In E.H. Hiebert & M.L. Kamil (Eds.), *Teaching and learning vocabulary: Bringing research to practice* (pp. 45–68). Mahwah, NJ: Erlbaum.

Duke, N.K., & Pearson, P.D. (2002). Effective practices for developing reading comprehension. In A.E. Farstrup & S.J. Samuels (Eds.), *What research has to say about reading instruction* (3rd ed., pp. 205–242). Newark, DE: International Reading Association.

Dunston, P.J., & Gambrell, L.B. (2009). Motivating adolescent learners to read. In K.D. Wood & W.E. Blanton (Eds.), *Literacy instruction for adolescents: Research-based practice* (pp. 269–286). New York: Guilford.

Elley, W.B. (1989). Vocabulary acquisition from listening to stories. *Reading Research Quarterly, 24*(2), 174–187.

Elley, W.B. (1992). *How in the world do students read? IEA study of reading literacy*. The Hague, The Netherlands: International Association for the Evaluation of Educational Achievement.

Feitelson, D., & Goldstein, Z. (1986). Patterns of book ownership and reading to young children in Israeli school-oriented and nonschool-oriented families. *The Reading Teacher, 39*(9), 924–930.

Gee, J.P. (1992). *The social mind: Language, ideology, and social practice*. New York: Bergin & Garvey.

Graves, M.F. (1987). The roles of instruction in fostering vocabulary development. In M.G. McKeown & M.E. Curtis (Eds.), *The nature of vocabulary acquisition* (pp. 165–184). Hillsdale, NJ: Erlbaum.

Graves, M.F. (2006). *The vocabulary book: Learning and instruction*. New York: Teachers College Press; Newark, DE: International Reading Association; Urbana, IL: National Council of Teachers of English.

Guthrie, J.T., & Davis, M.H. (2003). Motivating struggling readers in middle school through an engagement model of classroom practice. *Reading & Writing Quarterly, 19*(1), 59–85. doi:10.1080/10573560308203

Handsfield, L.J., Dean, T.R., & Cielocha, K.M. (2009). Becoming critical consumers and producers of text: Teaching literacy with Web 1.0 and Web 2.0. *The Reading Teacher, 63*(1), 40–50. doi:10.1598/RT.63.1.4

Harmon, J.M., Hedrick, W.B., & Wood, K.D. (2005). Research on vocabulary instruction in the content areas: Implications for struggling readers. *Reading & Writing Quarterly, 21*(3), 261–280. doi:10.1080/10573560590949377

Harmon, J.M., Katims, D.S., & Whittington, D. (1999). Helping middle school students learn with social studies texts. *Teaching Exceptional Children, 32*(1), 70–75.

Harmon, J.M., & Wood, K.D. (2001). The TAB book club approach: Talking (T) about (A) books (B) in content area classrooms. *Middle School Journal, 32*(3), 51–56.

Harmon, J.M., Wood, K.D., Hedrick, W.B., & Gress, M. (2008). "Pick a word—not just any word": Using vocabulary self-selection with expository texts. *Middle School Journal, 40*(1), 43–52.

Harmon, J.M., Wood, K.D., Hedrick, W.B., Vintinner, J., & Willeford, T. (2009). Interactive word walls: More than just reading the writing on the walls. *Journal of Adolescent & Adult Literacy, 52*(5), 398–408. doi:10.1598/JAAL.52.5.4

Irvin, J.L. (1998). *Reading and the middle school student: Strategies to enhance literacy* (2nd ed.). Needham Heights, MA: Allyn & Bacon.

Ivey, G., & Broaddus, K. (2001). "Just plain reading": A survey of what makes students want to read in middle school classrooms. *Reading Research Quarterly, 36*(4), 350–377. doi:10.1598/RRQ.36.4.2.

Jenkins, J.R., Stein, M.L., & Wysocki, K. (1984). Learning vocabulary through reading. *American Educational Research Journal, 21*(4), 767–787.

Kajder, S.B. (2005). "Not quite teaching for real": Preservice secondary English teachers' use of technology in the field following the completion of an instructional technology methods course. *Journal of Computing in Teacher Education, 22*(1), 15–21.

Kamil, M.L. (2004). Vocabulary and comprehension instruction: Summary and implications of the National Reading Panel findings. In P. McCardle & V. Chhabra (Eds.), *The voice of evidence in reading research* (pp. 213–234). Baltimore: Paul H. Brookes.

Kim, H., & Krashen, S. (1997). Why don't language acquirers take advantage of the power of reading? *TESOL Journal, 6*(3), 26–29.

Kinzer, C.K. (2010). Considering literacy and policy in the context of digital environments. *Language Arts, 88*(1), 51–61.

Kist, W., Doyle, K., Hayes, J., Horwitz, J., & Kuzior, J.T. (2010). Web 2.0 in the elementary classroom: Portraits of possibilities. *Language Arts, 88*(1), 62–68.

Krashen, S. (2005). Is in-school free reading good for children? Why the National Reading Panel report is (still) wrong. *Phi Delta Kappan, 86*(6), 444–447.

Krashen, S. (2009). *81 generalizations about free voluntary reading* (IATEFL Young Learners and Teenagers Special Interest Group Publication No. 2009-1). Kent, UK: International Association of Teachers of English as a Second Language.

Leu, D.J., Jr., Kinzer, C.K., Coiro, J.L., & Cammack, D.W. (2004). Toward a theory of new literacies emerging from the Internet and other information and communication technologies. In R.B. Ruddell & N.J. Unrau (Eds.), *Theoretical models and processes of reading* (5th ed., pp. 1570–1613). Newark, DE: International Reading Association.

Lubliner, S., & Smetana, L. (2005). The effects of comprehensive vocabulary instruction on Title I students' metacognitive word-learning skills and reading comprehension. *Journal of Literacy Research, 37*(2), 163–200. doi:10.1207/s15548430jlr3702_3

Manzo, A.V., Manzo, U.C., & Thomas, M.M. (2006). Rationale for systematic vocabulary development: Antidote for state mandates. *Journal of Adolescent & Adult Literacy, 49*(7), 610–619.

McKeown, M.G., Beck, I.L., Omanson, R.C., & Pople, M.T. (1985). Some effects of the nature and frequency of vocabulary instruction on the knowledge and use of words. *Reading Research Quarterly, 20*(5), 522–535.

Merkley, D.M., & Jefferies, D. (2000). Guidelines for implementing a graphic organizer. *The Reading Teacher, 54*(4), 350–357.

Miller, G.A., & Gildea, P.M. (1987). How children learn words. *Scientific American, 257*(3), 94–99. doi:10.1038/scientificamerican0987-94

Milligan, J.L., & Ruff, T.P. (1990). A linguistic approach to social studies vocabulary development. *The Social Studies, 81*(5), 218–220. doi:10.1080/00377 996.1990.9957528

Nagy, W.E. (1988). *Teaching vocabulary to improve reading comprehension.* Urbana, IL: National Council of Teachers of English; Newark, DE: International Reading Association.

Nagy, W.E., & Anderson, R.C. (1984). How many words are there in printed school English? *Reading Research Quarterly, 19*(3), 304–330.

Nagy, W.E., & Herman, P.A. (1987). Breadth and depth of vocabulary knowledge: Implications for acquisition and instruction. In M.G. McKeown & M.E. Curtis (Eds.), *The nature of vocabulary acquisition* (pp. 19–35). Hillsdale, NJ: Erlbaum.

Nagy, W.E., Herman, P.A., & Anderson, R.C. (1985). Learning words from context. *Reading Research Quarterly, 20*(2), 233–253.

Neuman, S.B., & Celano, D. (2001). Access to print in low-income and middle-income communities: An ecological study of four neighborhoods. *Reading Research Quarterly, 36*(1), 8–26.

Putman, S.M., & Kingsley, T. (2009). The Atoms Family: Using podcasts to enhance the development of science vocabulary. *The Reading Teacher, 63*(2), 100–108. doi:10.1598/RT.63.2.1

Ruddell, M.R., & Shearer, B.A. (2002). "Extraordinary," "tremendous," "exhilarating," "magnificent": Middle school at-risk students become avid word learners with the vocabulary self-collection strategy (VSS). *Journal of Adolescent & Adult Literacy, 45*(5), 352–363.

Rupley, W.H., & Slough, S. (2010). Building prior knowledge and vocabulary in science in the intermediate grades: Creating hooks for learning. *Literacy Research and Instruction, 49*(2), 99–112. doi:10.1080/19388070902780472

Schoenbach, R., Greenleaf, C., Cziko, C., & Hurwitz, L. (1999). *Reading for understanding: A guide to improving reading in middle and high school classrooms.* San Francisco: Jossey-Bass.

Spear-Swerling, L. (2005, August). Independent reading. *LD Online.* Retrieved September 18, 2010, from www.ldonline.org/spearswerling/ Independent_Reading

Stahl, S.A. (1999). *Vocabulary development.* Cambridge, MA: Brookline.

Stahl, S.A., & Fairbanks, M.M. (1986). The effects of vocabulary instruction: A model-based meta-analysis. *Review of Educational Research, 56*(1), 72–110.

Stanovich, K.E. (1986). Matthew effects in reading: Some consequences of individual differences in the acquisition of literacy. *Reading Research Quarterly, 21*(4), 360–407.

Sylvester, R., & Greenidge, W. (2009). Digital storytelling: Extending the potential for struggling writers. *The Reading Teacher, 63*(4), 284–295. doi:10.1598/RT.63.4.3

Taylor, B.M., Frye, B.J., & Maruyama, G.M. (1990). Time spent reading and reading growth. *American Educational Research Journal, 27*(2), 351–362.

Taylor, D.B., Mraz, M.E., Nichols, W.D., Rickelman, R.J., & Wood, K.D. (2009). Using explicit instruction to promote vocabulary learning for struggling readers. *Reading & Writing Quarterly, 25*(2/3), 205–220. doi:10.1080/10573560802683663

Vacca, R.T., Vacca, J.A.L., & Mraz, M.E. (2011). *Content area reading: Literacy and learning across the curriculum* (10th ed.). Boston: Allyn & Bacon.

Vasudevan, L. (2010). Literacies in a participatory, multimodal world: The arts and aesthetics of Web 2.0. *Language Arts, 88*(1), 43–50.

Walpole, S., & McKenna, M.C. (2004). *The literacy coach's handbook: A guide to research-based practice*. New York: Guilford.

White, T.G., Graves, M.F., & Slater, W.H. (1990). Growth of reading vocabulary in diverse elementary schools: Decoding and word meaning. *Journal of Educational Psychology, 82*(2), 281–290. doi:10.1037/0022-0663.82.2.281

Wood, K.D. (2002, May). *Meeting the needs of diverse learners: Focus on comprehension*. Paper presented at the 47th annual meeting of the International Reading Association, San Francisco.

Wood, K.D., Harmon, J.M., & Hedrick, W.B. (2004). Recommendations from research for teaching vocabulary to diverse learners. *Middle School Journal, 35*(5), 57–63.

LITERATURE CITED

de Maupassant, G. (1907). *The necklace*. Retrieved May 20, 2011, from bartleby .com/195/20.html

George, J.C. (1987). *Water sky*. New York: HarperTrophy.

Paulsen, G. (1987). *Dogsong*. New York: Puffin.

CHAPTER 5

Grouping Routines and Instructional Practices That Mediate Difficult Text

Rachel L. McCormack and Jeanne R. Paratore

Julia (pseudonym) is observing her student teacher, Ellena, as she teaches a reading lesson. Ellena is preteaching the vocabulary for a selection in a literature anthology. As she introduces each word, she asks the students to take a moment to think about the word. Then, she asks students to provide synonyms for it. Ellena jots down the students' responses on a semantic web that she has constructed on the board. At one point, Julia signals quietly for Ellena to stop and addresses the students:

Julia:	What do we call the words that we are putting around the web?
Student 1:	Synonyms.
Julia:	Yes! [gestures with her hands, sweeping them together in an arc]
Julia:	What do we call the words that are opposites? [sweeps her hands away from each other in an opposite arc]
Student 2:	Antonyms.
Julia:	Fantastic.
Julia:	[to Ellena] We're ready to move on.

With a nod, Julia signals to Ellena to proceed. Twice more during the vocabulary introduction, Julia checks in with her students. It does not appear to be disruptive or alter Ellena's cadence during the prereading segment of the reading lesson.

J ulia, a fifth-grade teacher in Puerto Rico and one of the many teachers with whom we have worked, has demonstrated that increasing instructional intensity pays off. She teaches Spanish-speaking

After Early Intervention, Then What? Teaching Struggling Readers in Grades 3 and Beyond (2nd ed.) edited by Jeanne R. Paratore and Rachel L. McCormack. © 2011 by the International Reading Association.

students in a school in which instruction is primarily in English. Her story continues later in this chapter.

During recent years, substantial attention has been directed toward intervention programs for students who struggle to learn to read in the first and second grades. Several approaches to early intervention have met with positive results (e.g., Ehri, Dreyer, Flugman, & Gross, 2007; Foorman, Francis, Shaywitz, Shaywitz, & Fletcher, 1997; Hiebert, 1983; Pinnell, 1985; Santa & Høien, 1999; Taylor, Strait, & Medo, 1994), indicating that teachers address difficulty in learning to read early and intensively, widespread failure can be prevented for many students. However, despite the success of such early intervention efforts, a considerable number of students continue to experience difficulty in reading beyond second grade. The National Assessment of Educational Progress (National Center for Education Statistics, 2010) found that only 67% of fourth-grade students achieved at or above the basic level of achievement in 2009. At the state level as well, large-scale testing typically indicates that large numbers of students are achieving below grade level in reading. For instance, in Massachusetts, where two of the studies in this chapter were conducted, results from the 2010 state assessment (Massachusetts Department of Elementary and Secondary Education, 2010) indicated that at the fourth-grade level, only 54% of fourth graders scored proficient or higher in English language arts. Disaggregation of results underscored the unevenness of achievement for particular types of learners: 58% of African American students, 62% of Hispanic/Latino students, 75% of students identified as having special learning needs, and 73% of students acquiring English as a second language achieved below the established benchmark.

The consequences of not learning to read at a level commensurate with one's peers are substantial. As described by Stanovich (2000), reading ability enables differential support of further vocabulary, knowledge, and cognitive development in and out of school. These knowledge bases then create further individual differences that result in differential performance as students grapple with different texts and tasks in and out of school.

In recent years, policymakers have raised the stakes for schools and students even higher by tying evidence of grade-level achievement to funding for institutions and promotion and graduation for individuals. Although consequences vary widely across states, Massachusetts provides one example: Failure to achieve the standard on the state's comprehensive assessment prohibits the awarding of a high school diploma. In school districts in which high percentages of students achieve below grade level, schools risk takeover by state educational officials.

Mediating Difficult Text: An Instructional Intervention

It was in this climate that our work with students who struggle beyond the early grades evolved (McCormack & Paratore, 2003). At the time that we planned and implemented the original study, one of the authors, Rachel, was one of two reading specialists in a local school, where part of her responsibility was to help classroom teachers bring every student to grade-level performance in reading. Although previous efforts at reading intervention in first and second grades had been judged to be relatively successful, a locally developed literacy performance assessment administered at the beginning of third grade indicated that many students continued to struggle in reading.

As we began to plan an instructional program for these students, we confronted two apparently conflicting research findings. Juel (1988, 1990) reports that students do best when they are taught with materials at their instructional levels (i.e., 90% or better accuracy in word identification) and most poorly when materials are at their frustration level (i.e., below 90% accuracy in word identification). This finding has led many teachers to continue the traditional practice of differentiating students' reading instruction by changing the text in which they read. Although differentiation allows students to read words in the text with relative ease, it may have an unexpected consequence: Easier texts may bar access to concepts, ideas, and linguistic structures otherwise acquired by reading grade-appropriate texts. As a result, when such texts represent the only or even the primary material routinely read by students in classrooms, these students may develop what Fielding and Roller (1992) referred to as "knowledge handicaps" (p. 680). That is, the lack of exposure to grade-level concepts, vocabulary, and syntax may prevent students from acquiring information that contributes to their development of language, comprehension, and writing.

We sought an instructional intervention that would allow us to reconcile these apparently conflicting findings, one that would provide students access to grade-appropriate language, ideas, and concepts and, at the same time, help them improve their ability to read unknown words and, therefore, advance toward independence in reading. We wanted students to engage in successful reading (Allington, 2002), but we wanted to accomplish this by mediating difficult text, enabling students to read with high levels of word reading accuracy rather than by changing the text we provided to students. We drew from evidence that students would need explicit, systematic, and intensive instruction in word study strategies

(Adams, 1990, 1998; Ehri, 1997; Torgesen, Wagner, & Rashotte, 1997). We also drew from evidence that instructional strategies such as preteaching vocabulary (Beck & McKeown, 1991), discussion of background knowledge (Pearson & Fielding, 1991), and repeated readings (Dowhower, 1987; O'Shea, Sindelar, & O'Shea, 1985; Rasinski, 1990; Samuels, 1979; Sindelar, Monda, & O'Shea, 1990) would allow students to read and reread text that might otherwise prove too difficult, and we considered the importance of explicit instruction in reading comprehension for readers of all levels of achievement (Anderson, Chinn, Waggoner, & Nguyen, 1998; Duke, Pearson, Strachan, & Billman, 2001; Pressley, 1998; Raphael, 1998).

As we clarified the intervention plan, we also refined our research focus and ended up with a single question to investigate: When students in the middle grades (3–5) read substantially below grade level, what are the effects of grouping students homogeneously for part of their literacy instruction and providing instruction using grade-level text in combination with explicit, systematic, and intensive instruction in both word and comprehension strategies? In the sections that follow, we describe three contexts in which we implemented our work, the procedures we followed, and the results we achieved. The first context is a suburban school district in the United States, the second is an urban school in the United States, and the third is an independent school in Puerto Rico.

The Intervention in Action: The First Context

South Elementary School is a suburban school of approximately 650 students in kindergarten through fifth grade. Most of the students are of European American descent, and most of the families are of middle-class socioeconomic status. Rachel had been a classroom teacher at South Elementary for more than 20 years and, during the year of the study, was one of two reading specialists in the school.

Identifying Students in Need of Extra Help

At the beginning of the school year, the second- and third-grade teachers, reading specialists, and special education teachers worked cooperatively to identify students who were likely to benefit from additional help in reading. To do so, they relied on three primary sources of evidence: (1) a locally developed reading performance assessment administered by the reading specialists to all third graders at the beginning of the school year, (2) the California Achievement Test (CAT-5), administered to all students in the school district at the end of grade 2, and (3) second- and third-grade teachers' observations and impressions of the students.

The reading performance assessment was designed by the reading specialists and administered individually to all 125 third graders during the first three weeks of the school year. The assessment included two measures: a running record (Clay, 1993) of an oral reading of a 255-word fable selected from the district-adopted published anthology for third grade, and an oral retelling immediately thereafter, analyzed using the standards established by Morrow (1989). In addition, the reading specialists collected and examined the results of the CAT-5 for more information about students' reading behaviors.

At the end of the third week of school, with all tests administered and all information gathered on each student, the classroom teachers, special education teachers, and reading specialists met. The team sought to identify students who would be likely to benefit from a special intervention in reading, based on the following criteria:

- They scored in the bottom quartile on the CAT-5.
- Classroom observations during either second or third grade indicated that they were having difficulty reading grade-level texts in either reading or content areas.
- On the reading performance assessment, they achieved a score below 90% on the running record and a score of 3 or lower on the oral retelling.

Based on a review and discussion of the evidence, the team identified 12 general education and six special education students who could benefit from extra help in reading.

Planning and Implementing the Intervention

The intervention plan was based on a flexible grouping model (Paratore, 1991, 2000). In the original iteration of the model, all students have access to the same grade-appropriate text, and the teacher differentiates instruction by forming small, needs-based groups in which students are provided with instruction and practice in the particular skills and strategies they need to successfully read and respond to the text.

During our classroom visits, we observed that in many cases when teachers implemented the model as it was originally designed, they did not always effectively differentiate instruction for students who were experiencing substantial difficulty in reading. Often, teachers were observed engaged in whole-class instruction for long periods of time, and even in classrooms where teachers formed small needs-based groups, we observed that teaching methods often did not include the types or intensity of decoding or comprehension instruction that could be expected to advance the lowest performing students toward greater independence in reading. As a result, some students received insufficient support and often failed to make appreciable gains, perhaps not because they lacked the ability to make progress, but rather because they lacked appropriate and effective instruction. In many instances, students seemed to spend more time listening and responding to text than actually reading it.

In planning the intervention for the 18 identified students, we held onto the basic tenets of the original grouping model, that access to grade-appropriate text was important for the development of vocabulary and concepts that influenced both comprehension and composition and also was important if all students were to have full access to the classroom literacy community. However, we deviated from the initial model by choosing to deliver instruction outside the classroom within a group of relatively homogeneous students. As the content of the instruction was largely similar to that which was occurring in the classroom, we called the group a pull-aside rather than a pull-out. In the pull-aside model, the students would read the same text as their higher performing classroom peers; however, their instruction would be beefed up with more systematic and intensive instruction in word study strategies, increased opportunities for repeated readings to build fluency, and more explicit and systematic instruction in comprehension monitoring strategies.

To carry out our plan, we needed the cooperation of the third-grade teachers and the special educators, which meant careful planning and a great deal of compromising. For example, all of the third-grade teachers had to agree to teach reading using the same literature at the same time, as the students would be pulled from four different classrooms. They also had to agree to keep the pacing of instruction consistent, which meant that the reading specialist had to keep a brisk pace. Finally, the teachers had to agree that when the students returned to their classrooms each day, they would be reintegrated into ongoing literacy instruction and be full participants in the classroom literacy community. In the case of the special education teachers, they had to agree to permit the reading specialist to take responsibility for teaching reading to students who had been identified as having special learning needs. This was a significant programmatic departure in this school, where up to this point, any student identified as needing special education services received instruction in reading from the special education teacher.

Clearly, this was a daunting proposition for the teachers involved. It meant that classroom teachers would give up some of their autonomy in choosing what their students would read and when they would read it. It also meant that lessons could not be executed on the fly. Strict adherence to the plan was necessary if the programs offered in the two separate settings were to remain cohesive.

Beginning the first week in October, the students were provided with the intervention in pull-aside instruction four days per week in one of two groups. The groups were formed on the basis of the classroom teachers' preference. Two of the four teachers volunteered to send their students during the first hour and teach reading in the classroom during that time. The other two delayed teaching reading until the second hour of the day, when they would send their students to the group.

In each group, there was a combination of general education and special education students. A typical session included the following activities: Before reading, students reviewed and practiced retelling what they had read the previous day. The students' inability to recall and retell information had been a major consideration when selecting them for the group, so this task received substantial emphasis. Next, the students were introduced to new vocabulary essential to the comprehension of the day's focal selection. Sight words were introduced, practiced, and added to the classroom word wall. Decodable words were introduced and practiced using appropriate word-making strategies and activities (Cunningham, 1995).

Following word study, students browsed through the selection and previewed text and illustrations, shared predictions, and posed questions. Next, the reading specialist read the text aloud while students followed along in their own copies of the book. As she read, the reading specialist used think-alouds to model comprehension-monitoring strategies, such as self-questioning, visualizing, and summarizing. After the read-aloud, the students shared their reactions, returned to and discussed their predictions, and attempted to answer any questions that they themselves had posed. Following the discussion, students read the selection with a peer using a variety of oral reading strategies, including echo reading, choral reading, Readers Theatre, and buddy reading. After peer reading, students reread a selected passage to the reading teacher individually or in pairs. They ended the reading hour by self-selecting books to read independently or in pairs. When the students returned to their classrooms, they rejoined the classroom literacy community. Along with their classroom peers, they recorded their responses to the focal selection in their reading journals, and then all of the students were given additional time to read self-selected books.

Monitoring Progress

We monitored the students' progress at three different intervals. First, as noted previously, almost every day student reread at least one page of text to the reading specialist; these rereadings were used to determine whether instructional strategies were effective in helping the students read difficult text on their own. Instruction was redirected or refined as necessary based on students' oral reading performances. Second, a running record of each student's oral reading was taken approximately every three weeks using "transition text"—that is, the same text they were reading but a chapter or selection not read previously. Third, in January, after approximately 12 weeks in the intervention program, the reading performance assessment was readministered to each of the 12 general education students. The purpose of readministering the assessment at this point was to determine if any of the students had made enough progress to be discharged from the intervention program. As weekly assessments had indicated that the special education students continued to require substantial support to read grade-level texts, they were not included in the readministration of the performance assessment.

The results of the reading performance assessment indicated that after the first 12 weeks of instruction, 6 of the 12 general education students had achieved grade-level norms, all surpassing 90% accuracy in word reading and exceeding a score of 7 on the retelling measure. Their classroom teachers also observed improvement in the students' reading performance on classroom tasks. Teachers noted that the students were able to read the science and social studies texts with relative ease and displayed more independence in literacy tasks in general. On the basis of this information, these six students were discharged from the intervention group and joined the classroom literacy community full time.

As for the other six students, although each achieved higher scores on the performance assessment, some even achieving at the grade-level benchmark, the students were not perceived by their classroom teachers to be experiencing the same level of success on routine classroom literacy tasks. As a result, the reading specialist and classroom teachers were not confident that the gains these students made would be maintained without continued support, so it was decided to keep them in the intervention program.

The Outcomes

We analyzed the results of the original group of 12 general education students and the six special education students who entered the intervention project in September. Recall that at the end of second grade, all 12 general education students had scored in the bottom quartile on the CAT-5. The mean percentile ranking achieved by the group was 21.5. At the end of third grade, the school district replaced the CAT-5 with the Iowa Test of Basic Skills (ITBS).

Although the tests are not directly comparable, they are similar in format and in the types of literacy tasks assessed. In addition, each test represents students in relation to national norms. On the ITBS, one student advanced to the second quartile, nine advanced to the third quartile, and two remained in the bottom quartile. The mean percentile ranking achieved by the group of 12 was 31.5. On the locally developed literacy performance assessment administered in September, the 12 general education students achieved a mean word reading accuracy score of 86% and a comprehension score of 3.7. In June, the mean word reading accuracy score was 97%, and the comprehension score was 9.4. In both September and June, students were tested on passages that were grade appropriate.

In the case of the six students with special learning needs, the changes in literacy performance were dramatic. In the September administration of the reading performance assessment, the students with special learning needs experienced substantial difficulty. None of these students was able to complete the reading of the fable, and in five cases, the assessment was stopped after 125 words. When the accuracy score for the 125-word abbreviated passage was calculated, the mean score was 72%. The June administration yielded dramatic gains for all six students. Each completed both the oral reading and the retelling. The mean word reading accuracy score was 93.8%, and the mean comprehension score was 9.6. The validity of these scores is supported by the students' performance on the Qualitative Reading Inventory–II. On the third-grade–level reading passage, five of the students performed at the instructional level in both word reading accuracy and comprehension.

The Intervention in Action: The Second Context

Mrs. Dahlene is a Title I teacher in a large urban school. Most of the students are economically poor, with 78% eligible for free or reduced-price lunch. Forty-five percent are children of color, primarily African American or Latino, and 25% speak English as a second language. On state testing, this school district scored within the cluster of five lowest performing districts in the state, despite the school and district's commitment to high literacy achievement for all students.

Identifying Students in Need of Extra Help

Mrs. Dahlene worked closely with two third-grade teachers. In both classrooms, she was responsible for the students on individualized educational plans (IEPs), but she also taught other students (i.e., non-IEP) who were low-performing readers. Typically, the instruction she provided to the struggling readers was substantially different from that given to their more able peers. She used reading materials of a lower reading level than those used by the classroom teacher, and most of her instructional time was focused on decontextualized word study activities. The students she worked with either convened at a table in the back of the classroom or in an office space outside the classroom.

Planning and Implementing the Intervention

Mrs. Dahlene convinced one of the third-grade classroom teachers, Mrs. Caron, to allow her to try an intervention similar to the one described in the previous section. She planned to use the district-adopted reading program anthology as the core text, the same text that the classroom teacher used with all of the students. Mrs. Dahlene and the classroom teacher coplanned their lessons using the same text. They agreed to keep detailed lesson plans, to help each other stay on track, and administer periodic running records on all students to document progress.

Monitoring Progress

Reading instruction followed a predictable format each day. Using Paratore's (1991, 2000) flexible grouping model, all students gathered for prereading activities. Then, Mrs. Dahlene pulled aside the lowest performing readers to spend more time in systematic phonics instruction, guide students through repeated readings of the selection after her initial read-aloud, and engage the students in discussion. The classroom teacher, meanwhile, worked with the more able readers. They read and reread the text alone and with partners, then they completed an assigned comprehension task with partners. The students then met with Mrs. Caron to discuss the selection and their cooperative learning activities and participate in direct instruction of a decoding or comprehension strategy.

Then, both groups reconvened for shared writing, group discussions of the selection, or individual writing in response journals. In addition, time was set aside each day for students to read other selections at their independent levels to practice the strategies taught in their groups.

The Outcomes

In September, Mrs. Dahlene and Mrs. Caron administered a performance assessment to every student in the class. The nine lowest performing students (out of a total of 24) achieved a mean word reading accuracy score of 81% and a mean comprehension score of 3 (of a possible 10 points). In May, those same students achieved a mean word reading accuracy score of 94% and a mean comprehension score of 8. In both administrations of the test, the level of text difficulty was grade appropriate. In addition to student outcomes, this implementation also yielded teacher outcomes.

Mrs. Dahlene commented that planning for this group of students was more rewarding and meaningful than for the other groups with whom she worked. Her observations of the students' actions and interactions in the classroom convinced her that they had a greater sense of belonging and connectedness to their peers. She also believed that the repeated readings of selections of the text were effective in helping the students build fluency and gain confidence in their reading. The periodic performance assessments confirmed her belief. The students with whom she worked made steady progress in word reading accuracy and comprehension of grade-level text. The classroom teacher was equally pleased with the effectiveness of the intervention. She noted that struggling readers became more fluent, more engaged during sustained silent reading, and generally more confident about reading.

The Intervention in Action: The Third Context

In the beginning of this chapter, we introduced Julia, a fifth-grade teacher practicing in an independent school in Puerto Rico. We met her while observing prospective cooperating teachers for undergraduate, preservice teachers.

Identifying Students in Need of Extra Help

Julia teaches three sections of English language arts per day in heterogeneously grouped classes of approximately 20 students each. The

Aldrich School (pseudonym) is an independent school with a pre-K–12 student population of approximately 800; 75% of the students are Puerto Rican, and 25% are European American, Asian American, European, or African. With the exception of one hour per day of instruction in Spanish, English is the language of instruction. The Aldrich School seeks to draw students with high levels of English-language proficiency; however, over the past few years, the number of students with limited English proficiency has grown. The school does not provide direct services for these students. Rather, it is the responsibility of the classroom teachers, almost all of whom are first-language Spanish speakers, to provide language interventions for their students. Julia is one such teacher. She has a degree in teaching English as a second language, which serves her well with this population of students.

The administrators at Aldrich discourage, but do not prohibit, Spanish speaking during English instruction, because they want students to have ample opportunities in the classroom to learn and use English. However, Julia's lessons, and the lessons of her peers, are peppered with Spanish when clarification is needed. The students also frequently draw on Spanish, especially if their ability to make themselves understood is affected by their English proficiency. They also routinely switch to Spanish when they are providing help to a peer.

Before we began to work with Julia, she taught her language arts classes in a whole-class format. Each day, she prepared students for the selection with a class discussion, during which she introduced the topic, developed vocabulary, and encouraged students to make predictions. Then, she read the entire selection aloud to the class, stopping every few pages to talk and ask the students questions. After the reading, the students answered questions on a worksheet.

We observed Julia closely during the read-aloud; although we knew that reading the text aloud to the whole class was not best practice, her ability to engage students and prompt deep thinking and understanding were consistently remarkable. She displayed an unbridled love for teaching and learning, skillfully posed "thick" questions and prompted her students to do the same, and had a seemingly intuitive sense of the importance of letting students in on her thinking as she worked with them to make sense of the texts they read. We realized that Julia would be a perfect fit as a mentor for one of our student teachers, if only we could convince her to make a few changes to her instructional routines.

When we met with Julia, we explained that we did not want her to change anything she did during the prereading part of her lesson but that we did want her to alter the reading of the selection. We asked her to form

Figure 5.1. Julia's Implementation of a Flexible Grouping Model

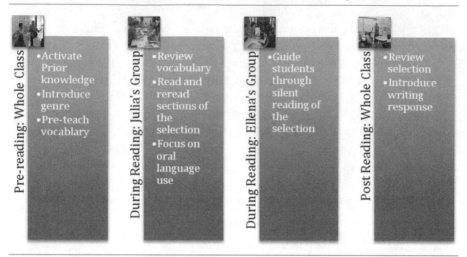

Pre-reading: Whole Class
- Activate Prior knowledge
- Introduce genre
- Pre-teach vocablary

During Reading: Julia's Group
- Review vocabulary
- Read and reread sections of the selection
- Focus on oral language use

During Reading: Ellena's Group
- Guide students through silent reading of the selection

Post Reading: Whole Class
- Review selection
- Introduce writing response

two groups of students during the reading of the text: The students who were identified as needing additional English-language instruction would work with Julia as a pull-aside group, while the rest of the class would work with the student teacher, Ellena (see Figure 5.1).

Planning and Monitoring the Intervention: Ellena's Group

In Ellena's group (see Figure 5.2), English was a second or third language for all but a few of the students (for some it was their first language), and their ability to read and write in English made it easy for them to read the text independently. Ellena guided the reading of the text by: (a) reviewing the vocabulary and concepts introduced in the whole-class prereading segment of the lesson, (b) teaching or reviewing a comprehension-monitoring strategy that would be helpful while reading, and (c) giving a focus question to think about while reading. The students read silently and asked Ellena questions if needed while she sat and read silently with them.

Planning and Monitoring the Intervention: Julia's Group

Julia's group (see Figure 5.3) comprised five or six students whose English-language proficiency was the most limited. Her group also included one

Figure 5.2. Ellena Works With Her Small Group

Figure 5.3. Julia Works With a Small Group of English Learners

or two students whose English was more proficient, so they could provide good English-language models for the others.

Julia used a consistent format each day. She began by reviewing the vocabulary and concepts and also used the opportunity to review the genre the students were reading and provide the students with explanations that they may have missed in the whole-class prereading discussion. She then guided students' reading by using various oral and silent repeated-readings techniques. Sometimes she asked the students to read a page silently, then she listened to them reread the same page chorally. At other times, she read sections aloud and asked the students to summarize or paraphrase, then reread with a partner. Whatever method she used, it always included substantial reading, followed by writing and a great deal of peer talk.

Monitoring Progress

As we searched for effective ways to describe and frame Julia's instruction, we found that her routine practices fit neatly into Teale's (2009) framework for instructional supports for English learners. That is, she consistently

- Extended explanations with redundant information, such as gestures, pictures, and other visual cues
- Provided extra attention to identifying and clarifying key and difficult vocabulary
- Consolidated text knowledge by paraphrasing and summarizing
- Provided additional time and practice with reading and writing activities
- Provided opportunities for extended linguistic interactions with peers and the teacher
- Strategically used her knowledge of the students' first language

In all of her teaching, Julia was especially focused on extending her students' understanding of focus ideas and concepts. Her body was in constant motion during her explanations, as she used signs and hand gestures and carefully observed the faces of her students. She constantly seemed to be asking herself, are the students understanding? Could she do anything else to help them understand?

The Outcomes

Julia was a reflective and enthusiastic participant in this intervention and readily shared with us the transformation she made in the months we were with her: "I'm learning about myself and my students every day." When we asked her to share with us the three most important things that she learned, she said the following:

1. "My instincts are good." Although Julia is trained in English as a second language, she was not particularly strategic about the instructional practices that she used; rather, her instruction most often seemed to emerge from solid intuition. She did what felt right, and through her discussions with us, she came to trust and follow her instincts.

2. "Reading the text aloud to the whole class is neither beneficial nor good practice." Building on practices familiar to her in both her own schooling and her observations of her colleagues, she had previously read every text aloud to the whole class. She explained that she thought that if she had to read the text aloud to some of the students, it would be more time efficient to read the text aloud to everyone. As she worked with alternative grouping formats and alternative strategies for mediating difficult texts, she developed a repertoire of strategies that demanded that students take greater responsibility for the text and, in turn, provided opportunities for students to extend their word reading accuracy, deepen their comprehension, and engage in book talk that provided opportunities to extend their oral English proficiency.

3. "Differentiating instruction does not necessarily mean changing the text." In one of our initial meetings, Julia expressed concern that she was not meeting the needs of the students by using a core text in her classes. However, when previously considering grouping needs, she assumed that she would have to change the text for each group, and she did not have access to a large curriculum library; moreover, she believed that the students using an easier text would miss out on the rigor of ideas in the higher level texts. Now, she said, she has an understanding of instructional strategies that effectively prepare her students to reread the text with accuracy and fluency, and she believed that she met individual needs without diminishing academic rigor.

What Have We Learned?

We began our work with a single question in mind: When students in the middle grades are reading substantially below grade level, what are the effects of grouping students homogeneously for part of their literacy instruction and providing instruction using grade-level text in combination with explicit, systematic, and intensive instruction in both word and comprehension strategies?

At the start, our work was motivated primarily by three factors. First, despite early intervention and effective classroom teaching in the earlier grades, many students continue to struggle in reading. Second, failing to learn to read in the early grades has long-term cognitive and intellectual consequences for students, leading many of them to school failure. Third, in the increasingly politically charged educational climate, the consequences for reading failure are compounded by threats of retention, denial of high school graduation, and reduced funding for schools and communities.

During the months of implementation, we became aware of a new and growing practice, one that further increased our interest in the outcomes of the work that we had underway. As we talked with teachers and visited classrooms in our regions, we found that teachers were increasingly returning to the grouping practices of the past. That is, using the practice that has become widely known as guided reading, teachers were grouping students by ability and meeting with five or six different groups each day, groups formed on the basis of the books that students could read with relative ease. Like ability grouping of the past, students in each guided reading group experienced a different reading curriculum, and different texts provided different opportunities to learn. That is, students in higher performing groups often read texts with interesting narrative plots or expository information; higher performing groups also read texts that were linguistically more interesting, with more sophisticated or unusual words and grammatical structures.

As we considered this practice, we understood the teachers' motivations. We, too, were concerned with the evidence that the shift away from ability grouping that took place during the 1980s and 1990s led many teachers to abandon grouping altogether and instruct students in strictly whole-class settings. We were also concerned with the evidence that for many students, the reading lesson had become, in fact, a listening lesson—a time when complex text was read aloud to them, and they were invited to discuss and write but rarely read. This practice, of course, might be effective in building language and comprehension, but unless a teacher was going to follow a student into adulthood, without independence in reading, eventually the learning would stop. So, although we understood teachers' motivations and shared their concerns, we had an additional concern: Students cannot learn what they are not taught. That is, failure to teach students to read and understand texts with high-level vocabulary, concepts, and ideas will likely deny them an equal opportunity to acquire the knowledge that they will need to continue to develop their cognitive and intellectual abilities, succeed in comprehending complex language and ideas, and become proficient at writing and sharing complex language and ideas. As the pendulum began to swing one more time back toward the practices of the past, our work took on even greater meaning for us.

So how do we make sense of our evidence? First, the fact that students in the first two contexts achieved high levels of performance on text that was judged to be too difficult for them reminded us that reading difficulty does not reside in the text alone, but that text difficulty interacts with the linguistic characteristics of the text and the actions of the teacher. Decades-old research in schema theory (Anderson & Pearson, 1984), vocabulary knowledge (Beck & McKeown, 1991; Beck, Perfetti, & McKeown, 1982), text structure (Meyer & Rice, 1984), and motivation theory (Wigfield & Asher, 1984) taught us that using readability formulas without attention to the ways and the contexts in which students are taught often leads us astray in choosing appropriate texts for them to read. Our work reaffirmed the need to pay attention to this earlier research. Systematic and routine use of time-honored strategies, including preteaching vocabulary, building background knowledge, reading aloud to diminish text difficulty, engaging students in rereadings, and guiding retellings with graphic organizers, paid off in making difficult text accessible to students and thereby allowing them to *read*, not just listen to, high-level text.

Second, we were reminded that meeting individual needs does not mean creating different tracks, nor does adhering to a common text mean one size fits all. Again, this was not a new finding, but in an educational climate of extreme pendulum swings, it is one that may need to be reaffirmed. Evidence tells us that tracking often has negative consequences for students, placing them on pathways that lead them to different destinations (Barr & Dreeben, 1983; Braddock & Dawkins, 1993; Collins, 1971; Oakes, 1985; Slavin, 1987; Wilcox, 1982). In reading instruction, the use of ability grouping typically means that some students read easy text, while others read more difficult text. When this constitutes all or even most of what happens routinely in classrooms, students often have very different instructional experiences (Allington, 1983; Hiebert, 1983). As a consequence, students may end up in very different places in relation to both the levels of reading proficiency they achieve and the types of future opportunities they have (Allington, 1991, 1994; Mehan, Villanueva, Hubbard, & Lintz, 1996). However, teaching to the whole class leads to similarly negative findings, resulting in lower rates of achievement for both higher and lower performing readers (Lou et al., 1996).

Yet there is a middle ground between whole-class instruction and tracking by ability. In the instructional model that we studied in the three different contexts, we recognized students' learning differences and grouped the students accordingly, so we could meet their particular needs, but we kept them on the same track as their higher performing peers in two ways. We instructed them using the same curriculum as their grade-level peers, and their classroom teachers made certain that these students were fully integrated into the classroom literacy curriculum. In short, we differentiated instruction but not curriculum. The payoff for students was improved reading fluency, which advanced them toward independence in reading and improved reading comprehension, which holds the potential for supporting their continued achievement not only in reading but also in schooling in general.

Third, we were reminded that in school contexts in which teachers take a collegial and cooperative stance, seemingly difficult and complex instructional arrangements can be implemented effectively.

Fourth, we were reminded of the remarkable power of good instruction. What we believe is important in our results is the fact that we did not formulate a new, creative, or special approach to teach struggling readers. Rather, we took instructional practices that have been well documented as effective, combined them into what we believed to be a balanced approach, and implemented them in a systematic and intensive way. We were heartened by the progress of all of the students, but we were especially encouraged by the substantial progress of the six students with special learning needs. Although the data are far too limited to allow us to generalize beyond this classroom, the students' progress and performance raised questions for us about the wisdom of the common practice of offering students with special learning needs instructional programs that are substantially different from those provided to their classroom peers. Once again, this is not a new finding. Over two decades ago, Allington and McGill-Franzen (1989) questioned the effectiveness of what they termed "different programs" but "indifferent instruction" (p. 75) for students identified as special education learners.

Yet, many years later, such practices persist, with seemingly little momentum in achieving large-scale programmatic change. As we reflect on what we did and what we learned, and as we attempt to sort out the circumstances that allowed these teachers to make a difference in the literate lives of the students they taught, we find a long list of contributing factors. We have distilled the list to three that we believe were critical in explaining students' success. First, the instructional model itself brought together much of what we have learned about the effective teaching of reading, and by so doing, it offered students explicit and systematic instruction in both word study and comprehension strategies and opportunities to practice the strategies they were learning in high-level texts. Second, although the instructional model framed one hour of literacy instruction, it was only part of what teachers and students did. In addition to the one-hour literacy lesson, the students also had daily opportunities to read and talk about books that they selected to read on their own, books as easy or difficult as they chose. In addition, they read across the content areas with and without instruction from the teacher. Third, the students were taught by teachers who were knowledgeable about the teaching of reading, who were effective classroom managers, and who were enthusiastic about their roles as teachers. In short, the students were taught by teachers who liked teaching and were constantly seeking to become better teachers. We suspect that each of these factors was equal in importance to the success we observed, and that if any one of the factors were to be taken away, the success we observed would likely be taken with it.

TRY IT!

In this chapter, the teachers grouped their students to differentiate instruction but did not differentiate the texts. In most instances, we observed them using narrative texts during their scheduled reading block.

1. Consider using the same model when using texts in social studies or science. At the outset, consider the content learning goals that you expect students to achieve. What do you want them to know and understand? Then, consider the actions that you will take to help them reach these learning goals. What vocabulary and concept knowledge will you develop with the whole class? What strategies (e.g., read-aloud, choral reading, partner reading) will you use to mediate text difficulty for low-performing readers? How will you support comprehension of both low-performing and capable readers?

2. After students complete the text in small, needs-based groups, consider the questions or statements that will prompt discussion when students reconvene as a whole class. Finally, how will you document students' content learning so that both they and you will know if they achieved the goals you set at the beginning?

REFERENCES

Adams, M.J. (1990). *Beginning to read: Thinking and learning about print.* Cambridge, MA: MIT Press.

Adams, M.J. (1998). The three-cueing system. In J. Osborn & F. Lehr (Eds.), *Literacy for all: Issues in teaching and learning* (pp. 73–99). New York: Guilford.

Allington, R.L. (1983). The reading instruction provided readers of differing reading abilities. *The Elementary School Journal, 83*(5), 548–559.

Allington, R.L. (1991.). The legacy of "slow it down and make it more concrete." In J. Zutell & S. McCormick (Eds.), *Learner factors/teacher factors: Issues in literacy research and instruction: 40th yearbook of the National Reading Conference* (pp. 19–30). Chicago: National Reading Conference.

Allington, R.L. (1994). Content coverage and contextual reading in reading groups. *Journal of Reading Behavior, 16*(1), 85–96.

Allington, R.L. (2002). What I've learned about effective reading instruction from a decade of studying exemplary elementary classroom teachers. *Phi Delta Kappan, 83*(10), 740–747.

Allington, R.L., & McGill-Franzen, A. (1989). Different programs, indifferent instruction. In D.K. Lipsky & A. Gartner (Eds.), *Beyond separate education: Quality education for all* (pp. 75–98). Baltimore: Paul H. Brookes.

Anderson, R.C., Chinn, C., Waggoner, M., & Nguyen, K. (1998). Intellectually stimulating story discussions. In J. Osborn & F. Lehr (Eds.), *Literacy for all: Issues in teaching and learning* (pp. 170–186). New York: Guilford.

Anderson, R.C., & Pearson, P.D. (1984). A schema-theoretic view of basic processes in reading comprehension. In P.D. Pearson, R. Barr, M.L. Kamil, & P.B. Mosenthal (Eds.), *Handbook of reading research* (Vol. 1, pp. 255–291). White Plains, NY: Longman.

Barr, R., & Dreeben, R. (with Wiratchai, N.). (1983). *How schools work*. Chicago: University of Chicago Press.

Beck, I.L., & McKeown, M.G. (1991). Conditions of vocabulary acquisition. In R. Barr, M.L. Kamil, P. Mosenthal, & P.D. Pearson (Eds.), *Handbook of reading research* (Vol. 2, pp. 789–814). White Plains, NY: Longman.

Beck, I.L., Perfetti, C.A., & McKeown, M.G. (1982). Effects of long-term vocabulary instruction on lexical access and reading comprehension. *Journal of Educational Psychology, 74*(4), 506–521. doi:10.1037/0022-0663.74.4.506

Braddock, J.H., II, & Dawkins, M.P. (1993). Ability grouping, aspirations, and attainments: Evidence from the National Educational Longitudinal Study of 1988. *The Journal of Negro Education, 62*(3), 324–336.

Clay, M.M. (1993). *An observation survey of early literacy achievement*. Portsmouth, NH: Heinemann.

Collins, R. (1971). Functional and conflict theories of educational stratification. *American Sociological Review, 36*(6), 1002–1019.

Cunningham, P.M. (1995). *Phonics they use: Words for reading and writing* (2nd ed.). New York: HarperCollins.

Dowhower, S.L. (1987). Effects of repeated reading on second-grade transitional readers' fluency and comprehension. *Reading Research Quarterly, 22*(4), 389–406.

Duke, N.K., Pearson, P.D., Strachan, S.L., & Billman, A.K. (2011). Essential elements of fostering and teaching reading comprehension. In S.J. Samuels & A.E. Farstrup (Eds.), *What research has to say about reading instruction* (4th ed.; pp. 51–93). Newark, DE: International Reading Association.

Ehri, L.C. (1997). Sight word learning in normal readers and dyslexics. In B.A. Blachman (Ed.), *Foundations of reading acquisition and dyslexia: Implications for early intervention* (pp. 163–190). Mahwah, NJ: Erlbaum.

Ehri, L.C., Dreyer, L.G., Flugman, B., & Gross, A. (2007). Reading rescue: An effective tutoring intervention model for language-minority students who are struggling readers in first grade. *American Educational Research Journal, 44*(2), 414–448. doi:10.3102/0002831207302175

Fielding, L.G., & Roller, C. (1992). Making difficult books accessible and easy books acceptable. *The Reading Teacher, 45*(9), 678–685.

Foorman, B.R., Francis, D.J., Shaywitz, S.E., Shaywitz, B.A., & Fletcher, J.M. (1997). The case for early reading intervention. In B.A. Blachman (Ed.), *Foundations of reading acquisition and dyslexia: Implications for early intervention* (pp. 243–264). Mahwah, NJ: Erlbaum.

Hiebert, E.H. (1983). An examination of ability grouping for reading instruction. *Reading Research Quarterly, 18*(2), 231–255. doi:10.1598/RRQ.18.2.5

Juel, C. (1988). Learning to read and write: A longitudinal study of 54 children from first through fourth grades. *Journal of Educational Psychology, 80*(4), 437–447. doi:10.1037/0022-0663.80.4.437

Juel, C. (1990). Effects of reading group assignment on reading development in first and second grade. *Journal of Reading Behavior, 22*(3), 233–254.

Lou, Y., Abrami, P.C., Spence, J.C., Poulsen, C., Chambers, B., & d'Apollonia, S. (1996). Within-class grouping: A meta-analysis. *Review of Educational Research, 66*(4), 423–458.

Massachusetts Department of Elementary and Secondary Education. (2010). *Spring 2010 MCAS tests: Summary of state results.* Malden, MA: Author.

McCormack, R.L., & Paratore, J.R. (Eds.). (2003). *After early intervention, then what? Teaching struggling readers in grades 3 and beyond.* Newark, DE: International Reading Association.

Mehan, H., Villanueva, I., Hubbard, L., & Lintz, A. (1996). *Constructing school success: The consequences of untracking low-achieving students.* New York: Cambridge University Press.

Meyer, B.J.F., & Rice, G.E. (1984). The structure of text. In P.D. Pearson, R. Barr, M.L. Kamil, & P. Mosenthal (Eds.), *Handbook of reading research* (Vol. 1, pp. 319–352). New York: Longman.

Morrow, L.M. (1989). Using story retelling to develop comprehension. In K.D. Muth (Ed.), *Children's comprehension of text: Research into practice* (pp. 37–58). Newark, DE: International Reading Association.

National Center for Education Statistics. (2010). *The nation's report card: Reading 2009: National Assessment of Educational Progress at grades 4 and 8* (NCES 2010-458). Washington, DC: National Center for Education Statistics, Institute of Education Sciences, U.S. Department of Education.

Oakes, J. (1985). *Keeping track: How schools structure inequality.* New Haven, CT: Yale University Press.

O'Shea, L.J., Sindelar, P.T., & O'Shea, D.J. (1985). The effects of repeated readings and attentional cues on reading fluency and comprehension. *Journal of Reading Behavior, 17*(2), 129–141.

Paratore, J.R. (1991). *Flexible grouping: Why and how?* Needham, MA: Silver Burdett Ginn.

Paratore, J.R. (2000). Grouping for instruction in literacy: What we've learned about what's working and what's not. *The California Reader, 33*(4), 2–10.

Pearson, P.D., & Fielding, L.G. (1991). Comprehension instruction. In R. Barr, M.L. Kamil, P.B. Mosenthal, & P.D. Pearson (Eds.), *Handbook of reading research* (Vol. 2, pp. 815–860). White Plains, NY: Longman.

Pinnell, G.S. (1985). Helping teachers help children at risk: Insights from the Reading Recovery program. *Peabody Journal of Education, 62*(3), 70–85. doi:10.1080/01619568509538485

Pressley, M. (1998). Comprehension strategies instruction. In J. Osborn & F. Lehr (Eds.), *Literacy for all: Issues in teaching and learning* (pp. 113–133). New York: Guilford.

Raphael, T.E. (1998). Balanced instruction and the role of classroom discourse. In J. Osborn & F. Lehr (Eds.), *Literacy for all: Issues in teaching and learning* (pp. 134–169). New York: Guilford.

Rasinski, T.V. (1990). Effects of repeated reading and listening-while-reading on reading fluency. *The Journal of Educational Research, 83*(3), 147–150.

Samuels, S.J. (1979). The method of repeated readings. *The Reading Teacher, 32*(4), 403–408.

Santa, C.M., & Høien, T. (1999). An assessment of Early Steps: A program for early intervention of reading problems. *Reading Research Quarterly, 34*(1), 54–79. doi:10.1598/RRQ.34.1.4

Sindelar, P.T., Monda, L.E., & O'Shea, L.J. (1990). Effects of repeated readings on instructional- and mastery-level readers. *The Journal of Educational Research, 83*(4), 220–226.

Slavin, R.E. (1987). *Ability grouping and student achievement in elementary schools: A best-evidence synthesis.* Baltimore: Center for Research on Elementary and Secondary Schools, Johns Hopkins University.

Stanovich, K.E. (2000). *Progress in understanding reading: Scientific foundations and new frontiers.* New York: Guilford.

Taylor, B.M., Strait, J., & Medo, M.A. (1994). Early intervention in reading: Supplemental instruction for groups of low-achieving students provided by first-grade teachers. In E.H. Hiebert & B.M. Taylor (Eds.), *Getting reading right from the start: Effective early literacy interventions* (pp. 107–121). Boston: Allyn & Bacon.

Teale, W.H. (2009). Students learning English and their literacy instruction in urban schools. *The Reading Teacher, 62*(8), 699–703. doi:10.1598/RT.62.8.9

Torgesen, J.K., Wagner, R.K., & Rashotte, C.A. (1997). Approaches to the prevention and remediation of phonologically based reading disabilities. In B.A. Blachman (Ed.), *Foundations of reading acquisition and dyslexia: Implications for early intervention* (pp. 287–304). Mahwah, NJ: Erlbaum.

Wigfield, A., & Asher, S.R. (1984). Social and motivational influences on reading. In P.D. Pearson, R. Barr, M.L. Kamil, & P. Mosenthal (Eds.), *Handbook of reading research* (Vol. 1, pp. 423–452). White Plains, NY: Longman.

Wilcox, K. (1982). Differential socialization in the classroom: Implications for educational opportunity. In G. Spindler & L. Spindler (Eds.), *Doing the ethnography of schooling: Educational anthropology in action* (pp. 268–309). New York: Harcourt Brace.

Focusing the Lens: Self-Monitoring and Comprehension for Struggling Readers

CHAPTER 6

Accessible Comprehension Instruction Through Question–Answer Relationships

Taffy E. Raphael and Kathryn H. Au

Many teachers of students in the upper elementary grades have indicated to us that their students can decode words accurately and even read aloud with expression. However, when these students are asked questions about what they have just read, they are unable to answer. These students have often come from primary classrooms where they experienced early intervention in the form of intensive instruction in word identification but very little instruction in reading comprehension. Teachers who receive these students face the challenging task of helping them get up to speed with comprehending text—quickly. Question–answer relationships (QARs), introduced to the literacy education field almost 30 years ago (Raphael, 1982), can provide a means of improving students' reading comprehension in an efficient and effective manner. QAR has become a popular way of explaining tasks associated with questioning activities, which are among the most common forms of interaction in classrooms. From primary grades through advanced graduate-level courses, the language of QAR provides a way to make visible and concrete how reader knowledge and text information intersect, contributing to comprehension, critical thinking, and knowledge development.

In this chapter, we explore ways that using the language of QAR can help teachers build students' reading comprehension abilities in a full, well-rounded manner. Specifically, we show how the language of QAR can be used to give students the benefits of two equally important yet seemingly disparate approaches: literature-based instruction and cognitive strategy instruction. We argue that students need and deserve both kinds of instructional experiences and that the language of QAR can be used as a bridge to connect the two. We begin by describing what we believe to be a serious challenge to successful comprehension instruction: the false competition between critical components of a comprehensive

After Early Intervention, Then What? Teaching Struggling Readers in Grades 3 and Beyond (2nd ed.) edited by Jeanne R. Paratore and Rachel L. McCormack. © 2011 by the International Reading Association.

literacy curriculum. We provide a brief overview of these components before turning to a description of the role of QAR.

Teachers cited in this chapter are either individuals we have worked with or composites of several individuals. Composites are indicated by the use of Ms. with a last name. Full names are used for actual individuals.

The Importance of Balance

Our proposal to use QAR to help students connect what they are learning from both literature-based and cognitive strategy instruction stems in part from an ongoing concern for promoting a balanced approach to literacy education (Madda, Griffo, Pearson, & Raphael, 2011; Pearson, Raphael, Benson, & Madda, 2007). We believe that it is particularly important to promote a balanced approach in schools with a high proportion of students from diverse cultural and linguistic backgrounds (Au & Raphael, 2010). These schools tend to be susceptible to simplistic solutions based on alarmist views about the failures of America's public schools.

An example in the recent past was the proposal that training in phonemic awareness would solve students' problems in learning to read (Adams & Brown, 2003). This proposal found favor in the context of the back-to-basics emphasis promoted by the federal government under No Child Left Behind of 2001. A current example is the suggestion that teaching mostly nonfiction and removing most fiction from the curriculum will boost reading achievement (Wiggins, 2010). Wiggins's advice was based on two premises: Most of the reading that adults do is nonfiction, and fiction bores boys. This advice was influenced by the Common Core State Standards Initiative, which emphasizes nonfiction through reading in the content areas (Council of Chief State School Officers, 2010), and by a recent upsurge of interest in promoting the reading of boys (Brozo, 2010).

Simplistic solutions that pit one form of important knowledge building and strategic thinking against another equally important one do not serve any student well but are particularly undermining to students who depend on school for learning. For more than half a century, literacy educators have known that reading involves both personal response and knowledge-building components (Rosenblatt, 1976). For decades, literacy educators have seen panic over student achievement lead to overemphasis on only part of the picture for literacy instruction (Flesch, 1955/1986; New York State Education Department, 2009). What educators experience is a "manufactured crisis" and misguided solutions (Berliner & Biddle, 1995).

Comprehensive Comprehension Curriculum

We can draw on the existing research base to fulfill our responsibilities as literacy educators. but we must push back against those who cherry-pick among that research as a consequence of misguided interpretations, naïveté, or a narrow or lack of understanding of what it means to comprehend. Decades of research (Barr, Kamil, Mosenthal, & Pearson, 1991; Israel & Duffy, 2009; Kamil, Mosenthal, Pearson, & Barr, 2000; Pearson, Barr, Kamil, & Mosenthal, 1984; Sipe, 2008) underscore knowledge building and engagement as hallmarks of the successful reader. As depicted in Figure 6.1, the research delineates the importance of the workings of the text (e.g., how it is structured, literary elements that authors use) and the readers' approach to making sense of the text (e.g., stances that readers assume throughout the reading process, strategies that support their sense making). Instruction in these aspects of comprehension needs to occur across school subjects within a classroom and grade level and across multiple years of schooling.

Research on text reflects the deep understandings of and multiple approaches for introducing students to how narrative (c.g., Graesser, Golding, & Long, 1991) and expository texts (e.g., Weaver & Kintsch, 1991)

Figure 6.1. Components of Comprehension Instruction

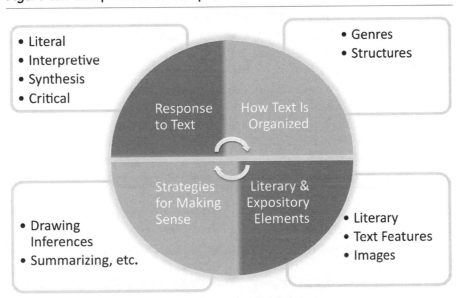

are organized, from macrolevels related to genres to microlevels that convey how writers construct paragraphs or subsections of text (e.g., problem–solution, explanation). This research also is reflected in research on the use of graphic organizers to guide note-taking or text construction, as well as instruction focused on text features such as keywords and headers. Research on text elements expands the research on organization to focus on literary elements, text features, and images that work together to convey meaning.

Research on literary stances (e.g., Langer, 1995; Sipe, 2008) within the framework of reader response theory documents the relationship between readers and text as they enter a text (informational or narrative) world, move through that world or step back from it to reflect as they are reading, and leave the text world to take a more objective look at what they have experienced and how the text worked to create that experience. Such research brings added dimensions to considering what successful, engaged readers do before, during, and after reading and the related strategies that they could employ within each stance.

Research on comprehension strategies provides readers with a set of means to an end. That is, strategies provide a way of helping students control their journey through the text world, so they can accomplish their particular goals, whether personal or otherwise directed. Strategies have been characterized in various ways by federal agencies (e.g., National Assessment for Education Progress guidelines; American Institutes for Research, 2008), researchers (Snow, 2002), and those writing for practitioners (e.g., Harvey & Goudvis, 2000). Delineations of categories vary, but there is little disagreement that core strategies involve making inferences (e.g., predictions, visualizations), identifying important information, summarizing, monitoring, and questioning. Some systems include predictions within making inferences, whereas others separate the two into separate categories. Similarly, some may include questioning within monitoring, while others consider the two as more distinct. Regardless of how the pie is divided (e.g., number of or names of the slices), there is remarkable agreement about the ingredients and what the whole pie looks like.

Ironically, professional conversations about meaning making tend to isolate these four components of the relevant knowledge base. The components often compete for instructional time and thus are seen as alternative approaches rather than part of a coherent whole, especially for students who are identified as struggling readers. This can lead to such absurd recommendations as Wiggins's (2010), that literacy educators essentially omit teaching with narrative text, and all the instructional opportunities that such texts offer, suggesting that such instruction is irrelevant to success in school or life.

Although less dramatic, teachers can lose balance even within a so-called "balanced" curriculum if strategies are overemphasized rather than taught as simply tools for learning, literary understanding and appreciation, and personal growth. We have seen teachers turn *Strategies That Work: Teaching Comprehension to Enhance Understanding* (Harvey & Goudvis, 2000), a book that can provide valuable insight into individual comprehension strategies, into a guide for reading instruction that teaches strategies in isolation and as isolated tools. Similarly, we have seen Calkins's curriculum for writing instruction (Calkins et al., 2006) instantiated as a joyless routine of tasks, rather than teaching genre as a part of the author's toolkit for meeting personal goals for writing for a particular audience and purpose. We have also seen literature instruction turned into a dry emphasis on identifying literary elements or deadly, dull, daily prompted responses, rather than teaching students to traverse the text world as a mirror and window into our own lives and the lives of those we may never meet and places we may never visit (Galda, 1998).

Although we have come a long way from Durkin's (1978) research showing comprehension instruction as consisting of simply mentioning, we have not served our students well by overemphasizing strategy instruction at the expense of maintaining the big picture and balancing this instruction within a comprehensive comprehension curriculum. Further complicating the matter is the complexity of making the relationships among strategies, stances, text organization, and text elements clear to students, as these relationships are invisible to the naked eye. Instruction relies on language that is accessible to students across developmental levels and to teachers who work within a range of disciplines. Students need clear frameworks to understand why they are being taught particular aspects of comprehension, how and where this knowledge is relevant, and when and how to use their current knowledge to develop new or deeper understandings.

Just as metacognitive knowledge is seen as critical to effective use of strategies and text organization (i.e., the what, how, when, and why of what is learned; Paris, Lipson, & Wixson, 1983), it is equally critical to success across all four components of the comprehensive curriculum. Further, students need to see the connections of this relevant knowledge among instruction in language arts, learning in the disciplines, and use beyond school contexts. QAR provides the opportunity to create a shared language for creating bridges among these constructs.

QAR: A Language for Instructional Coherence and Sustainability

We believe in the importance of coherence within and across grade levels, and sustainability of the instructional focus through powerful frameworks that help students see connections over time and across disciplines, as well as between in- and out-of-school purposes (Newmann, Smith, Allensworth, & Bryk, 2001). Moreover, we believe it is critical to maintain a clear and steady focus on the goal of this instruction: promoting learning, personal growth, and satisfaction, not only in terms of success as a student but also to become literate individuals who use what they have learned for achievement, personal fulfillment, and advocacy. For both instruction in and the use of core comprehension constructs, teachers and students benefit when they have a shared language for talking about these largely unobservable constructs, a language that is appropriate for use over time within classrooms and grade levels across school subjects, as well as across grade levels.

The language of QAR is one way to create consistency, a bridge across disciplinary and temporal contexts. One year of comprehension instruction—and by extension, anything less—even by a highly skilled and experienced teacher who uses a common language like QAR is insufficient. In our experience, this finding holds for all schools. However, it is especially salient in schools serving a high proportion of students who may struggle with reading and writing. These students require multiple years of consistent instruction in all aspects of comprehension—the more years, the better. Both the framework and the language used within this framework contribute to each teacher's ability to create a coherent experience for students throughout schooling.

Researchers such as Newmann and his colleagues (2001) have found that coherence is at the core of schools that are effective in raising students' achievement levels. Coherence is at the heart of what Au and Raphael (2011) has termed a "staircase curriculum" (p. 2). The staircase curriculum is one in which teachers hold a clear vision of the excellent graduating reader and writer—the top step—and each grade-level teacher has a clear understanding of the goals their students must achieve to remain on the staircase and reach this vision. Each stair is steep enough to ensure progress, and there are no cracks in the staircase through which a student might fall (or in the vernacular of school, fail).

Language introduced through QAR provides a way for teachers across time to distinguish between information found "In the Book" from information that is available "In My Head," a distinction at the foundation of learning, or knowledge building. The two terms serve as metaphors for discussing external and internal sources of information. *Book* stands for any source (e.g., text, images, media) that is external to the reader, while *Head* stands for the knowledge one can access without using external resources. Book information, when learned, can become Head knowledge. As Vygotsky (1978) has argued, an individual's learning begins within the social realm, that is, the individual's interactions with others. What begins as external knowledge, essentially becomes internal when learned. Readers' engagement with an external source (e.g., questioning the author) leads to meaning construction and learning (McKeown, Beck, & Worthy, 1993). Similarly, epistemology, or the study of knowledge, suggests that knowledge development comes from the internalization and successful control over content and ideas that were once external. One of the primary goals of schooling is, of course, the development of knowledge.

Thus, we argue that the importance and staying power of QAR comes not from its rather limited use as a strategy for designating where an answer came from (Raphael, 1986) but from its role as a language or vocabulary, creating the bridge for linking knowledge development, sources of knowledge, and the changing nature of information; what was once an In the Book relationship eventually can become information In My Head, just as what was once known may escape us and require that we return to the book for the information we need (Raphael & Au, 2005; Raphael, Highfield, & Au, 2006). The language of QAR allows teachers and students to specify the relationship as well as the strategies that they can use to achieve their goal.

How to Get Started With Teaching QAR

Instruction in QAR begins by introducing the core terms, the basic language of QAR, through a series of paired comparisons (see Figure 6.2) so that students learn the category scheme and terms. The instruction then spirals up into its more sophisticated and valuable use as a vocabulary for talking about knowledge and its development and the nature of readers' engagement with the text.

That QAR provides a shared language is a central concept to effective QAR instruction. More often than we would have expected, we have encountered teachers who have made comments such as, "I'm done teaching QAR. We did this in October." "I always use QAR! My students tell me what the QAR is whenever they answer a question, but they seem bored with it." "My students can tell me the QARs, but now what should I do with it?" These comments are characteristic of teachers who view

Figure 6.2. Paired Comparisons for Question–Answer Relationships

QAR as an end goal rather than a common language to be used in the classroom, extending the initial instruction into use within the language arts and learning in other school subjects. The purpose of QAR instruction is not so that students can "get the QAR right" but rather that students come to understand the relationship among sources of information that are key to building knowledge. Regardless of students' age levels, reading abilities, and dispositions, the QAR language remains consistent. This is one reason why, when used within and across grade levels within a school, QAR helps build bridges across instructional contexts, leading to increased curricular coherence.

QAR instruction flows through five focus areas, repeated for each subsequent paired comparison:

1. Sources of knowledge

2. Meaning of core terms

3. Language of QAR modeled in authentic situations (e.g., read-alouds, inquiry projects, book club or literature circles)

4. Check students' understandings and modify instruction as needed

5. Use the language across school subjects and across grade levels as appropriate

Of these five focal areas, the third and the fifth are the ones that often are underdeveloped or even left out of the process.

The First Paired Comparison

In the first paired comparison, students are introduced to the idea that information related to a text source can be thought of as either external to the text source (i.e., In My Head) or internal to the text source (i.e., In the Book). Instruction in this first comparison lays the foundation for the purposes for learning the QAR language. These purposes relate to helping students think and talk about the relationship among the core contributors to meaning making:

- What the reader brings to the text through background knowledge, life experiences, and prior reading
- The content of the text or multiple texts, including conventional print materials, digital texts, and graphic images
- The purpose for reading as reflected in the kinds of questions that are driving the reading, whether self-generated or asked by others, such as the teacher

The language provides a way of talking about how knowledge develops—how new information today becomes background knowledge in the future.

For example, students in Tammy Nakagawa's class collaboratively generated a list of external resources from which they could get information (see Figure 6.3). The teacher recorded their ideas in the right column of the chart paper and placed a small box in front of each item on the list. They then talked about which of these resources could be read, marking the relevant ones with the letter R. Students were then given one minute to make a list of information that they had in their heads. Using that list, they then discussed where the information had come from the original external sources for what was now their own knowledge. This rich, highly interactive conversation focused on the strategy component of the comprehensive comprehension curriculum. The discussion underscored the distinction between internal knowledge in our heads, external sources of information that we draw on for information, which of those external sources were accessed by reading, and the constantly changing state of the relationship. Knowledge does not reside In the Book and In My Head permanently; it changes as individuals come to own knowledge that had once been external, or even as individuals may forget information that once resided comfortably in memory.

In addition to providing a way to characterize knowledge development, QAR instruction provides a way of clarifying the purpose of the questions, invoking background knowledge, and moving the reader back into the text. First graders in Jen McCoy's Chicago classroom described QAR as

Figure 6.3. Students' Collaborative List of External Sources

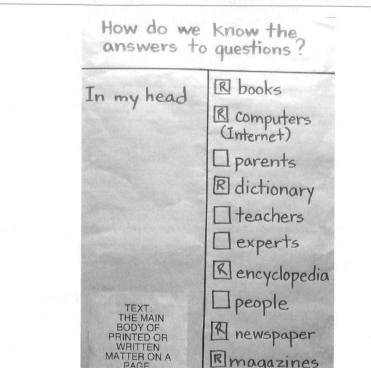

a way to know "how our question and the answer get along." They can talk about how ideas are in their own heads or in the books they listen to or read on their own. When Jen asks her students questions, she does not simply ask them to identify the QAR after the question has been answered. She sometimes prefaces by saying to the students, "I know some of you may have the information you need to answer this question in your head, but I'm asking it as an In the Book QAR. I want you to be able to justify your answer by showing us where in the book you found the information." Or, sometimes she will say to the students, "I know that this could be an In the Book QAR, but I'll bet that some of you may have this information in your heads by now!" Jen sets the stage for continued discussion that will connect the strategies that the students use for seeking information to purposes for reading, and their personal response as they assume different stances throughout the reading process.

QAR language is used to scaffold students' use of strategies for engaging in inquiry, whether using a single text or multiple sources.

Fourth-grade students in a classroom in Chicago use QAR to support their strategy use during their student-led book club discussions, creating a bridge between their text comprehension and their response to the literature, both fiction and informational. In one activity, each book club group has five sentence strips. Toward the end of their individual book club discussions, each group is charged with creating at least one and up to three questions that would lead to interesting and important whole-class discussion. The questions are to grow out of their book club discussions and be worthy of more sustained conversation among the entire class. Students then post their sentence strips next to the chart, as displayed in Figure 6.4. Sometimes the students are asked to post the question on the side of the chart that reflects the QAR that they thought would be used, while other times they post them randomly, and part of the whole-class discussion involves the most appropriate source for responding.

The task requires that students consider the inferences they have drawn based on text information, predictions they have made, summaries of key ideas, inquiry questions that the reading has prompted, connections to other texts and life experiences, and so forth. Also, the questions require the students to consider issues that they genuinely would be interested in pursuing with their peers outside their individual book club groups.

The examples above demonstrate the power of QAR language to create bridges among comprehension strategies, text organization and literary knowledge, and the stances that the students have assumed

Figure 6.4. Fourth-Grade Students' Inquiry Activity

during reading, even when using only the In the Book and In My Head QARs. Teachers use these concepts to develop questions that probe for high levels of literacy and to help students learn appropriate strategies to answer questions. Students learn how to create questions that push their own and their peers' high-level thinking. Introducing students to the two categories provides a way into talking about where information comes from, the broad array of information sources used to comprehend text, and how information builds in our heads using these many external sources over time. The appropriate amount of instructional time spent on these two primary categories depends on the students' age and amount of prior experience with QAR, from a few minutes (i.e., middle school students with extensive experience) to several months (i.e., early primary students with no prior experience).

The Four Core QARs

When students can explain the difference between In the Book and In My Head QARs, use the language in classroom academic conversations with confidence, and recognize when the task requires going to the text or using background knowledge, they are ready for the next level of QAR instruction. This involves learning about the four core QARs: Right There, Think & Search, Author & Me, and On My Own, each introduced within a paired comparison as indicated in Figure 6.2. The first pair focuses students' attention on the difference between Right There and Think & Search QARs, both specific categories within In the Book; the second pair distinguishes between Author & Me and On My Own, both In My Head QARs.

In the Book Paired Comparisons

The paired comparisons for In the Book—Right There and Think & Search—are displayed in Figure 6.5. These two QARs differ in terms of the key phrase in the definition for Right There. Notice that the final line of the definition refers to information that is "'right there' in the same place."

This concept of place changes developmentally as students mature in their reading abilities. In texts designed for early readers, often a sentence begins and ends on the same line. Looking across sentences may represent a challenge for those just learning to read, so "in the same place" usually refers to information contained within a single sentence. As readers mature, the construct of same place tends to expand to mean the same paragraph, the same page, or sometimes the same text.

Figure 6.5. "In the Book" Question–Answer Relationships Defined

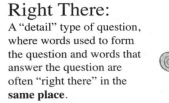

Right There:

A "detail" type of question, where words used to form the question and words that answer the question are often "right there" in the **same place**.

Think & Search:

The answer is in the text, but readers have to "think & search" to find the answer, sometimes within a paragraph or across paragraphs, sections, chapters, and texts.

Figure 6.6. Emerging to Sophisticated Readers

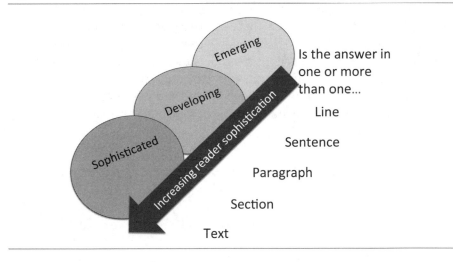

Is the answer in one or more than one...

Line

Sentence

Paragraph

Section

Text

Emerging

Developing

Sophisticated

Increasing reader sophistication

The definition of Think & Search QARs conveys the range of places where one can search for information in and across texts, using the qualifier "sometimes" to indicate that place can vary, and thus the level of thinking about and searching for text information may increase in complexity with longer and multiple texts. Place, in the language of QAR, must remain fluid and open to redefinition. As displayed in Figure 6.6, Think & Search in primary grades can mean looking for information in different sentences or paragraphs. Think & Search in intermediate grades generally involves looking across paragraphs, pages, or sections of text and can get into multiple text sources. In middle school, Think & Search generally involves students looking across sections and multiple texts. Sometimes students initiate the change to the definition of *place*. Students in one fourth-grade classroom noted that it did not seem like much of a Think & Search when they were looking at different sentences in the same paragraph. Their teacher agreed, and collaboratively, they decided that they would consider same place as being within a single paragraph. Other times, the teacher raises the possibility of expanding the definition for *place* with the students. We have found that it rarely matters who brings it up, as long as the students are ready developmentally for reconsidering how *place* is defined for distinguishing between Right There and Think & Search QARs.

In My Head Paired Comparisons

The third paired comparison expands In My Head QARs into Author & Me and On My Own, with definitions for each displayed in Figure 6.7. Both QARs represent questions that require readers to respond by using background knowledge. The distinction between the two comes down to the amount of significant, actionable information that the reader uses from the text to determine the appropriate background knowledge to access. On My Own questions require little to no information from the text for readers to construct a complete and appropriate answer. These QARs

Figure 6.7. "In My Head" Question–Answer Relationships Defined

Author & Me:
The information to answer the question comes from my background knowledge, but to even make sense of the question, I'd need to have read and understood the text.

On My Own:
The question relates to the text, but I could probably answer this one even if I had never read the text. All the ideas and information come from my background knowledge.

are designed to build reader knowledge prior to reading or draw on the readers' experiences during the reading process, such as the following:

- "The essay we are about to read was written midway through the U.S. Civil War, in about 1863. What was happening within the country at that time that might have influenced the writer? What would you want to know about the author's background to help you critically analyze his points?"

- "The characters in this story had to make some fairly tough decisions. Think about a time when you faced a tough decision and then turn to your partner to talk about it."

- "We've read several folk tales now and have been studying key elements that make up a folk tale. What do you expect you will encounter in the folk tale that we are about to read, titled…?"

All On My Own QARs share the central factor that the reader does not depend on deep understanding of the text information to participate fully in discussion related to the question.

In the first example, a student who has knowledge of the Civil War era from studying U.S. history in school, watching historical period movies in our out of school, or reading informational or historical fiction relevant to that era can participate actively in the discussion without having read the essay or understood any of the essay's core ideas. In the second example, students can talk extensively about making a tough decision without referring to the text or using any text information. In the third example, readers can draw on their prior experience within the genre but will not need specific information from the text to answer the question. On My Own QARs are often used before reading to access, activate, or build relevant knowledge or set a purpose for reading (e.g., K in K–W–L; Ogle, 1986). However, they are, or should be, rare during and after reading, as that instruction should guide students to make meaningful and significant connections between their own lives and knowledge and the text world they have entered.

Author & Me QARs create a bridge between the cognitive strategies that students use to construct the author's intended meaning and personal responses created to make text-to-self and self-to-text connections. Although the information used to answer the question comes from the reader's own knowledge base and life experiences, knowing what to access and why involves understanding the text. Author & Me QARs underscore the connection between the text and the reader's world:

- "In the arena, Katniss was faced with what seemed to be an intolerable choice for a 14-year-old. What does her solution say about trust? How big a risk do you think she was taking when she made the offer to Peeta?"

- "Using [name of essayist]'s essay as a model, create a similar argument in an essay arguing to change one of the following school policies: (a) the time fourth graders go to lunch, (b) the availability of playground equipment for fourth and fifth graders, or (c) changing the age requirement for open library access."

- "What do you think would have happened differently if the brother and sister in the story had read the directions through before starting the game?"

Notice that in each of these examples, students would be unable to answer the question (implied or explicit) using only external sources. The information needs to come from the students' knowledge base. However, in the first example, they would need to know both what Katniss's decision was and how it related to the trust that she and another character in the story had developed. In the second, the students would need to understand the structure used by a particular essayist and then adapt it to create their own argument. In the third, they would need to know the significance of the directions to the story and reconstruct the story with that significant event changed.

Just as In The Book QARs reflect developmental differences as readers mature in their control over the reading process, In My Head QARs vary developmentally but do so according to the decreasing dependence that readers have on the external source for actionable knowledge. Some students may think of the first question as an Author & Me, just as we did in offering it as an example. The logic is that the author is providing significant information in the form of evidence that Peeta and Katniss came to trust one another, could trust their lives to one another, and were willing to die by eating the poison berries rather than be forced to harm one another. Students would draw on that information from the text to construct their answers.

However, some students may argue that they know the text so well that everything they need to answer the question is in their head and that further, they are going to contrast Peeta and Katniss with Romeo and Juliet, also from their own knowledge. Thus, to them, QAR is an On My Own. How should their teacher respond? One option is for the teacher to tell the student that he or she is wrong, because it is an Author & Me. Another, and to us a far more reasonable one, is to celebrate the way in which the student has used QAR language to form his or her argument and move on. Such a position underscores that the goal of QAR instruction is not to get the QAR right but to understand conceptually the relationship among ideas, bridging among cognitive strategies, literary elements, and the organization of text for deep personal engagement in response to what has been read.

QAR Language and the Reading Cycle

Thus far, our focus has been on what to teach about QAR so that students learn the core vocabulary for use in day-to-day classroom activity conveyed as part of a coherent and comprehensive comprehension curriculum. In this section, we use the relationship between the language of QAR and the stances reflected in the reading cycle to illustrate how QAR functions in classroom conversations.

As we noted earlier, Langer (1995) describes the four stances that readers assume throughout the reading process, whether reading informational or narrative texts. The stances reflect the reader's relationship to the world created by the text and parallel the reading cycle of before, during, and after reading. The reading cycle should not be thought of as a linear process happening before reading an entire text, followed by during reading as if a text is always completed in a single reading event, and after as if once readers leave a text world, they do not return. Rather, imagine an authentic reading situation, perhaps a novel read over a course of a week, prior to going to sleep, during lunch or coffee breaks, on the train when commuting, and when relaxing on a weekend. Similarly, one can imagine reading a professional text while in the office between meetings, before going into the office, and after dinner. We enter and leave the text world throughout our engagement with that text. Although the cycle of before, during, and after can occur in a linear way, it is not typical.

With the nonlinear nature of the reading cycle in mind, consider Langer's (1995) stances. Prior to reading, skilled readers consider what the text world is like. If they have read nothing yet, they draw on background knowledge (e.g., other texts by the same author, similar genres or topics) using On My Own QARs as they consider the text world. A reader who has put down the text and is now returning to it, or one using significant information from the text (e.g., table of contents, headers, charts, images), draws on Author & Me QARs by building from previous readings to anticipate or predict upcoming ideas and events before entering the text world.

Once the reader enters the text world, Langer (1995) describes the stances as moving through and stepping back, using Right There, Think & Search, and Author & Me QARs. As readers move through the text, they use all the resources that they can bring to bear to make sense of what they are reading: identifying key information (Right There or Think & Search), making inferences (Author & Me), summarizing (Think & Search), monitoring to check predictions (Author & Me), and so forth. In effect, readers make self-to-text connections that facilitate meaning construction. However, while in the text world, readers also step back and reflect on how the text content is changing their own knowledge and perceptions, not only of the text world but also of their own. In doing so, readers invoke a range of responses (Author & Me) that enhance their engagement with the text.

Upon leaving the text world, readers engage in critical response to what they have read, strategies that support Author & Me QARs. Readers revisit characters' motivations and how plots have played out. The stories may change the way readers think about something in their own lives. They engage in critical analysis of the quality of the text, moving beyond whether the text was a good read (e.g., "I liked this, because…," "This was useful, because…") to considering the quality of the narrative, the argument, or the information itself.

The language of QAR provides a bridge among the four areas depicted in Figure 6.2 to help teachers create a coherent and comprehensive comprehension curriculum. Students must understand the relationship among their own knowledge, purposes for reading (i.e., the implied or explicit questions that drive the reading event), and text information, ideas, and concepts. This relationship is made visible and concrete through QAR. Comprehension strategies can be explained in terms of how they help uncover and address these relationships (e.g., summarizing strategies are useful for Think & Search QARs but not so useful for On My Own, strategies for making inferences or predicting are useful for Author & Me QARs but not so much for Right There). Personal response strategies provide an array of approaches to making reader–text connections (Author & Me). For success in creating Think & Search QARs, students need to know how texts are organized and literary elements are used. Omitting any of the four core areas of the comprehensive curriculum, or teaching them without using the full range of texts that reflect how our culture conveys the history of the human experience, shortchanges readers in significant ways. Simply knowing how to identify the QARs is insufficient. The goal of QAR instruction must be to build a language to convey the complex constructs that comprise successful comprehension.

QAR: Beyond Instruction to Extension and Application

Ms. Richman's fourth graders are familiar with QAR's category system and understand that QAR helps them communicate clearly across a variety of instructional settings. This came in handy during book club activities. Students often are asked to create two or three questions that they believe would lead to interesting whole-class or small-group discussions. Ms. Richman noticed the students falling into a pattern of generating questions that reflected superficial connections to the ideas in the texts. Typical questions included the following:

- "I disagreed with how [character's name] handled the situation. Have you ever disagreed with a friend?"
- "Do you think living in [historical era, country, etc.] would be harder or easier than today?"
- "What did you think of [character, content, or event]?"

To address the problem, Ms. Richman displayed several samples and asked students to indicate what kind of QARs the sample questions represented. Students categorized them as mostly On My Own. Using QAR language, she called students' attention to the differences between what they were asking (i.e., On My Own) and the kinds of questions that lead to meatier, text-connected discussions during and after reading (i.e., Author & Me, Think & Search). She reminded the students that she wanted them to consider connections or contrasts/conflicts among ideas across the multiple texts that they had read as well as between what they had read and what they already knew. The discussion was a turning point in the students' questioning practices and raised the overall quality of the discussion.

Concluding Comments

We believe that one of the primary goals of education is to create educated citizens who are able to use what they have learned—the processes, strategies, content knowledge, and dispositions—to achieve success and personal satisfaction. Fundamental to this goal is access to information, which demands high levels of literacy. In this chapter, we argue for the importance of a common language that supports teachers across disciplinary areas and grade levels in teaching students literacy processes and content knowledge, as well as a deep understanding of how this knowledge and important strategies and skills develop across time. We believe that QAR can provide one path to accomplish this goal. The goal of QAR instruction, as we mentioned throughout the chapter, is not about students routinely identifying the QAR they used to answer a question. Rather, it is the language that is learned to highlight relationships among the reader, texts, and tasks and how those relationships contribute to the development of knowledge and use of that knowledge to accomplish one's goals over a lifetime.

TRY IT!

1. Using the first paired comparison and relatively short age-appropriate text, introduce your students to the QAR language of In the Book and In My Head through a think-aloud activity.

2. Introduce the idea that "In the Book" is a metaphor for sources that are external to your own knowledge using a chart similar to the one in Figure 6.3. Cocreate a similar chart, asking students to name sources of information where they can get ideas or information, which of these they use in or out of school, and which ones they can read.

3. Use the QAR language of In the Book and In My Head during teaching for at least three different school subjects (e.g., in math for story problems, in social studies, in reading instruction) to illustrate the value of this language across the school day.

4. After a text has been read (e.g., story, read-aloud, textbook segment), have students divide into teams of four. Ask each team to create two interesting questions that can be used to talk about the text, one that asks readers to use information from their head and one that asks them to use information from what was read.

REFERENCES

Adams, G.N., & Brown, S.M. (2003). *The six-minute solution: A reading fluency program.* Frederick, CO: Sopris West.

American Institutes for Research. (2008). *Reading framework for the 2009 National Assessment of Educational Progress.* Washington, DC: National Assessment Governing Board, U.S. Department of Education.

Au, K.H., & Raphael, T.E. (2010). Using workshop approaches to support the literacy development of ELLs. In G. Li & P.A. Edwards (Eds.), *Best practices in ELL instruction* (pp. 207–221). New York: Guilford.

Au, K.H., & Raphael, T.E. (2011). The staircase curriculum: Whole-school collaboration to improve literacy achievement. *The NERA Journal, 46*(2), 1–8.

Barr, R., Kamil, M.L., Mosenthal, P., & Pearson P.D. (Eds.). (1991). *Handbook of reading research: Vol. 2*. New York: Longman.

Berliner, D.C., & Biddle, B.J. (1995). *The manufactured crisis: Myths, fraud, and the attack on America's public schools*. Cambridge, MA: Perseus.

Brozo, W.G. (2010). *To be a boy, to be a reader: Engaging teen and preteen boys in active literacy* (2nd ed.). Newark, DE: International Reading Association.

Calkins, L., Cruz, M.C., Martinelli, M., Chiarella, M., Kesler, T., Gillette, C., et al. (2006). *Units of study for teaching writing, grades 3–5*. Portsmouth, NH: Heinemann.

Council of Chief State School Officers. (2010). *Common core state standards for English language arts and literacy in history/social studies, science, and technical subjects*. Washington, DC: Author. Retrieved July 23, 2010, from www.corestandards.org/the-standards/english-language-arts-standards

Durkin, D. (1978). What classroom observations reveal about reading comprehension instruction. *Reading Research Quarterly, 14*(4), 481–533. doi:10.1598/RRQ.14.4.2

Flesch, R. (1986). *Why Johnny can't read and what you can do about it* (First Perennial Library ed.). New York: Harper & Row. (Original work published 1955)

Galda, L. (1998). Mirrors and windows: Reading as transformation. In T.E. Raphael & K.H. Au (Eds.), *Literature-based instruction: Reshaping the curriculum* (pp. 1–11). Norwood, MA: Christopher-Gordon.

Graesser, A.C., Golding, J.M., & Long, D.L. (1991). Narrative representation and comprehension. In R. Barr, M.L. Kamil, P.B. Mosenthal, & P.D. Pearson (Eds.), *Handbook of reading research* (Vol. 2, pp. 171–205). White Plains, NY: Longman.

Harvey, S., & Goudvis, A. (2000). *Strategies that work: Teaching comprehension to enhance understanding*. York, ME: Stenhouse.

Israel, S.E., & Duffy, G.G. (Eds.). (2009). *Handbook of research on reading comprehension*. New York: Routledge.

Kamil, M.L., Mosenthal, P.B., Pearson, P.D., & Barr, R. (Eds.). (2000). *Handbook of reading research: Vol. 3*. New York: Longman.

Langer, J.A. (1995). *Envisioning literature: Literary understanding and literature instruction*. New York: Teachers College Press.

Madda, C.L., Griffo, V.B., Pearson, P.D., & Raphael, T.E. (2011). Balance in comprehensive literacy instruction: Evolving conceptions. In L.M. Morrow & L.B. Gambrell (Eds.), *Best practices in literacy instruction* (4th ed., pp. 37–63). New York: Guilford.

McKeown, M.G., Beck, I.L., & Worthy, M.J. (1993). Grappling with text ideas: Questioning the author. *The Reading Teacher, 46*(7), 560–566.

Newmann, F.M., Smith, B., Allensworth, E., & Bryk, A.S. (2001). Instructional program coherence: What it is and why it should guide school improvement policy. *Educational Evaluation and Policy Analysis, 23*(4), 297–321. doi:10.3102/01623737023004297

New York State Education Department. (2009). *Federal education policy and the states, 1945–2009: A brief synopsis* (Rev. ed.). Albany: Author. Retrieved February 18, 2011, from www.sifepp.nysed.gov/edpolicy/research/res _policymakers.shtml

Ogle, D.M. (1986). K–W–L: A teaching model that develops active reading of expository text. *The Reading Teacher, 39*(6), 564–570.

Paris, S.G., Lipson, M.Y., & Wixson, K.K. (1983). Becoming a strategic reader. *Contemporary Educational Psychology, 8*(3), 293–316. doi:10.1016/0361-476X(83)90018-8

Pearson, P.D., Barr, R., Kamil, M.L., & Mosenthal, P. (1984). *Handbook of reading research*. New York: Longman.

Pearson, P.D., Raphael, T.E., Benson, V.L., & Madda, C.L. (2007). Balance in comprehensive literacy instruction: Then and now. In L.B. Gambrell, L.M. Morrow, & M. Pressley (Eds.), *Best practices in literacy instruction* (3rd ed., pp. 30–54). New York: Guilford.

Raphael, T.E. (1982). Teaching children question-answering strategies. *The Reading Teacher, 36*(2), 186–191.

Raphael, T.E. (1986). Teaching question answer relationships, revisited. *The Reading Teacher, 39*(6), 516–522.

Raphael, T.E., & Au, K.H. (2005). QAR: Enhancing comprehension and test taking across grades and content areas. *The Reading Teacher, 59*(3), 206–221.

Raphael, T.E., Highfield, K., & Au, K.H. (2006). *QAR now: A powerful and practical framework that develops comprehension and higher-level thinking in all students*. New York: Scholastic.

Rosenblatt, L.M. (1976). *Literature as exploration* (3rd ed.). New York: Noble and Noble.

Sipe, L.R. (2008). *Storytime: Young children's literary understanding in the classroom*. New York: Teachers College Press.

Snow, C.E. (2002). *Reading for understanding: Toward a research and development program in reading comprehension*. Santa Monica, CA: RAND.

Vygotsky, L.S. (1978). *Mind in society: The development of higher psychological processes* (M. Cole, V. John-Steiner, & S. Scribner, Eds.). Cambridge, MA: Harvard University Press.

Weaver, C.A., & Kintsch, W. (1991). Expository text. In R. Barr, M.L. Kamil, P. Mosenthal, & P.D. Pearson (Eds.), *Handbook of reading research* (Vol. 2, pp. 230–245). White Plains, NY: Longman.

Wiggins, G. (2010, December). Wiggins wonders: Ban fiction from the curriculum. *21st Century Fluency Project*. Retrieved February 18, 2011, from thecommittedsardine.net/blogpost.cfm?blogID=1663

Supporting Students Who Struggle With Comprehension of Text: Using Literature Discussion Groups in Grades 3–6

Shannon C. Henderson and Linda J. Dorn

The students in Priscella Leibig's fourth-grade class have been participating in literature discussion groups (LDGs) all semester (all names are pseudonyms). Today, they are talking about *Honeysuckle House* (2004) by Andrea Cheng. This is a story about Sarah, a Chinese American girl whose best friend Victoria suddenly moves away, and Tinj, an immigrant from China who transfers to Sarah's school. The teacher tries to pair the two girls because of their common cultural roots. However, Sarah misses Victoria and resents Tinj's presence in her life. The book has strong themes, and Ms. Leibig's students are clearly focused on the topics of friendship, cultural differences, loss, and relationships.

Ms. Leibig opens the discussion with her prompt, "Who would like to begin our discussion?" The students understand the importance of conversational moves for developing and sustaining dialogue. Daniel begins the topic, and two other students extend the theme of loss to a new level:

Daniel: Sarah should just move on with her life and make friends with Tinj.

Jaylon: It's like in *Old Yeller* when Travis had to shoot Old Yeller. He lost his friend, and when Elizabeth gave him this little speckled pup, he really couldn't take it, because it didn't feel as special as Old Yeller did to him.

Kayla: It's like Old Yeller was Victoria and Victoria moved, and when the new speckled pup came along, Travis was Sarah, and the new speckled pup was Tina. Then, at the end of *Old Yeller*, Travis was beginning to like the new speckled pup, and at the end of *Honeysuckle House*, Sarah was starting to like Tinj.

After Early Intervention, Then What? Teaching Struggling Readers in Grades 3 and Beyond (2nd ed.) edited by Jeanne R. Paratore and Rachel L. McCormack. © 2011 by the International Reading Association.

The students continue to build on the themes of friendship and loss while using conversational moves to keep the discussion in motion. Ms. Leibig's role is that of participant observer, joining in at times to enrich the discussion or prompting the students to think at a deeper level. Near the end, Ms. Leibig asks, "What do you think was the author's purpose in writing this story?" Brandon responds, "It's about how close two people can be in friendship and how another person can make you feel after a friend has moved away." Jaylon's comment captures the central theme: "The author wanted to teach us about relationships and how you can deal with it if a friend moves away." The other students expand on the idea of relationships and the associated consequences. Daniel concludes the discussion with words of advice: "When something happens in the past, you shouldn't hold on to it for the rest of your life. You need to know when to let go and move on." The discussion has been thoughtful, one in which literacy (the book) and language (the conversations) were the primary tools for shaping literate knowledge.

From Dorn, L.J., & Soffos, C. (2005). *Teaching for deep comprehension: A reading workshop approach.* Portland, ME: Stenhouse. Reprinted with permission.

Despite the progress to improve the literacy achievement of students in U.S. schools over the past 20 years (Lee, Grigg, & Donahue, 2007; Salahu-Din, Persky, & Miller, 2008), the majority of students do not meet grade-level reading and writing benchmarks (National Center for Education Statistics, 2010). In the early grades, a primary focus of instruction has been on the development of early reading skills (e.g., phonemic awareness, phonics, sight words) and has largely ignored developing comprehension processes. Yet, struggling readers beyond third grade with good decoding skills may have difficulty making sense of the information and ideas they encounter while reading (Buly & Valencia, 2002).

The fourth-grade students participating in the small-group discussion from Ms. Leibig's class are engaged in a LDG designed to develop the students' understanding of the text they are reading and to scaffold their comprehension to higher levels. The structure of these groups reflects the understanding that comprehension is a fluid, context-sensitive process that requires a dynamic, flexible approach to instruction that enables all students to participate in rich and meaningful conversations about text.

Teaching and learning are reciprocal processes; therefore, teachers must be sensitive observers of students' reading behaviors and be able to respond according to students' needs. This is especially important for struggling readers who have habituated inappropriate reading behaviors that can be resistant to instruction. Although we know that effective classroom teachers provide a differentiated curriculum that is responsive to students' strengths and needs, in too many cases, the core curriculum is delivered in a standard format that treats students as though they all possess the same levels of knowledge and experience. This is especially troubling, as the number of struggling readers in the upper grades can be traced back to the quality of classroom instruction in earlier grades (Snow, Burns, & Griffin, 1998).

The Individuals with Disabilities Education Improvement Act of 2004 introduced provisions that allowed for documentation of how a student responds to instruction as an alternative means of diagnosing learning disabilities. This process, termed Response to Intervention, shifted the focus from identification of reading disabilities to prevention. As a result, many schools have begun a process of providing differentiated instruction for those students who struggle with literacy and monitoring students' response to the instruction at prescribed intervals. The differentiated instruction is most often conceptualized using a tiered framework with classroom interventions (often referred to as Tier 1 interventions) serving as the first line of defense in preventing reading failure (Dorn & Henderson, 2010; Dorn & Schubert, 2008).

Unfortunately, many classroom teachers are struggling in their efforts to differentiate instruction for those students who are encountering difficulties with reading and writing while still ensuring high-quality core instruction. As a solution, schools encourage and sometimes mandate the use of packaged programs. In this chapter, we argue that packaged programs are ineffective for addressing the comprehension needs of struggling readers. Then, we present seven research-based principles that have been shown to support students' comprehension of text. Finally, we share how teachers can implement LDGs during readers' workshop while providing individual scaffolds for the students who are not responding to group instruction.

The Problems With Packaged Programs

Our work in schools has revealed that classrooms are brimming with packaged intervention programs, whereby the teacher or an instructional aide pulls together a small group of students and proceeds through a series of prescribed lessons. Although the teachers may be collecting data and monitoring their students' progress, we see little evidence that teachers are modifying the program sequence to adjust their instruction to meet students' needs. In too many cases, if a student is not making progress, the failure is attributed to the student rather than the instruction or the program. Furthermore, a student's failure to respond to the program might be followed by more intense remediation with another packaged approach. Many of these prescribed solutions are grounded in a simplistic approach that views learning through a deficit model and ignores the complexity of the human brain in constructing knowledge.

Another problem with the use of packaged intervention programs is that although the programs may improve a student's proficiency on particular subskills (e.g., phonics, sight words, fluency, answering text questions), this knowledge may not transfer to authentic reading and writing tasks. In other words, the student might meet exit criteria associated with the program but, upon return to the classroom, have little knowledge of how the skills transfer to authentic reading and writing activities.

To complicate matters even further, students who are accurate readers but poor comprehenders are commonly overlooked (Biancarosa & Snow, 2004; Moje, 2010); concomitantly, few interventions focus on developing crucial comprehension processes. This is due, in large part, to the widely held view that if we teach students to decode and develop their vocabulary knowledge through listening comprehension, then reading comprehension will follow (Gough & Tunmer, 1986). Moreover, even when students are identified as having comprehension problems, interventions have typically focused on teaching word parts, isolated vocabulary, strategies, fluency (privileging accuracy and automaticity), retelling, and answering literal-level questions. If students are not taught how to comprehend at higher levels, then the consequences may be immense. At minimum, students may have difficulty in meeting the expectations of the new Common Core State Standards (Council of Chief State School Officers, 2010) that require them to:

- Cite textual evidence to support analysis of what the text says
- Determine a theme or central idea of a text and how it is conveyed
- Provide a summary distinct from personal opinions or judgments
- Explain how an author develops the point of view
- Compare different text genres and media
- Read and comprehend a variety of genres around a topic or subject

Why Do Students Struggle With Comprehension?

We all struggle with comprehension, depending on our reading abilities, the text we are reading, and our purpose for reading it (Snow, 2002). For example, consider this excerpt from a commercial flight manual:

If the ailerons or spoilers are jammed, force applied to the Captain's and the First Officer's control wheels will identify which system, ailerons or spoilers, is usable and which control wheel, Captain's or First Officer's, can provide roll control. If the aileron control system is jammed, force applied to the First Officer's control wheel provides roll control from the spoilers. The ailerons and the Captain's control wheel are inoperative. If the spoiler system is jammed, force applied to the Captain's control wheel provides roll control from the ailerons. The spoilers and the First Officer's control wheel are inoperative. (Delta Air Lines, 2010, p. 9.20.3)

Most of us can accurately decode the words and read the text with fluency. In fact, most could provide a retelling of what we just read. However, unless you know something about flying, we would wager that you have little understanding of the content and most certainly are unable to apply the knowledge to another text or situation.

Most students, when introduced to a new genre of text or an unfamiliar subject, experience a degree of disequilibrium. The difference is that good readers monitor when they do not understand, and they possess the motivation and/or task persistence to accomplish their purpose for reading. Further, good readers have developed a repertoire of strategies that they can employ to achieve their purpose for reading when comprehension breaks down.

Reflecting on the flight manual excerpt, our first and most efficient strategy was to go to an expert and ask him to define and explain the terms *control wheel* (yoke; turns the plane and makes it go up and down), *ailerons* (on the outer part of the wing; rolls the airplane, so you can turn right and left), and *spoilers* (on top of the wing; destroy lift and cause drag to slow and help turn the airplane). Had we not had that strategic response available in our repertoire, we may have gone to the Internet and searched a few of the terms that we concluded might be important in developing our understanding (e.g., if the aileron control fails, the First Officer will turn the airplane using the spoilers; however, if the spoiler control fails, the Captain will turn the plane using the ailerons). Most certainly, it would not have mattered how many times we reread the passage, as we would not have been able to understand the content of the passage without the specific vocabulary knowledge and at least some prior understanding of flight principles. Imagine if we had tried to fix up our comprehension by applying the strategies of visualizing, inferring, or making a prediction! To select and effectively apply any of those strategies, we would first need at least an elementary understanding of the content.

Comprehension is neither stable nor an absolute ability. As teachers, we must keep in mind that the ability to comprehend varies across readers, texts, and contexts (Snow, 2002). Consider your students when they encounter difficulty with comprehension during independent reading. Is it because they do not monitor for meaning or because they lack the motivation or task persistence to attend to the text? Or, maybe they monitor when meaning breaks down but have limited strategies for working out the problem. Perhaps they have knowledge of various comprehension strategies, yet they lack the flexibility for solving the problem with efficiency and ease? Could it be that they are fluent readers in one type of text, but when introduced to an unfamiliar genre, they struggle with understanding? We find that many teachers spend weeks explicitly focused on teaching one comprehension strategy, yet they do not provide their students with opportunities and support to apply flexible strategies during independent reading. It takes a knowledgeable and responsive teacher to provide students with the instruction that they need at the precise moment that the opportunity presents itself. When it occurs it is almost magical—evidence of an effective teacher at the top of her game.

How Can We Support Students Who Struggle With Comprehension?

Research supports that teachers of strong comprehenders teach their students how to comprehend (Taylor, Pearson, Clark, & Walpole, 2000), particularly through the process of think-alouds as they model for students what they do as good readers. In our work with the comprehensive intervention model (CIM; Dorn & Henderson, 2010), we have found that reading comprehension improves when teachers create conditions for developing students' declarative (i.e., what to do), procedural (i.e., how to do it), and conditional knowledge (i.e., when and where to do it; Paris, Lipson, & Wixson, 1983) while also providing differentiated instruction that enables the students to transfer their newly acquired knowledge across changing contexts.

Because comprehension is a complex process, teachers must develop an understanding of the theories and practices that have been empirically supported by research and use these to increase their expertise in working with students. With this understanding, teachers must then reflect on how well the student is responding to instruction as they engage in moment-to-moment decisions that will best facilitate the student's ability to comprehend not only the text under consideration but also how to apply this knowledge when reading independently.

Research-Based Principles for Supporting Reading Comprehension

We have found that a readers' workshop framework that includes LDGs incorporates seven research-based principles for facilitating students' reading comprehension. First, we will describe the seven principles; then, we will share authentic examples from the LDG framework that align with these principles.

Principle 1: Text Selection

Text selection commands center stage when making instructional decisions related to comprehension instruction. Teachers must ask themselves, does the text encourage student thinking? Is it at an appropriate reading level? Are there big ideas or themes? Is there plenty of detail? Can students accomplish their purpose for reading? Does it raise new questions? Does it make you want to read or learn more? Does the text provide opportunities to teach what the students need to learn next? Duke, Purcell-Gates, Hall, and Tower (2006) purport the importance of content-rich texts and emphasize that they can come in many genres and include illustrations, graphics, and forms. In the early grades, we encourage teachers' text selection to focus heavily on particular genres or text structures for LDGs (e.g., personal narrative, biography, folk tale, mystery, cause and effect, comparison). However, as students move up in grade level, book selection should shift and begin to focus on topics, content, and responding to essential questions that may require students to read texts from myriad genres having multiple text structures (Burke, 2010; Guthrie, Wigfield, & Perencevich, 2004).

Principle 2: Activation of Background Knowledge or Providing Prior Knowledge

What students bring to the reading event has a profound influence on their ability to comprehend what they have read (R. Anderson & Pearson, 1984; Kintsch, 2004; Kintsch & van Dijk, 1978; Spiro, 2004). Therefore, the more students know about the topic they are preparing to read, the more deeply they can understand it and think about it (Gunning, 2008). In addition, readers' knowledge of genre or how a particular text is structured helps them organize and better understand the content of the text (Donovan & Smolkin, 2002; Kamberelis, 1999; Purcell-Gates, Duke, & Martineau, 2007). Comprehension suffers when readers cannot synthesize new and old information (Keene & Zimmermann, 2007; Otero & Kintsch, 1992) and when they are unable to select relevant background knowledge and apply that knowledge to the text in question (R. Anderson & Pearson, 1984). Additionally, if students do not have the background knowledge necessary to comprehend the text under consideration, then it is imperative for the teacher to provide the prior knowledge necessary for them to do so.

Principle 3: Setting a Purpose for the Reading

Skillful readers approach text with a purpose for reading (Snow, 2002). They may not be consciously aware of it, and it may change over the course of a reading, but a reader's purpose will influence how he or she interacts with text information and subsequently how he or she comprehends it (R. Anderson & Pearson, 1984; Pressley, 2002; Wolfe, 2001). Therefore, we must ensure that students know independently how to set flexible purposes for reading, select an appropriate text to achieve their purpose, and monitor and evaluate whether their purpose is being met or whether they must do something further to achieve it. Authentic purposes may include reading for enjoyment, reading to accomplish a task, or reading for information.

Unfortunately, much of the instruction related to purpose setting that we observe is focused on assessment outcomes (e.g., constructing a retelling, summarizing, answering teacher questions). Although important, these purposes are usually imposed and evaluated by the teacher rather than the student. Transitioning students from relying on teacher purpose setting to individual purpose setting may pose a significant challenge, but it is a necessary step to developing thoughtful and independent readers.

Principle 4: Teaching Genre Explicitly

Knowledge of genre and text structures plays a role in constructing an understanding of text (Baumann & Bergeron, 1993; Garner & Bochna, 2004; Meyer, Brandt, & Bluth, 1980; Purcell-Gates et al., 2007; Williams, 2005) and assists students in making inferences (Duke, Pressley, & Hilden, 2004; Hansen, 1981), making accurate predictions (McIntyre, 2007), and selecting strategic actions (Pressley et al., 1994). Further, knowledge of specific genres frees up working memory so that readers can process text at higher levels of comprehension.

Research supports the practice of teaching genre by having students read many books in the particular genre to identify its characteristics (Youngs & Barone, 2007) and having students map the structure of the text using graphic organizers (Alvermann & Boothby, 1986). However, it is important to note that not all students need similar instruction in a particular genre (Mullins, Martin, Kennedy, & Foy, 2007; Park, 2008). Teachers must be careful observers to determine which text structures students have well under control and which require additional instruction, then differentiate their instruction accordingly.

Principle 5: Embedded Strategy Instruction for Skillful Reading

We teach students strategies so that they become skillful readers (Afflerbach, Pearson, & Paris, 2008), and research suggests that instruction in small repertoires of comprehension strategies improves students' comprehension on standardized tests (V. Anderson, 1992; Brown, Pressley, Van Meter, & Schuder, 1996; Gersten, Fuchs, Williams, & Baker, 2001). However, the goal of strategy instruction should not be for students to learn strategies per se but to facilitate the unconscious strategic actions that undergird students' ability to construct reasonable interpretations of text (Afflerbach et al., 2008; Pressley, 2002). When students monitor that understanding has broken down, they must have available the resources to select and apply strategic actions that are in accordance with their purpose for reading (e.g., prediction is not particularly helpful when reading a recipe, but possibly visualizing the described process is).

Another consideration when teaching strategies is that reading demands change over time, and not all strategies are applicable to every discipline. As students move up through the grade levels, they must learn to approach texts in discipline-specific ways (Moje, 2010; Shanahan & Shanahan, 2008). For example, chemists, mathematicians, historians, and literary scholars approach texts differently and rely on specific strategies to navigate discipline-specific texts. Early instructional efforts that initially focus on highly generalized strategies may be increasingly problematic as students advance through the grades. To prepare students to navigate highly specialized texts, teachers should ensure that students possess specific strategic actions that are relatively unique to the discipline they are studying (Shanahan & Shanahan, 2008).

Principle 6: Group Discussions of Text

Quality discussion in classrooms appears to impact students' vocabulary and use of comprehension strategies (Kong & Fitch, 2002) and is linked to gains in reading comprehension (Murphy, Wilkinson, Soter, Hennessey,

& Alexander, 2009). However, not all discussions are created equal. Data from a meta-analysis by Soter and colleagues (2008) indicate that the most productive discussions are

- Structured and focused yet not dominated by the teacher
- When students hold the floor for extended periods of time
- When students are prompted to discuss texts through open-ended or authentic questions
- When discussion incorporates a high degree of teacher uptake (i.e., questions in which the teacher incorporated and built on students' comments)

Moreover, Soter et al. suggest that during discussions, a certain amount of "modeling and scaffolding on the part of the teacher is necessary to prompt elaborated forms of individual reasoning from students" (p. 389).

Principle 7: Writing About the Reading

Writing instruction has been found to help students make connections between what they read, know, understand, and think and improve comprehension of text (Carr, 2002). Two national reports, *Reading Next—A Vision for Action and Research in Middle and High School Literacy* (Biancarosa & Snow, 2004) and *Writing to Read: Evidence for How Writing Can Improve Reading* (Graham & Hebert, 2010), identify intensive writing as a critical element of any literacy program. Specifically, Graham and Herbert report that when students write about the texts they read, whether writing an extended response that involves either a personal reaction to the text or a personal experience that related to it, there was a strong and consistently positive impact on reading comprehension. We offer three core recommendations: (1) have students write about the texts they read, (2) teach students the writing skills and processes that go into creating text, and (3) increase how much students write.

To be clear, each of these recommendations result in improvements not only to reading skills but also specifically to reading comprehension. However, we warn that the study also reveals that having lower achieving students write about text without teaching them how to do so may not be effective (Graham & Hebert, 2010; Graham & Perin, 2007; National Institute of Child Health and Human Development, 2000). Therefore, teachers must take special care to ensure that struggling readers understand how to write about text in ways that facilitate their comprehension of it.

Meeting the Needs of Struggling Readers With LDGs

In our work in schools, we use a CIM (Dorn & Henderson, 2010; Dorn & Soffos, 2011) as a Response to Intervention method. The CIM includes four layers of complementary support, with classroom instruction (Tier 1) as the first line of defense against reading failure. In the CIM, the classroom program embraces a readers' workshop approach with an emphasis on LDGs and conversational moves for facilitating students' deeper comprehension of texts. The readers' workshop framework begins with a whole-group minilesson, followed by small reading groups (guided reading or LDG), and concluding with a whole-group debriefing period. During the LDG time, the teacher meets with a small group of students, who read and discuss several texts that are organized within a genre unit of study (Dorn & Soffos, 2005). If a student is not responding to instruction, the teacher provides tailored support within the framework for scaffolding the student's learning.

The LDG framework includes a predictable yet flexible format for supporting students' reading comprehension before, during, and after reading (see Figure 7.1). In this final section, we describe the use of genre units within the LDG framework and include details for how teachers can differentiate this approach for struggling readers in grades 3–8. The LDG framework incorporates a focused unit of study that occurs over a sustained period of time around a particular genre. The genre units are associated with state frameworks and aligned with the National Assessment of Educational Progress (National Center for Education Statistics, 2010) and the Common Core State Standards (Council of Chief State School Officers, 2010); for example, a fourth-grade unit might concentrate on persuasive texts during reading, writing, and language workshops with opportunities during the LDGs to delve more deeply into this genre.

Component 1: Introduction of Genre Unit

Genre units enable students to acquire deeper understandings about how texts are organized. As readers acquire knowledge of how text is structured, they build cognitive frameworks that enable them to organize incoming information quickly and unconsciously and attend to that which is most important to their purpose for reading. As a result, the brain is freed from attending to lower level tasks and can actively engage in higher level comprehension processes.

Figure 7.1. 10-Step Format for Genre Study Over Time

1. The teacher introduces the genre to be studied.
2. The teacher reads aloud a book that typifies the genre so that students can appreciate the language and style of the author. This book serves as the mentor text that will be used for modeling and teaching concepts and strategies throughout the study of the particular genre.
3. The teacher returns to the mentor text, possibly rereading on a subsequent day, and prompts students to think about characteristics of the text. The teacher and students coconstruct an anchor chart that reflects the genre's characteristics that they have noticed.
4. The teacher and students chart the story using an enlarged text map that will serve as an anchor when students are independently reading other texts in the particular genre.
5. The teacher meets with small groups of students, based on their reading skill, shares with the students several texts in the genre, and provides a brief book talk on each one.
6. The students vote on which book they wish to read first, second, third, and so forth.
7. The students read silently and record their thinking about the text in their response logs. The teacher conducts one-to-one conferences as the students read.
8. The individual literature discussion groups meet with the teacher to fill in a group text map, which will be copied and placed in the students' individual response logs for reference when reading other books in the genre and to prepare for book discussions.
9. The students write about their reading in their reading response logs.
10. The students continue to read other books in the specified genre, and the teacher guides the students to create a text map that compares features of different texts within the genre unit.

Note. Adapted from Dorn, L.J., & Soffos, C. (2005). *Teaching for deep comprehension: A reading workshop approach.* Portland, ME: Stenhouse.

The first step in the LDG format is to introduce and share a description of the genre to be studied. The teacher then introduces a mentor text as an exemplary model of the genre. After the teacher reads the book to the students, the teacher and students revisit the description and add to or revise it based on their experiences with the mentor text. Next, the teacher introduces a large version of a text map for the genre and engages the group in completing the text map based on the genre characteristics of the mentor text (see Figure 7.2). The description is revisited and added to, if appropriate. Finally, the students place a copy of the revised description and a blank text map behind the Genre Study section in their response logs.

As the students acquire more experience with the genre, they build a knowledge base for understanding how authors organize their texts to

Figure 7.2. Narrative Text Map for a Mentor Text

Title: Baseball Saved Us   Author: Ken Mochizuki

Introduction: In 1942, a boy and his family must live in an internment camp in the desert

Event: They decided to make a baseball field	Event: They started playing baseball games	Event: The Championship Game
Elaboration: • filled in holes • made baseball uniforms • made bleachers • friends sent balls, gloves & bats	Elaboration: • picked teams • the boy wasn't very good at first	Elaboration: • the other team was winning • the boy looked at the guard and got mad • the boy made a home run
Event: The family went home after the war	Event: Baseball Season Starts	Event: The first game of the season
Elaboration: • No one would talk to him or eat by him at school	Elaboration: • The boy makes some friends • Call him "Shorty" • Playing at camp made him better at baseball	Elaboration: • The boy was nervous • People called him "Jap" • He hit a homerun

Conclusion: The team won their first game and he was really part of the team.

help readers comprehend their messages. This is essential information for linking reading and writing processes and for promoting deeper comprehension.

Component 2: Strategy Instruction (Minilesson)

Effective teachers are mindful that a skillful reader is not consciously aware of strategic actions occurring in their brain as they read (Afflerbach et al., 2008). However, these teachers also recognize that skillful readers monitor whether their purpose for reading is being achieved and are able to apply strategies flexibly when it is not. Therefore, the goal of strategy instruction in the LDG is not for students to become aware of the strategies they are using but rather for the strategies to become unconscious mental activities that occur as students are engaged in reading a text.

During readers' workshop, teachers model their thinking using a mentor text from the specific genre under study. Unlike other approaches that work from the outside in (i.e., name the strategy, then teach it), the teachers work from an inside-out approach (Villaume & Brabham, 2002), in which the strategy (or strategies) is authentically encountered when rereading a section from the mentor text. Once encountered, the strategy used to facilitate comprehension is identified and collaboratively recorded on an anchor chart for subsequent reference. The emphasis of the strategy instruction focuses on conveying how the strategy better helped the reader understand the text or how the strategy can be applied to fix comprehension when understanding breaks down.

This approach to strategy instruction is especially critical for struggling readers who experience difficulty in transferring learning from one context to another. In readers' workshop, teachers meet with students individually during their independent reading of the text to ensure that the strategies taught in explicit minilessons are being transferred to authentic reading experiences. Although developing metacognitive awareness of strategies is not the end goal, students are prompted to notice how a particular strategy helps them when they encounter difficulty or recognize that their purpose for reading is not being accomplished. Students then record their thinking about the strategic process in their response logs.

Component 3: Previewing and Selecting Books Within the Genre Unit

Choice is an important factor in reading motivation; however, struggling readers need the teacher's guidance in selecting appropriate texts. The students' success lies with the teacher's ability to preselect books that students will be able to read with minimal assistance, which implies that the teacher must understand the students' strengths and needs plus know how a particular book will support or challenge the readers.

Once the teacher has selected the appropriate books within the genre unit, he or she identifies three or four books for the first unit of study within the LDG format. The teacher motivates the students to read the books by providing a brief introduction to each book in the unit. Then, the teacher reminds the students of how good readers preview books (a strategic activity that was previously taught during the minilessons) to acquire information about the book and make good decisions about book choices. The teacher guides the students to apply previewing behaviors, for instance, reading the front and inside flaps and the back cover; reading excerpts of reviews, endorsements, and literary awards; reading the first page or lead paragraph; scanning the table of contents; and looking at the illustrations, figures, photographs, or other visual features. Next, the students rate each book in order of reading preference, and the teacher prompts the students to articulate their rationale for each book choice.

Component 4: Setting a Purpose for Reading and Using a Reading Response Log

After the books are selected, the teacher provides a book orientation and sets a purpose for reading the first book in the genre unit. The teacher instructs the students to use comprehension strategies to help themselves when reading, and to flag places where they encounter difficulty. The teacher explains how students can use their response logs as a resource, for instance, to jot down questions, take notes, record vocabulary, sketch ideas, or make comments about the text. For struggling readers, the response log is especially important, as it provides students with a place to capture their thoughts in preparation for the LDG. The students can use their response logs at any time during or after the reading. In Figure 7.3, we provide an example of a reader's entry regarding questions he recorded about the book he was reading.

Figure 7.3. A Student's Reading Response Log Entry

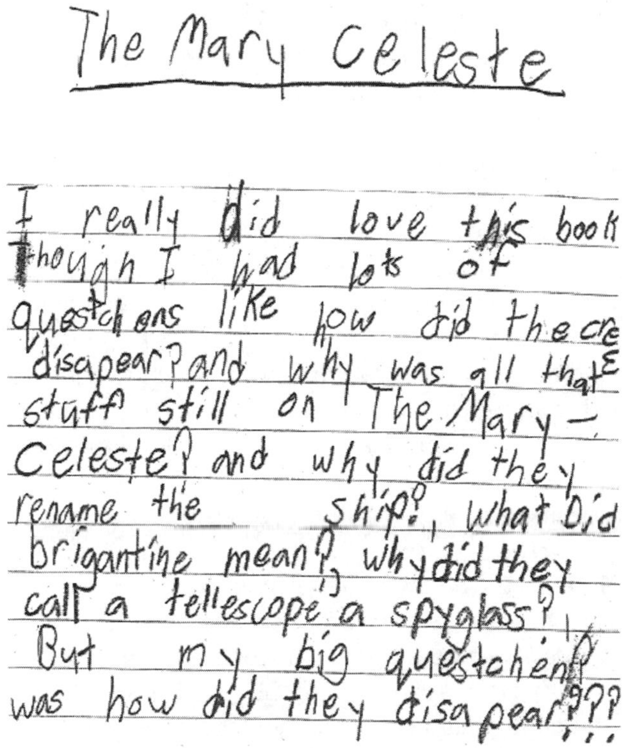

The Mary Celeste

I really did love this book though I had lots of questchons like how did the cre disapear? and why was all that stuff still on The Mary — Celeste? and why did they rename the ship?, what Did brigantine mean?, why did they call a tellescope a spyglass?, But my big questchen was how did they disapear???

Component 5: Silent Reading and Teacher Conference

Once students are settled in a comfortable spot and reading independently, the teacher conducts one-on-one conferences with them. The initial interaction of the one-on-one conference is always to check on students' comprehension of the text. If things are going well, then the teacher uses this time to guide the student's thinking to a higher level. However, if the student is encountering difficulty, then the teacher prompts the student to locate the place where his or her comprehension began to break down and assists in identifying and applying an appropriate strategy to reconstruct the meaning.

During independent reading time, students are engaged in strategic activities that support their thinking and prepare them for group discussion. While some students may only need a few sticky notes and their response logs to participate in higher levels of discussion, other students may require the support of text maps and specific prompts provided by the teacher to scaffold them to think deeply about the text and participate fully in the literature discussion.

Component 6: Discussing the Book

The talk in the LDG is a collaborative event bounded by a common experience around a shared text (for descriptions of book clubs, see Raphael, Pardo, & Highfield, 2002; Raphael et al., 2003). An important goal of the LDG is to lift the understanding of the group through interactive dialogues and conversational chains that keep the discussion in motion. These discussions can occur after the students have completed the text or at strategic places during the reading, but generally the duration and frequency of the discussions is dependent on the individual needs of the group and the length and complexity of the book. Typically, teachers differentiate their support by meeting more frequently with students struggling with comprehension to promote active engagement with text and interrupt any misconceptions that may have developed during their independent reading.

However, regardless of the group, all students come prepared to participate fully in the discussion. Teachers model and instruct students in how to flag places in the text where they wish to share their perspectives, provide commentary, and pose questions—and hold them accountable for doing so. Teachers also model and teach students how to use a response log to record their written responses to the reading (see Component 7: Writing About Reading) and expect students to have their logs readily available, so students are able to share their thinking and personal responses recorded across multiple readings of the text. Conversational moves, such as agreeing or disagreeing with each other, expressing confusion when puzzled, seeking or giving clarification, comparing ideas, offering evidence, expressing opinions, generalizing to new situations, and making connections, are taught and supported. During the discussion, the teacher is sensitive to how the students are responding to one another and prompts them to build discourse chains within the group; for example, she might ask, "Can anyone tell us more about that? Do you agree or disagree with Tanya's interpretation?" The teacher monitors the students' comprehension and redirects the discussion if the talk gets off task. The teacher's participation in the book discussion is regulated according to observations of the students' use of conversational moves to facilitate deeper understandings from the text experience.

Differentiated support for the discussion groups is provided during one-on-one conferences if necessary to support students' participation in the discussion. Teachers may assist them in flagging relevant places in the text, reflect on previous discourse moves with the students, or assist them in their written responses to the text. The goal for instruction is not only to deepen students' comprehension of text but also to instruct in such a way that students are able to fully engage and readily profit from the core classroom curriculum.

Component 7: Writing About Reading

The value of writing to increase reading achievement is well documented by research (Graham & Hebert, 2010). In the LDG, the students each keep a reading response log, which is organized into three major categories. The first section, My Thinking, is where students write about their reading, including personal reactions, analyzing and interpreting the text, writing summaries, recording notes, asking questions, and other meaningful responses to the text. In the second section, Powerful Language, students record examples of language acquired through their reading, such as interesting words, figurative language, and powerful phrases. In the third section, Genre Study, students record genre-specific information, such as definitions of genre and associated characteristics, text maps, and drawings.

If a student needs additional assistance, the teacher might type a prompt on a label and place this in the student's My Thinking section of the reading response log. Figure 7.4 is an example of how a teacher might provide a written prompt to scaffold a struggling reader to write about the reading.

Figure 7.4. A Teacher's Prompt to Scaffold the Student's Ability to Write About the Reading

> Jimbo and Tank learn many lessons
> from their experiences in the story.
> Think about what they learned from Mr.
> Munday, Apollo and Josh Gibson.
> How do you think these experiences
> changed Jimbo and Tank

Mr. Munday taught Jimbo and Tank
many lessons especially not to sneak
into base ball games.
   Apollo taught Tank and Jimbo not chew
tobacco, and you can also be
friends with anyone.
   Tank and Jimbo both learned how
to hit and throw a ball. They also
learned to be a team and not take it
in your own hands.
   To be a polite person - that do not steal
from anyone and to help people
out.

Component 8: Text Mapping Across Texts Within the Genre

When students can recognize genre and text conventions, they can use this knowledge to guide their comprehension. The final step in the LDG consists of coconstructing a text map across the different books within the genre unit. Texts have certain conventions that distinguish them as a particular genre. For example, a tall tale generally contains heroes and heroines, unusual obstacles to overcome, and exaggerated events. Realistic fiction, by contrast, contains more realistic characters that encounter universal problems in a believable story line; and informational text is intended to communicate facts in a clear and concise format. Having students map across a genre helps develop the cognitive structures that will assist them when reading other texts (see Figure 7.5 for an example of a biography text map). By having knowledge of many text structures, students can quickly recognize the type of text they are reading. This

Figure 7.5. Sample Text Map of a Biography Unit of Study

Biography: The story of a real person that was written by someone else

Name of Person (Book Title)	Date of Birth and Death	Major Contributions	Childhood Experiences	Adulthood Experiences	Most Famous for
Dr. Martin Luther King, Jr	1929–1968 Born in Atlanta, GA	Helped end segregation	Martin couldn't play with his white friends because he was black	Married Coretta, had two children, became a minister	I Have a Dream speech, peaceful protests, helped to end segregation
George Washington Carver	1864–1943	Agricultural scientist, inventor, professor	Stolen as a baby and sold into slavery	Taught at a college, performed experiments	Crop rotation to help soil stay fertile; products made from peanuts
Eleanor Roosevelt	1884–1962	Helped the poor; believed in equal rights	Mom and dad died, grandmother was strict, sent her to boarding school	Was First Lady of USA; Chairperson of United Nations	First Lady of USA; her work with the poor
Albert Einstein	1879–1955	Scientist, math, physics, inventor, professor, violin player	Shy, didn't talk until he was 4 years old	Discovered theory of gravity, speed of light, believed in peace	Genius, scientist in math and physics, $E = MC^2$
Jackie Robinson	1919–1972	Great athlete and civil rights leader	Dad left family; was youngest of five children	Played baseball for Dodgers; Hall of Fame; civil rights leader	A great baseball player, first African American in Major League
Clara Barton	1821–1912	Helped soldiers to recover from war wounds; established Red Cross	Helped nurse her brother back to health; shy, smart, good horseback rider	Teacher, nurse, volunteer	Began Red Cross in USA; president of Red Cross for 20 years

enables them to unconsciously organize the incoming information, thus freeing up cognitive resources that can now be allocated to building deeper understandings.

Closing Thoughts on Intervention for the Struggling Reader

In this chapter, we presented a framework for implementing LDGs within readers' workshop. We believe that struggling readers are entitled to the same high-quality instruction as their grade-level peers. However, we recognize that some students require more precise scaffolding in one-on-one situations with an observant teacher to gain the maximum benefits from group instruction. In the LDG framework, the one-on-one conference provides the struggling reader with personalized guidance and highly tailored feedback to ensure a successful group experience. Further, the teacher collects more systematic data on the struggling reader to capture evidence of how the student's knowledge is transitioning from the external (i.e., prompts, charts, tools) to the internal (i.e., mental processes) through assisted instruction.

An essential element of the LDG is the writing about reading component. If a student is not responding to instruction, the teacher scaffolds the student's learning with additional support to ensure a successful and motivating learning experience. For instance, if a student is struggling with writing about reading, the teacher might place a prompt in the student's response log to assist with organizing the thinking process (see Figure 7.4). This scaffolding approach is in contrast to the typical intervention model, whereby struggling readers are placed in a remediation program that is based on a deficit theory.

Strategies used to comprehend texts are taught in authentic ways in the LDG framework, including during interactive conversations around high-quality books. For struggling readers, the teacher might add a new section, My Strategies, to the response log and use this scaffold during one-on-one conferences to promote the student's metacognition and self-reflection. However, it is important for teachers to recognize that the goal of reading is to understand and enjoy the text and that good readers employ a flexible range of strategies for achieving the deepest understanding.

Returning to the scenario with which we began the chapter, Ms. Leibig's fourth-grade discussion group, the students were at different reading levels, yet all were active participants in the discourse. During authentic discussions about books, the students learned how to build on one another's ideas and use language as a tool for constructing literate knowledge. Ms. Leibig's role was to create an environment that ensured a meaningful and motivating experience for all students. Throughout this chapter, we argued that instruction for struggling readers beyond third grade should mirror the high-quality experiences of their grade-level peers. Thus, the role of instruction is to differentiate support to guarantee that all students achieve their highest potential in literacy.

TRY IT!

In this chapter, we support the use of LDGs to differentiate and support the comprehension efforts of struggling readers. Organizing LDGs around a particular genre is a powerful way to support students who struggle with comprehending text. Consider incorporating the described approach as a means of differentiating instruction for students who are struggling with comprehension using the following as a guide to prepare for the 10-step format for genre study over time (Figure 7.1).

1. Choose a genre to study in depth with your students using grade-level standards and student interest.

2. Gather myriad texts in the specific genre (10–20 if possible).

3. Examine multiple texts within the specific genre to identify consistent features and structure. Have students really get to know it!

4. Select one text to serve as your mentor text, which will serve as the basis for all of your modeling and teaching in the genre.

5. Create a large version of the text map to fill out with students after reading the mentor text.

6. Read the mentor text several times. Determine which comprehension strategies or text features you wish to reveal, model, and teach.

7. Acquire composition books to serve as students' reading response logs, in which they can record their use of strategic actions, powerful words and phrases, and their thinking about the stories.

8. Group appropriate texts within the genre for students to select from for their small-group discussions.

9. Generate prompts to promote higher levels of thinking and engagement around the selected texts.

10. Prepare book introductions for each of the selected texts to share with your students.

REFERENCES

Afflerbach, P., Pearson, P.D., & Paris, S.G. (2008). Clarifying differences between reading skills and reading strategies. *The Reading Teacher, 61*(5), 364–373. doi:10.1598/RT.61.5.1

Alvermann, D.E., & Boothby, P.R. (1986). Children's transfer of graphic organizer instruction. *Reading Psychology, 7*(2), 87–100. doi:10.1080/0270271860070203

Anderson, R.C., & Pearson, P.D. (1984). A schema-theoretic view of basic processes in reading comprehension. In P.D. Pearson, R. Barr, M.L. Kamil, & P.B. Mosenthal (Eds.), *Handbook of reading research* (Vol. 1, pp. 255–291). White Plains, NY: Longman.

Anderson, V. (1992). A teacher development project in transactional strategy instruction for teachers of severely reading-disabled adolescents. *Teaching and Teacher Education, 8*(4), 391–403. doi:10.1016/0742-051X(92)90064-A

Baumann, J.F., & Bergeron, B.S. (1993). Story map instruction using children's literature: Effects on first graders' comprehension of central narrative elements. *Journal of Reading Behavior, 25*(4), 407–437.

Biancarosa, G., & Snow, C.E. (2004). *Reading next—A vision for action and research in middle and high school literacy: A report to Carnegie Corporation of New York.* Washington, DC: Alliance for Excellent Education.

Brown, R., Pressley, M., Van Meter, P., & Schuder, T. (1996). A quasi-experimental validation of transactional strategies instruction with low-achieving second-grade readers. *Journal of Educational Psychology, 88*(1), 18–37. doi:10.1037/0022-0663.88.1.18

Buly, M.R., & Valencia, S.W. (2002). Below the bar: Profiles of students who fail state reading assessments. *Educational Evaluation and Policy Analysis, 24*(3), 219–239. doi:10.3102/01623737024003219

Burke, J. (2010). *What's the big idea? Question-driven units to motivate reading, writing, and thinking.* Portsmouth, NH: Heinemann.

Carr, S.C. (2002). Assessing learning processes: Useful information for teachers and students. *Intervention in School and Clinic, 37*(3), 156–162. doi:10.1177/105345120203700304

Council of Chief State School Officers. (2010). *Common core state standards for English language arts and literacy in history/social studies, science, and technical subjects.* Washington, DC: Author. Retrieved November 18, 2010, from www.corestandards.org/the-standards/english-language-arts-standards

Delta Air Lines. (2010, June 14). 737-732/-832. In *Operations manual* (Vol. 2, 8th rev., p. 9.20.3). Atlanta, GA: Author.

Donovan, C.A., & Smolkin, L.B. (2002). Children's genre knowledge: An examination of K–5 students' performance on multiple tasks providing differing levels of scaffolding. *Reading Research Quarterly, 37*(4), 428–465. doi:10.1598/RRQ.37.4.5

Dorn, L.J., & Henderson, S.C. (2010). The comprehensive intervention model: A systems approach to RTI. In M.Y. Lipson & K.K. Wixson (Eds.), *Successful approaches to RTI: Collaborative practices for improving K–12 literacy* (pp. 88–120). Newark, DE: International Reading Association.

Dorn, L., & Schubert, B. (2008). A comprehensive intervention model for preventing reading failure: A Response to Intervention process. *Journal of Reading Recovery, 7*(2), 29–41.

Dorn, L.J., & Soffos, C. (2005). *Teaching for deep comprehension: A reading workshop approach.* Portland, ME: Stenhouse.

Dorn, L.J., & Soffos, C. (2011). *Interventions that work: A comprehensive intervention model for preventing reading failure in grades K–3.* Boston: Allyn & Bacon.

Duke, N.K., Pressley, M., & Hilden, K. (2004). Difficulties with reading comprehension. In C.A. Stone, E.R. Silliman, B.J. Ehren, & K. Apel (Eds.), *Handbook of language and literacy: Development and disorders* (pp. 501–520). New York: Guilford.

Duke, N.K., Purcell-Gates, V., Hall, L.A., & Tower, C. (2006). Authentic literacy activities for developing comprehension and writing. *The Reading Teacher, 60*(4), 344–355. doi:10.1598/RT.60.4.4

Garner, J.K., & Bochna, C.R. (2004). Transfer of a listening comprehension strategy to independent reading in first-grade students. *Early Childhood Education Journal, 32*(2), 69–74. doi:10.1007/s10643-004-1071-y

Gersten, R., Fuchs, L.S., Williams, J.P., & Baker, S.K. (2001). Teaching reading comprehension strategies to students with learning disabilities: A review of research. *Review of Educational Research, 71*(2), 279–320. doi:10.3102/00346543071002279

Gough, P.B., & Tunmer, W.E. (1986). Decoding, reading, and reading disability. *Remedial and Special Education, 7*(1), 6–10. doi:10.1177/074193258600700104

Graham, S., & Hebert, M. (2010). *Writing to read: Evidence for how writing can improve reading: A report from Carnegie Corporation of New York*. Washington, DC: Alliance for Excellent Education.

Graham, S., & Perin, D. (2007). *Writing next: Effective strategies to improve writing of adolescents in middle and high schools: A report to Carnegie Corporation of New York*. Washington, DC: Alliance for Excellent Education.

Gunning, T.G. (2008). *Developing higher-level literacy in all students: Building reading, reasoning, and responding*. Boston: Allyn & Bacon.

Guthrie, J.T., Wigfield, A., & Perencevich, K.C. (Eds.). (2004). *Motivating reading comprehension: Concept-oriented reading instruction*. Mahwah, NJ: Erlbaum.

Hansen, J. (1981). The effects of inference training and practice on young children's reading comprehension. *Reading Research Quarterly, 16*(3), 391–417.

Kamberelis, G. (1999). Genre development and learning: Children writing stories, science reports, and poems. *Research in the Teaching of English, 33*(4), 403–460.

Keene, E.O., & Zimmermann, S. (2007). *Mosaic of thought: The power of comprehension strategy instruction* (2nd ed.). Portsmouth, NH: Heinemann.

Kintsch, W. (2004). The construction–integration model of text comprehension and its implications for instruction. In R.B. Ruddell & N.J. Unrau (Eds.), *Theoretical models and processes of reading* (5th ed., pp. 1270–1328). Newark, DE: International Reading Association.

Kintsch, W., & van Dijk, T.A. (1978). Toward a model of text comprehension and production. *Psychological Review, 85*(5), 363–394. doi:10.1037/0033-295X.85.5.363

Kong, A., & Fitch, E. (2002). Using book club to engage culturally and linguistically diverse learners in reading, writing, and talking about books. *The Reading Teacher, 56*(4), 352–362.

Lee, J., Grigg, W.S., & Donahue, P.L. (2007). *The nation's report card: Reading 2007* (NCES 2007-496). Washington, DC: National Center for Education Statistics, Institute of Education Sciences, U.S. Department of Education.

McIntyre, E. (2007). Story discussion in the primary grades: Balancing authenticity and explicit teaching. *The Reading Teacher, 60*(7), 610–620. doi:10.1598/RT.60.7.1

Meyer, B.J.F., Brandt, D.M., & Bluth, G.J. (1980). Use of top-level structure in text: Key for reading comprehension of ninth-grade students. *Reading Research Quarterly, 16*(1), 72–103.

Moje, E.B. (2010). Comprehending in the subject areas: The challenges of comprehension, grades 7–12, and what to do about them. In K. Ganske & D. Fisher (Eds.), *Comprehension across the curriculum: Perspectives and practices K–12* (pp. 46–72). New York: Guilford.

Mullins, I.V.S., Martin, M.O., Kennedy, A.M., & Foy, P. (2007). *PIRLS 2006 international report: IEA's Progress in International Reading Literacy Study in primary schools in 40 countries.* Chestnut Hill, MA: TIMSS & PIRLS International Study Center, Boston College.

Murphy, P.K., Wilkinson, I.A.G., Soter, A.O., Hennessey, M.N., & Alexander, J.F. (2009). Examining the effects of classroom discussion on students' comprehension of text: A meta-analysis. *Journal of Educational Psychology, 101*(3), 740–764. doi:10.1037/a0015576

National Center for Education Statistics. (2010). *The nation's report card: Reading 2009: National Assessment of Educational Progress at grades 4 and 8* (NCES 2010-458). Washington, DC: National Center for Education Statistics, Institute of Education Sciences, U.S. Department of Education.

National Institute of Child Health and Human Development. (2000). *Report of the National Reading Panel. Teaching children to read: An evidence-based assessment of the scientific research literature on reading and its implications for reading instruction: Reports of the subgroups* (NIH Publication No. 00-4754). Washington, DC: U.S. Government Printing Office.

Otero, J., & Kintsch, W. (1992). Failures to detect contradictions in a text: What readers believe versus what they read. *Psychological Science, 3*(4), 229–235. doi:10.1111/j.1467-9280.1992.tb00034.x

Paris, S.G., Lipson, M.Y., & Wixson, K.K. (1983). Becoming a strategic reader. *Contemporary Educational Psychology, 8*(3), 293–316. doi:10.1016/0361-476X (83)90018-8

Park, Y. (2008). *Patterns in and predictors of elementary students' reading performance: Evidence from the data of the Progress in International Reading Literacy Study (PIRLS).* Unpublished doctoral dissertation, Michigan State University, Ann Arbor.

Pressley, M. (2002). Metacognition and self-regulated comprehension. In A.E. Farstrup & S.J. Samuels (Eds.), *What research has to say about reading instruction* (3rd ed., pp. 291–309). Newark, DE: International Reading Association.

Pressley, M., Almasi, J., Schuder, T., Bergman, J., Hite, S., El-Dinary, P.B., et al. (1994). Transactional instruction of comprehension strategies: The Montgomery County, Maryland, SAIL program. *Reading and Writing Quarterly, 10*(1), 5–19.

Purcell-Gates, V., Duke, N.K., & Martineau, J.A. (2007). Learning to read and write genre-specific text: Roles of authentic experience and explicit teaching. *Reading Research Quarterly, 42*(1), 8–45.

Raphael, T.E., Florio-Ruane, S., Kehus, M.J., George, M., Hasty, N.L., & Highfield, K. (2003). Constructing curriculum for differentiated instruction: Inquiry in the teachers' learning collaborative. In R.L. McCormack & J.R. Paratore (Eds.), *After early intervention, then what? Teaching struggling readers in grades 3 and beyond* (pp. 94–116). Newark, DE: International Reading Association.

Raphael, T.E., Pardo, L.S., & Highfield, K. (2002). *Book club: A literature-based curriculum* (2nd ed.). Lawrence, MA: Small Planet Communications.

Salahu-Din, D., Persky, H., & Miller, J. (2008). *The nation's report card: Writing 2007: National Assessment of Educational Progress at grades 8 and 12* (NCES 2008-468). Washington, DC: National Center for Education Statistics, Institute of Education Sciences, U.S. Department of Education.

Shanahan, T., & Shanahan, C. (2008). Teaching disciplinary literacy to adolescents: Rethinking content-area literacy. *Harvard Educational Review, 78*(1), 40–59.

Snow, C.E. (2002). *Reading for understanding: Toward a research and development program in reading comprehension.* Santa Monica, CA: RAND.

Snow, C.E., Burns, M.S., & Griffin, P. (Eds.). (1998). *Preventing reading difficulties in young children.* Washington, DC: National Academies Press.

Soter, A.O., Wilkinson, I.A., Murphy, P.K., Rudge, L., Reninger, K., & Edwards, M. (2008). What the discourse tells us: Talk and indicators of high-level comprehension. *International Journal of Educational Research, 47*(6), 372–391. doi:10.1016/j.ijer.2009.01.001

Spiro, R.J. (2004). Principled pluralism for adaptive flexibility in teaching and learning to read. In R.B. Ruddell & N.J. Unrau (Eds.), *Theoretical models and processes of reading* (5th ed., pp. 654–659). Newark, DE: International Reading Association.

Taylor, B.M., Pearson, P.D., Clark, K., & Walpole, S. (2000). Effective schools and accomplished teachers: Lessons about primary-grade reading instruction in low-income schools. *The Elementary School Journal, 101*(2), 121–165.

Villaume, S.K., & Brabham, E.G. (2002). Comprehension instruction: Beyond strategies. *The Reading Teacher, 55*(7), 672–675.

Williams, J.P. (2005). Instruction in reading comprehension for primary-grade students: A focus on text structure. *The Journal of Special Education, 39*(1), 6–18. doi:10.1177/00224669050390010201

Wolfe, P. (2001). *Brain matters: Translating research into classroom practice.* Alexandria, VA: Association for Supervision and Curriculum Development.

Youngs, S., & Barone, D. (2007). *Writing without boundaries: What's possible when students combine genres.* Portsmouth, NH: Heinemann.

LITERATURE CITED

Cheng, A. (2004). *Honeysuckle House.* Asheville, NC: Front Street.

Gipson, F. (1956). *Old Yeller.* New York: Harper & Row.

CHAPTER 8

Helping Students Understand Expository Text About History by Applying the Action Cycle Approach

Robert W. Gaskins

As students progress through school, they face an increasing amount of expository text (Moje, 2010), which is particularly noteworthy, because research consistently indicates that expository texts pose significant challenges that narrative texts do not (e.g., Armbruster, 1984; Gajria, Jitendra, Sood, & Sacks, 2007; Martin & Duke, 2011). As Alvermann, Simpson, and Fitzgerald (2006) suggest, expository texts "can require ways of thinking and knowing that are different from those used when reading narrative texts" (p. 451). Thus, unsurprisingly, expository text is found by many students to be more difficult to comprehend than narrative texts (e.g., Gersten, Fuchs, Williams, & Baker, 2001). Consequently, focusing attention on methods that facilitate students' understanding of content area material is of critical importance, especially for struggling readers who often experience difficulty with comprehension, including the comprehension of expository texts (e.g., Gajria et al., 2007; Gersten et al., 2001).

This chapter begins with a review of research and theory related to the comprehension of expository texts commonly used during content area instruction. The review sets the stage for the remainder of the chapter, which focuses on the action cycle approach, which is an instructional approach that applies the ideas presented in this research literature in a novel manner and has produced promising results facilitating the comprehension of struggling readers in expository texts (R. Gaskins, 2009; R. Gaskins & Galloway, 2008, 2009).

After Early Intervention, Then What? Teaching Struggling Readers in Grades 3 and Beyond (2nd ed.) edited by Jeanne R. Paratore and Rachel L. McCormack. © 2011 by the International Reading Association.

The Importance of Organized Knowledge

In striving to facilitate students' comprehension of expository texts, the major focus of literacy educators has been on teaching strategies to students (e.g., Fisher, Brozo, Frey, & Ivey, 2007; Tierney, Readence, & Dishner, 1995; Vacca & Vacca, 2007). The evidence compiled on the benefits of applying research-based strategies clearly indicates that this practice is a productive one. Reviews of the research literature consistently suggest that there are six to eight research-based strategies that help students, including struggling readers, comprehend texts (e.g., Dole, Duffy, Roehler, & Pearson, 1991; Duke & Pearson, 2002; Gajria et al., 2007; Gersten et al., 2001; McNamara, 2007).

However, in content-rich material pertaining to specific disciplines, strategy instruction can only go so far in facilitating comprehension (Moje, 2010). When reviewing the factors typically identified as making content area texts difficult to understand (e.g., unfamiliar content, specialized vocabulary, density of ideas, abstract concepts, varied and unfamiliar text structures), issues pertaining to the content itself are at the heart of those items. As such, although strategies can provide a productive means of approaching the content in expository texts, strategies cannot substitute for inadequate or inaccurate content knowledge. Ultimately, deeper and more complex understanding of content-rich material requires deeper and more complex content knowledge. Consequently, the most central issue in helping students understand expository texts is helping students develop their content knowledge (Alexander & Jetton, 2000; Walsh, 2003), an issue that Hiebert and Martin (2009) argue could be enhanced by having knowledge at the center of the literacy curriculum.

In considering how to build students' content knowledge, it is valuable to review research on expertise of understanding the nature of experts' knowledge in their areas of specialization. Research on expertise reveals that experts not only know a lot more than novices but also, and even more important, experts' knowledge is organized around central concepts or big ideas in their areas of expertise (Alexander, 2006; Bransford, Brown, & Cocking, 1999; Donald, 2002). This organization provides experts with a strong framework for understanding new data related to their areas of specialization and helps them quickly identify the most important ideas in the data and focus their attention on those ideas. In addition, experts' well-organized knowledge structures enable them to readily fill in gaps in incoming information. All of these advantages of organized knowledge facilitate understanding (e.g., Alexander & Jetton, 2000; Donovan & Bransford, 2005).

Although it would be wonderful if one set of organizing principles could provide a framework of big ideas that would work across disciplines, in fact, each discipline has its own set of key concepts (e.g., Dewey, 1902/1956; Prawat, 1991; C. Shanahan, 2009; T. Shanahan & Shanahan, 2008). Given the value of understanding these big ideas for structuring one's thinking about ideas in a discipline, it makes sense to organize the curriculum around these big ideas and help students develop an understanding of the core concepts that organize each discipline (Alexander & Jetton, 2000; Erickson, 2001). In that way, teachers can help students establish central concepts as hooks on which to attach ideas within the discipline and thereby facilitate students' understanding of expository texts in content area material. Indeed, some educators are now designing instructional programs that are directed toward these goals (e.g., Donovan & Bransford, 2005; Guthrie, Wigfield, & Perencevich, 2004; Levstik & Barton, 2005; Pearson, 2006; Romance & Vitale, 2001).

Helping Students Develop Organized Knowledge

In light of early research on organized knowledge, in the late 1980s, the leaders of Benchmark School began to review the research literature in the content area disciplines of science and social studies to determine the key ideas in each subject area. Soon after, they led discussions among the teachers at the school about the theory and research regarding organized knowledge, the perspectives of experts in each subject area about what the big ideas were in each discipline, and how these insights might direct our curricula and instruction. The core concepts in each discipline became known as the essential understandings, and soon our content area instruction was organized around helping students internalize these central ideas to facilitate their understanding of science and social studies (see I. Gaskins, 2005; I. Gaskins, Satlow, Hyson, Ostertag, & Six, 1994; Pressley, Gaskins, Solic, & Collins, 2006).

In analyzing the effectiveness of this approach, we have found that centering our content area teaching around the instruction of essential understandings, while continuing to teach students to apply relevant strategies, helps students begin to see subject areas as meaningfully organized around big ideas rather than as a series of complex and disjointed facts. In addition, students begin to recognize connections within disciplines that they had not recognized before; for example, the study of ecosystems could inform the study of the circulatory system, because both systems are related by the overriding principle that all parts of a system are interrelated, and if you change one part of the system, it affects the whole system. Most important, we have found that this approach facilitates students' understanding of content area material.

As exciting as these results have been, my colleagues and I continually reflect on how to make our instruction even more beneficial to our students. Most important for this chapter, as I was teaching social studies a few years ago, I had an idea about how to rewrite the original 10 essential understandings pertaining to social studies to form five interconnected core concepts that would function not as individual hooks on which to organize students' thinking but as an integrated framework that could help students structure their understandings of history in an even more cohesive fashion. The idea was to create something akin to a story grammar used to facilitate students' comprehension in narrative texts (Mandler & Johnson, 1977; Stein & Glenn, 1979), only this version would be applied to expository texts pertaining to human actions across history. Like the narrative story grammar framework, the new structure would provide a framework of how events typically unfold in this domain. However, beyond that, each key concept within the structure was designed to promote further analysis and deeper understanding within the broader structure relevant to the study of human history. By connecting the core concepts into an integrated whole, a framework was created that reflects the findings that expert knowledge is not only organized but connected (Donovan & Bransford, 2005), as well as "cohesive and well-integrated" (Alexander, 2003, p. 11).

The New Essential Understandings in Social Studies

The new conceptual framework was developed after the completion of an extensive review of the literatures pertaining to human motivation (e.g., Csikszentmihalyi, 1990; Deci & Ryan, 2002; Maslow, 1999) and human history (e.g., Diamond, 1997; Fernández-Armesto, 2001; Trigger, 2003). The five interconnected statements were designed to help students predict, understand, and analyze the causes and consequences of human actions across history. The following statements comprise the new essential understandings:

1. *Humans take actions to meet their needs*—To understand why humans do what they do, the most fundamental issue is to identify the underlying issues that motivate people to take action. To be sure, many individuals have presented competing explanations of what motivates human actions (e.g., Alexander & Winne, 2006; Schunk, Pintrich, & Meece, 2007); however, one general means of reflecting a wide range of perspectives is to state that we take action to meet our needs (e.g., Deci & Ryan, 2002; Maslow, 1999). In an effort to keep this discussion straightforward and manageable for our students,

these ideas were consolidated into the needs to (a) keep our bodies healthy and safe (i.e., survival needs), (b) figure out our identities in social groups and feel like we belong (i.e., social needs), and (c) determine how we fit into the universe (i.e., big-picture needs). After establishing these needs, I discovered that they are essentially the same as the issues that Smith (2001) identifies as the core challenges faced by the human species.

2. *The physical features of a place affect the actions that humans take to meet their needs*—Although human needs are at the root of human actions, by themselves, human needs cannot explain why a group or an individual takes a specific action. Thus, for example, even though the human need for survival indicates that all humans will create shelters for protection, the need for survival alone does not reveal how a specific shelter will look at a particular place and time. To understand specific actions, we need to understand the elements that compose the context in which those actions take place. The physical features (i.e., the characteristics of a place that occur naturally) are an essential part of that context (e.g., Geography Education Standards Project, 1994). Returning to the shelters example, knowing the physical features of a particular place at a particular time will provide tremendous insight into the materials and designs that will characterize the shelters found there.

   To help students develop a consistent set of physical features on which to attend, the students are always asked to consider the same seven features, which are a derivation of the physical features found across most geography texts: climate, topography and landforms, soil, mineral resources, bodies of water, vegetation, and animals. This set provides an outline for taking notes and a well-established foundation for reflecting on human actions.

3. *The human features of a place affect the actions that humans take to meet their needs*—The human features (i.e., the characteristics of a place created by humans) are another critical set of components that comprise the context in which an action takes place (e.g., Geography Education Standards Project, 1994). As with the physical features, understanding the human features of a place at a particular time, primarily the culture but also population and other demographic information, provides insights into what shapes the specific actions of a group or an individual. In the case of shelters, the human features affect such issues as the choice of materials, the details

of construction, the function of the structure, and the aesthetic elements of the building.

As is the case with the physical features, students are taught a consistent set of human features on which to reflect as we consider each new unit and scenario. These features form an outline for taking notes and identifying key issues to consider in discussions and assignments. In particular, students learn a core group of issues referred to as the aspects of culture, which are a set of issues (e.g., food, tools and technology, government, economy, education, religion) clustered into three categories related to their primary function in helping fulfill one of the human needs (see Figure 8.1). To be sure, one can argue with the categorization of certain issues; however, the system seems to fulfill its purpose quite well. The categorization system has been effective in helping students organize and remember an extensive list of issues. Students also are taught that all of the issues are interconnected, and thus, every issue is ultimately connected to each category. Finally, it should be noted that for certain discussions, students may be asked to focus on only a core set of issues, most commonly, "the big five" (i.e., economic, political, social, and religious and cosmological structures as well as technological developments; see Figure 8.2).

4. *Human actions (and natural events) have consequences that can affect the physical features of a place*—All actions and events have consequences that affect the world in some way. The effects can range from negligible to profound, highly localized to widespread, and short to long term. In addition, the effects may impact physical features, human features, or both. However, what is assured is that human actions (and natural events) will have some kind of effect. As an example, technological advances in transportation and communications have had consequences that have affected both physical and human features of the world. Related to physical features, advancements in transportation and communication have led to disruptions of soil, vegetation, and animals as structures, such as roads, airports, factories, warehouses, and communications, have been built. Further, these advancements have contributed to global warming because of increased emissions.

5. *Human actions (and natural events) have consequences that can affect the human features of a place*—As was just mentioned, all actions and events have consequences, and some of those effects will result in changes in the human features of a place. Continuing

Figure 8.1. The Human Features of a Place

The two human features on which we focus are

1. *Population and related factors—Population* is the number of people living in a place. Knowing the number of people living in a place as well as other information about the makeup of the group helps us understand how people live in that place and why they meet their needs the way they do.

2. *Culture—Culture* is the way a group of people live. Stated differently, *culture* is the pattern of thoughts and actions, and the products of those thoughts and actions, that are shared by a group of people and serve as guidelines for taking action to meet their needs. The aspects of culture are

   a. *Survival—*What the group has determined to be the best ways to maintain existence as individuals and as a group:
      i. Food
      ii. Housing
      iii. Clothing
      iv. Tools and technology
      v. Jobs and economy
      vi. Transportation
      vii. Health and medicine
      viii. Military

   b. *Social—*What the group has determined to be the best ways for people to interact so that they have a sense of identity in the group and feel they belong:
      i. Communication
      ii. Leadership and government
      iii. Values and traditions
      iv. Education
      v. Sports and recreation

   c. *Big picture—*What the group has determined to be the best ways to understand how the world works and, in the process, how they fit in and have meaning in the universe:
      i. Myths, spiritual beliefs, and religion
      ii. Scientific studies

---

with the previous example, advancements in transportation and communication have led to widespread changes in the everyday lives and cultures of people all over the world. More specifically, these advancements have led to changes in, for example, industries, social interaction, and economies. These final two essential understandings help students recognize that actions and events lead to changes that affect the future by altering the physical and human features on which subsequent actions are based.

Figure 8.2. Core Issue Version of the Aspects of Culture: "The Big Five"

Survival—What the group has determined to be the best ways to maintain existence as individuals and as a group:
1. Economic structure
2. Technological developments

Social—What the group has determined to be the best ways for people to interact so that they have a sense of identity in the group and feel they belong:
3. Political structure
4. Social structure

Big picture—What the group has determined to be the best ways to understand how the world works and, in the process, how they fit in and have meaning in the universe:
5. Religious and cosmological structure

The Action Cycle

Although these five essential understandings form a conceptual framework that helps students predict, remember, understand, and explain the causes and consequences of human actions, I designed one further structure to help students visualize the cyclical nature of the essential understandings and the relationship between concepts. This visual representation of the essential understandings is known as the action cycle (see Figure 8.3).

In the action cycle, human needs sit outside of the cycle of actions and events, continually propelling the wheel forward, because we must incessantly address these needs, since they cannot be permanently met (R. Gaskins, 1999). These needs are filtered through the physical and human features that make up the context of that particular time and place, then manifest themselves in actions that address the issues that are the focus of our immediate attention. These actions lead to consequences that affect the physical or human features of the place, and those consequences create a new context for subsequent actions. This pattern continues throughout history.

Each action cycle represents the causes and consequences of a group's actions, or an individual's actions in an alternate version with a modified representation of the context. In fact, the action cycle can represent groups of any size, from individuals to factions within a small community to superpowers around the globe. Given this arrangement, at any given time in a region, there are multiple interrelated action cycles. To be sure, one group's actions influence other groups in the area. In the action cycle diagram (Figure 8.3), the influence of an outside group (e.g., another group

Figure 8.3. The Action Cycle

Essential Understandings (EUs)

Human Needs

EU 1: Humans take actions to meet their needs:

- *Survival needs*—We need to keep our bodies healthy and safe.
- *Social needs*—We need to figure out our identities in the group and feel like we belong.
- *Big picture needs*—We need to figure out our identities in the universe and feel like we belong.

Context

EU 2: The physical features of a place affect the actions that humans take to meet their needs:

- Use the seven central physical features as a structure to help find out which physical features affected the action taken.

EU 3: The human features of a place affect the actions that humans take to meet their needs:

- Consider the influence of factors related to population and other demographic issues on the action taken.
- Use the aspects of culture as a structure to help find out which human features affected the actions taken.

Human Needs

Human needs are at the root of human action.

Context

- Physical features
- Human features—The actions that humans take are shaped by the context in which they occur.

Action

There are a range of possible actions that can come from a particular context. All actions have consequences.

Consequences

The consequences of an action or event change aspects of the context, which creates a different setting for future actions.

Consequences

EU 4: Human actions (and major natural events) have consequences that can affect the physical features of a place:

- Use the seven central physical features as a structure to help find out which physical features were affected by the action (or natural event).

EU 5: Human actions (and major natural events) have consequences that can affect the human features of a place:

- Consider any changes to the population or other demographic issues.
- Use the aspects of culture as a structure to help find out which human features were affected by the action (or natural event).

An Action Taken by Someone Outside the Group or a Natural Event

Sometimes an outside group takes actions that have consequences that affect the context of the target group. Or, sometimes a natural event (e.g., climate change, natural disaster) has consequences that affect the context of the target group.

or country) is represented at the bottom left corner, leading directly toward consequences. This location on the diagram is also where the impact of natural events (e.g., climate change, natural disaster) is represented.

Given the graphic nature of the action cycle and the fact that it represents the entire conceptual framework of the essential understandings, this diagram has become the primary reference that students use to comprehend texts and structure their thinking in discussions and written work in social studies. Each student has a copy of the action cycle in his or her binder, and each classroom in which this instruction occurs has a large action cycle chart prominently displayed on the wall.

The Action Cycle Instructional Approach

Although the conceptual framework established in the essential understandings and expanded in the action cycle is at the heart of what we teach in social studies classes, it is the entire instructional approach in which this framework resides that helps students get engaged with the content, ask questions, apply the framework, improve their understanding of the content, and transfer the use of the framework to new materials. Alexander (1997) states that expertise requires the development of (a) principled knowledge (i.e., organized knowledge), (b) strategic processing, and (c) interest and motivation. Thus, these guidelines were used as a framework for the overall instructional approach:

- The overarching action cycle instructional approach is built on a conceptual framework designed to help students organize their thinking about content related to social studies (i.e., principled knowledge).
- Students are explicitly taught to apply the conceptual framework using a gradual release of responsibility model (i.e., strategic processing; Pearson & Gallagher, 1983).
- The entire program applies a guided inquiry approach that keeps the instruction purposeful, interesting, and fun (i.e., interest, motivation).

In planning their instruction, teachers using this approach follow the same four basic steps: (1) generate questions, (2) make predictions, (3) develop knowledge, and (4) integrate ideas. Throughout the instructional process, teachers review both the essential understandings and the action cycle and, as necessary, cue students to apply them to facilitate their completion of each step. As with the action cycle, the instructional sequence is cyclical, with the integration of ideas (step 4) leading directly into the generation of questions (step 1) and the start of a new instructional sequence.

Step 1: Generate Questions

Each unit of study and section within a unit begins with teachers leading students to generate questions that initiate the upcoming investigation. For example, Why did England want to start a colony in Virginia? Why did the colonists choose the location that they did for the colony that became known as Jamestown? What issues and events led to the start of the American Civil War? (Stated more specifically in the language of the action cycle, Why did the Confederacy take the action of seceding from the Union? What aspects of the physical and social context created the conditions that set the stage for the decision to secede?) Why is the Battle of Gettysburg widely considered to be the turning point of the American Civil War? What actions did the Lakota Sioux of the 18th and 19th centuries take to meet their survival needs? Why did they take those particular actions? What were the consequences of the introduction of the horse to Lakota Sioux society? At the beginning of the year, the teacher takes the lead in this process. However, as the year progresses, students become increasingly comfortable with the essential understandings and the questions that this framework implies, and as a result, the students begin to assume the lead role in the question generation process.

Another key component of this initial phase of an instructional cycle is an effort to provide an introduction that will spark students' interest in the content and prime the question generation process. As one example, before considering the impact of the horse on Lakota Sioux society, students were provided with a picture of a dog pulling a travois laden with items. Students were told that when the Lakota first lived on the Great Plains, the animal they chose to help them with their work was the dog, as opposed to a bigger or stronger animal. The students were provided time to reflect on the picture and the information that had been provided. Then, they were asked to consider what questions they had about this situation. As you might guess, drawing on their background of seeing Plains Indians on horseback, the first questions they asked were, "Why did they use dogs?" and "Why didn't they use horses?" At that point, the students' curiosity was piqued, and we were off and running. As a general practice, through both the introduction and the question generation process, we seek to get students invested in the content. Over time, we want them to take ownership of the investigations and learn to find genuine satisfaction in the inquiry process and the content.

Step 2: Make Predictions

After establishing a set of guiding questions, students use the essential understandings and the action cycle to predict answers to the guiding questions. Usually, students begin by making predictions individually. Then, they form small groups to share their ideas, ask each other questions to clarify why they have predicted as they have, and discuss which predictions seem most reasonable and why. Small-group work is followed by whole-class discussion, in which the teacher works to keep the pace brisk while hearing from each group. At this time, if students have not done so already, the teacher clarifies how the predictions follow from the framework provided by the essential understandings and the action cycle. Then, the core predictions are transformed into purposes for reading. This step is another important component in building interest, ownership, and motivation for engaging with the readings. Students genuinely look forward to discovering whether their hypotheses are on target.

Step 3: Develop Knowledge

At this stage, students typically consult resources to determine the answers to the guiding questions and evaluate the accuracy of their predictions. Often, pictures are reviewed and sometimes videos are added. I have also written a fair number of texts to consolidate interesting information found in sources that would have been too advanced and complex for most elementary and middle school students. Like historians, students seek evidence to support or refute particular predictions. When resources provide mildly or significantly different perspectives, teachers initiate discussions about the basis for making sense of disparate information and the general issues involved in attempting to discern the validity of historical data. In this step of the process, students use blank charts relating to the physical features of a place, the human features of a place, and the "big five" aspects of culture (or derivations of those charts, depending on the circumstance) as a means of taking notes. Essentially, these charts serve as frameworks within which to structure students' developing understandings.

Step 4: Integrate Ideas

Finally, students integrate all that they have learned in a cumulative fashion within the section or unit. In other words, teachers and students work together, usually as a whole class, to establish what seem to be the most important ideas, determine how the ideas fit together within the conceptual framework provided by the essential understandings and the action cycle, and discuss how, by using the action cycle as a conceptual framework, this new information seems to suggest other connections and further questions to be explored. At this stage in the process, students sometimes are asked to demonstrate their understandings in writing or through the completion of a project. This happens consistently at the end of units in the form of quizzes and final projects, and more informally but fairly consistently, at the end of a section within a unit. The purpose of the latter tasks is to help teachers and students evaluate current understandings as well as to provide students with practice responding to written questions that require them to make connections and synthesize what they are learning. The action cycle provides the structure for these activities.

The Action Cycle in Action

The action cycle can be applied in a range of different types of units in social studies (as well as other subjects, but that discussion extends beyond the purview of this chapter). In what follows, I present three types of units as examples. The units focus on developing an understanding of

1. How a group of people lived and why they lived that way (e.g., the study of the Lakota Sioux culture before settlers arrived).

2. The causes and consequences of a significant action in history (e.g., the decision by England to establish a colony in Virginia).

3. The causes and consequences of the actions of groups in conflict (e.g., the study of the American Civil War).

Lakota Sioux Culture

One expansive unit that we teach in elementary school as part of the study of the United States introduces students to Native American nations found in different regions across North America before European traders and American settlers arrived. This unit helps students appreciate the diverse range of cultures found across the continent as well as the ingenuity of each of these groups. In addition, the close connection that each group shares with the land provides an excellent opportunity for students to observe quite clearly the interconnection between human needs, physical features, and human features. Consequently, this unit reinforces the utility of the essential understandings and the action cycle very well.

In the study of each nation, the content is taught in the same general order: Review the universal nature of human needs, establish the physical features of where the group lived, engage in a comprehensive investigation of the human features of the group (constantly noting the direct relationship between the physical features and the human features), and consider the consequences of the group's way of life on the environment. We also investigate innovations and outside influences (or events) that led to changes in the physical features of the place, the group's way of life, or both. The essential understandings and the action cycle are consistently reviewed and used as a framework throughout the process.

Because these studies focus on exploring the many facets of how each group lived at that time, students gather information about each aspect of culture (see Figure 8.1). In the sample lesson provided in Figure 8.4, students learn about the physical features of the Great Plains, which sets the stage for a thorough review of the human features of the Lakota Sioux. It is worth mentioning that lessons often stretch across more than one class period.

Figure 8.4. Instructional Plan for the Lesson on the Physical Features of the Great Plains

Generate Questions
- *Introduction*—Provide pictures of the environment in which the Lakota Sioux lived in the 17th, 18th, and 19th centuries, as well as pictures of how these people lived during this time period. In addition, provide a few artifacts for the students to examine.
- Share that we will be studying the Lakota Sioux before the settlers arrived.
- *Introduce the task*—"Using the pictures and artifacts as well as your background knowledge, I would like you to record your current beliefs and hypotheses about how the Lakota Sioux lived during this time period."
- *Review*—"Before you do that, consider what information you need to know to have a thorough understanding of a culture. What are your ideas and why do you feel that way?" Briefly review the idea of using the essential understandings and the action cycle as a framework for understanding how people live, why they live that way, the actions that they take, and the consequences of those actions.
- Restate the task about beliefs and hypotheses and have the students work independently and in small groups to record their ideas. Then, summarize their ideas as a whole class. Record responses on the smartboard here and throughout the lessons during whole-class discussions.
- *Generate questions*—"What questions do you want answered about how the Lakota Sioux lived during this time?"
- *Focus on one question*—"What question do you think we should answer first?" "Why do we almost always start our units by determining the physical features of the place?"

(*continued*)

Figure 8.4. Instructional Plan for the Lesson on the Physical Features of the Great Plains (Continued)

- *Review*—"What do we mean by physical features?" "What are the major physical features that we study?"

Make Predictions
- Have the students return to the pictures. Provide a blank physical features chart.
- *Task*—"Using the pictures and your background knowledge, predict what you think the physical features would be like where the Lakota Sioux lived at this period of time." Have them work independently and then in small groups.
- Discuss their answers as a whole class, with you summarizing and asking them to explain the reasoning behind their predictions.

Develop Knowledge
- *Task*—"Read the handout [a text written by the author that provides a relatively concise overview of the Great Plains during this time period as it pertains to all of the physical features in question] and take notes using the blank physical features chart to answer our purpose question." Have students work independently and then discuss in small groups.

Integrate Ideas
- Discuss the physical features as a whole group, with representatives from the small groups sharing the groups' ideas. Consolidate what was learned into the most critical information.
- *Written task*—"Answer the question, How does knowing the physical features of a place help you understand how a group lived in that place?"
- *Looking ahead*—"Now that we know the physical features, what are the most fundamental questions that we want answered to understand how the Lakota Sioux lived at that time?" "Why do we typically begin a study of a group's culture by considering issues related to survival?" "What is the first question that we should address?"

Generate Questions
- *New questions established*—"What did the Lakota Sioux eat?" "Why did they eat those things; that is, how are the items connected to the physical features?"

Note. This lesson is part of the unit on the Lakota Sioux.

The Settlement of Jamestown

The settlement of Jamestown provides a fascinating study in the intersection of multiple cultural influences. Helping students understand why things unfolded as they did, as opposed to simply teaching them names, dates, and facts, has kindled a host of stimulating questions within the students with whom I have worked. In this case, questions such as those listed in Figure 8.5 provide a good framework for the investigation

Figure 8.5. Guiding Questions for the Unit on the Settlement of Jamestown

- Why did England want to start a colony in Virginia?
- Why was Jamestown established on the spot where it was?
- Why did the initial colonists struggle so greatly to survive there?
- What were the issues that caused conflict between the colonists and the Powhatans?
- How did the colonists live? (Study the aspects of culture for the colonists.)
- How did the Powhatans live? (Study the aspects of culture for the Powhatans.)
- What finally changed the fortunes of the colonists and enabled the colony to get established and start to grow?
- Why didn't the native inhabitants, most notably the Powhatans, get rid of the colonists at Jamestown when they had the chance?
- What were the short- and long-term consequences of the establishment of Jamestown for England?
- What were the short- and long-term consequences of the establishment of Jamestown for the Powhatans?

of this colony. To be sure, the goal is for students to generate the questions that will direct the inquiry process. Even so, it is always wise to have an outline of questions prepared, so you can shape the direction of the study as much as is necessary to address your overarching objectives.

In the study of Jamestown, once we discuss the colonists establishing the colony on the James River, conversations rather quickly move into questions that involve the interaction between the colonists and the Powhatans. This situation suggests using the action cycle to address issues from more than one perspective, which is discussed in the next section. However, the initial question (Why did England want to start a colony in Virginia?) illustrates how a significant action that focuses primarily on one group can be addressed. When considering why England wanted to establish a colony in Virginia, it is necessary to reflect on the physical features of England in the early 1600s as well as English leaders' understanding at that time of the physical features of Virginia. In addition, certain aspects of the culture of England in the early 17th century are especially relevant in answering this question. In this case, as with similar questions, economic, technological, political, social, and religious considerations are the most essential set of issues to review. Thus, the example lesson connected to this question reflects this abbreviated list of aspects of culture (see Figure 8.6).

Figure 8.6. Instructional Plan for the Lesson Addressing the Question, Why Did England Want to Start a Colony in Virginia?

Generate Questions
- *Introduction*—"On December 20, 1606, three small ships left the docks of London, England. Few paid any attention to their departure. The intention of the 100+ colonists and 40 or so crew members was to start a colony in the New World for England. Upon their departure, none knew the tremendous difficulties that lay ahead of them, nor could they have had any idea how profoundly their actions would affect history as they established the Jamestown colony."
- Present an array of children's books on Jamestown.
- *Introduce the task*—"Using the books to spark your memories, record your current understanding about Jamestown. I don't want you to read the books; just look at the covers and pictures." Have students work independently and in small groups before discussing and recording the ideas in a whole-class setting.
- *Generate a question*—"Any time we study a significant action in history, what is the most fundamental question that we want to answer?" (Why did they do that?)
- "Trying to start a colony was expensive, and there was no guarantee that it would be successful. So, why were they willing to invest a great deal of money (and almost certainly, many lives) when there was no assurance that they would get any return? That is the key question."
- *Review*—"What are the factors that we have been studying that help explain why people do what they do?" (the first three essential understandings or the human needs and context segments of the action cycle) "Thus, where do you think we should focus our attention in investigating this question?" (needs, physical features, human features) "To answer our why question, what smaller questions do we need to answer first?" (physical features of England at the time, English leaders' understanding of the physical features of Virginia at the time, human features of England at the time)

Make Predictions
- *Task*—"Consider what you know about the factors that shape why humans do what they do. Based on those ideas, why do you think England wanted to start a colony in the New World? Work individually and then in small groups to record your ideas and be sure to explain your reasoning."
- Discuss the students' ideas as a whole group and record the ideas.

Develop Knowledge
- *Task*—"Read the text provided [written by the author] and take notes to answer our purpose question. Use the following three frameworks to record your notes: (1) a blank physical features form to take notes on the physical features of England at the time, (2) a blank physical features form to take notes on what the English leaders believed to be the physical features of Virginia at the time, and (3) a blank human features chart focused on the 'big five' aspects of culture: economic, technological, political, social, and religious issues." Have students work independently and then in small groups.

Integrate Ideas
- Come together as a whole class and have students report what they learned. Consolidate the information into the most important points.

(continued)

Figure 8.6. Instructional Plan for the Lesson Addressing the Question, Why Did England Want to Start a Colony in Virginia? (Continued)

- Review how this information establishes the context in which the action of deciding to start a colony took place. Use the action cycle to demonstrate how what they just learned fits into the cycle.
- *Looking ahead*—"Now that we have a better understanding of why England wanted to establish a colony in Virginia, what seems to be a reasonable question to explore next?" (What happened when they got there?) "When we want to understand what a group of people did in a particular place, what is the first question that we usually ask?" (What are the physical features of the place?)

Generate Questions
- *New question established*—"What were the physical features at the Jamestown colony?"

Note. This lesson is part of the unit on the settlement of Jamestown.

Considering Multiple Perspectives on the American Civil War

The American Civil War is one of the most compelling periods in the history of the United States. The story of how this nation grew apart, descended into bitter and bloody conflict, and struggled to heal after the war is epic. It is also a story that illustrates the impact of a range of physical and human features on the actions and outcomes related to this conflict. When studying the Civil War, as with any intriguing, multifaceted, and complex historical event, the question is not so much what to address but what to leave out. As always, the optimal breadth and depth of your investigation depends on the students you are teaching. However, providing at least a solid amount of depth is important, because that is when investigations get interesting and, thus, when students have the opportunity to recognize the joy of historical inquiry (e.g., Levstik & Barton, 2005).

The American Civil War is also a story that demonstrates the importance of considering each event, with its multitude of actions, from more than one perspective to obtain a richer understanding of what occurred and why. This, then, is an excellent example of when it is necessary to use more than one action cycle. In this case, most often it will be relevant to have one action cycle that represents the perspective of the Union and another that represents the Confederacy. For example, when considering why the Battle of Gettysburg is widely recognized as the turning point in the Civil War, it is important to consider separately the state of the Union and Confederate causes entering that battle and exiting it (see Figure 8.7). In addition, it is important to consider separately

Figure 8.7. Instructional Plan for the Lesson on the Significance of the Battle of Gettysburg

Generate Questions

- *Introduction*—"We have recently read about the First Battle of Bull Run or Manassas and the realization following this battle that this war was not going to end quickly. We have also read a general overview of the battles that followed from 1861 into 1863. Next, we will focus on the battle that is widely considered to be the turning point of the American Civil War—Gettysburg."
- *Generate a question*—"When I tell you that people consider this the turning point of the war, what is the first question that comes to mind?" "Why do people believe it was the turning point?" "What does it mean to be called the turning point?" If they are not sure, explain that it means that there was a significant change from what was happening before the battle to what happened after the battle. It means that there was a change in fortunes for both sides.
- *Connection*—"To understand why the Battle of Gettysburg is considered the turning point of the war, it helps to think about the action cycle. If the Battle of Gettysburg is the central action that we are considering, and 'turning point' means that there was a significant change from before the event to after, in terms of the action cycle, what do we need to know to answer this question?" Students need to know what happened before Gettysburg, which is essentially the context leading up to the Battle of Gettysburg, and what happened after Gettysburg, which is the short- and long-term consequences of the battle and corresponding events related to the war.
- "In looking at the context leading up to the battle and the consequences of the battle, we need to remember that the context and consequences were different for the Union and the Confederacy." An example is the different contexts and consequences for the two teams playing in the Super Bowl.
- "So, what should we consider first?" (the context for both sides before Gettysburg) "One way to do that is to ask, What was the condition of the Union and the Confederacy heading into the Battle of Gettysburg? In other words, how were things going for each side?"
- "If we are looking at the context [point to it on the action cycle], what issue are we looking at?" (the physical and human features of each group)
- "In this case, we will only take a very general look at the physical features and focus most of our energy on the basic condition of the human features of both sides. Most significant, we will look at the 'big five' but add one more issue: the military. We will add that issue, because the condition of the armies is a critical issue in war. So, we are asking, How were things going for the Union right before Gettysburg, and how were things going for the Confederacy?"

Make Predictions

- "Based on our readings so far in this unit, you already have a general idea about the state of the Union and the Confederacy before the Battle of Gettysburg. Even so, there is probably more that you suspect is true, but you are not sure."
- *Task*—"Using a blank page with 'physical features' at the top and a blank human features chart with space for notes about the big five and military issues, write down how you think the Union was doing before the Battle of Gettysburg. You

(continued)

Figure 8.7. Instructional Plan for the Lesson on the Significance of the Battle of Gettysburg (Continued)

can use the readings we have done and the maps we have used that are in your binder." Have students work independently and then in small groups. Next, discuss as a whole class.
• *Task*—"Complete the same task in the same way about the Confederacy."

Develop Knowledge
• "Read the handouts [written by the author, including compiled maps] and take notes on the state of the Union and the Confederacy just before the Battle of Gettysburg. Use new sets of the physical and human features charts used to make predictions [these are provided]." Have students work independently and then in small groups.

Integrate Ideas
• Come together as a whole class and have students report what they learned. Consolidate the information into the most important points.
• *Task*—"Write a brief statement about the state of the Union and the Confederacy heading into the Battle of Gettysburg. Based on this information, write your thoughts about why this battle was especially important for both sides."
• Review how this information fits into the action cycle and sets the stage for the battle (i.e., the action).
• *Looking ahead*—"Now that we know the context for the Battle of Gettysburg, what makes sense to discuss next?" (What happened at the Battle of Gettysburg?)

Generate Questions
• *New question established*—"What happened at the Battle of Gettysburg?"

Note. This lesson is part of the unit on the American Civil War.

the actions that were taken by each side that contributed to the short- and long-term consequences that followed this confrontation, as well as the cumulative effect of a series of factors that seem to find this event as a convenient fulcrum. To be sure, elementary students do not need to become versed in military tactics, nor do they need to commit troop movements during the battle to memory. However, having a general sense of central characters, the most important decisions they faced, and the actions they took in the face of great challenge helps bring this human drama to life for the students and makes it resonate with greater meaning.

Conclusion

Reading is a multifaceted task that presents a range of challenges for students who struggle with processing texts. These challenges inhibit the comprehension of texts, whether the texts are narrative or expository. However, expository texts are widely considered to be even more difficult to comprehend than narrative texts. Consequently, determining means of helping struggling readers improve their comprehension of expository text is a critical goal.

In this chapter, I described an instructional practice that draws from literature on literacy, expertise, psychology, and history. At the center of the approach is a conceptual framework (i.e., the action cycle) that presents an integrated and cohesive set of core concepts that can structure students' understanding of content area materials related to human actions. Data from a five-year research and development project conducted with struggling readers indicate that instruction in the action cycle approach helps students improve their abilities to approach tasks strategically, make predictions, remember text information, and make connections between ideas within the text (Gaskins, 2009; R. Gaskins & Galloway, 2008, 2009). I look forward to continuing to explore this line of research.

TRY IT!

1. There are a number of ways to apply the action cycle approach. Three are presented in this text. These applications should work well in whole-class, small-group, and individual settings. Experiment with this approach and determine what works best with your students based on their individual strengths and challenges.

2. Although the instructional plans provided here do not feature the use of digital resources, you may want to consider the use of such resources in activities applying the action cycle approach. Not only can you use texts, images, maps, and videos that are found online, but also you can experiment with creating class blogs, wikis, or nings to both facilitate and evaluate students' developing understanding of the content.

REFERENCES

Alexander, P.A. (1997). Mapping the multidimensional nature of domain learning: The interplay of cognitive, motivational, and strategic forces. In M.L. Maehr & P.R. Pintrich (Eds.), *Advances in motivation and achievement* (Vol. 10, pp. 213–250). Greenwich, CT: JAI.

Alexander, P.A. (2003). The development of expertise: The journey from acclimation to proficiency. *Educational Researcher, 32*(8), 10–14. doi:10.3102/0013189X032008010

Alexander, P.A. (2006). *Psychology in learning and instruction*. Boston: Allyn & Bacon.

Alexander, P.A., & Jetton, T.L. (2000). Learning from text: A multidimensional and developmental perspective. In M.L. Kamil, P.B. Mosenthal, P.D. Pearson, & R. Barr (Eds.), *Handbook of reading research* (Vol. 3, pp. 285–310). Mahwah, NJ: Erlbaum.

Alexander, P.A., & Winne, P.H. (Eds.). (2006). *Handbook of educational psychology* (2nd ed.). Mahwah, NJ: Erlbaum.

Alvermann, D., Simpson, M., & Fitzgerald, J. (2006). Teaching and learning in reading. In P.A. Alexander & P.H. Winne (Eds.), *Handbook of educational psychology* (2nd ed., pp. 427–455). Mahwah, NJ: Erlbaum.

Armbruster, B.B. (1984). The problem of "inconsiderate text." In G.G. Duffy, L.R. Roehler, & J. Mason (Eds.), *Comprehension instruction: Perspectives and suggestions* (pp. 202–217). New York: Longman.

Bransford, J.D., Brown, A.L., & Cocking, R.R. (Eds.). (1999). *How people learn: Brain, mind, experience, and school*. Washington, DC: National Academy Press.

Csikszentmihalyi, M. (1990). *Flow: The psychology of optimal experience*. New York: Harper & Row.

Deci, E.L., & Ryan, R.M. (Eds.). (2002). *Handbook of self-determination research*. Rochester, NY: University of Rochester Press.

Dewey, J. (1956). *The child and the curriculum and The school and society*. Chicago: University of Chicago Press. (Original works published 1902 and 1915, respectively)

Diamond, J. (1997). *Guns, germs, and steel: The fate of human societies*. New York: W.W. Norton.

Dole, J.A., Duffy, G.G., Roehler, L.R., & Pearson, P.D. (1991). Moving from the old to the new: Research on reading comprehension instruction. *Review of Educational Research, 61*(2), 239–264.

Donald, J.G. (2002). *Learning to think: Disciplinary perspectives*. San Francisco: Jossey-Bass.

Donovan, M.S., & Bransford, J.D. (2005). Introduction. In M.S. Donovan & J.D. Bransford (Eds.), *How students learn: History, mathematics, and science in the classroom* (pp. 1–28). Washington, DC: National Academies Press.

Duke, N.K., & Pearson, P.D. (2002). Effective practices for developing reading comprehension. In A.E. Farstrup & S.J. Samuels (Eds.), *What research has to say about reading instruction* (3rd ed., pp. 205–242). Newark, DE: International Reading Association.

Erickson, H.L. (2001). *Stirring the head, heart, and soul: Redefining curriculum and instruction* (2nd ed.). Thousand Oaks, CA: Corwin.

Fernández-Armesto, F. (2001). *Civilizations: Culture, ambition, and the transformation of nature*. New York: Touchstone.

Fisher, D., Brozo, W.G., Frey, N., & Ivey, G. (2007). *50 content area strategies for adolescent literacy*. Boston: Allyn & Bacon.

Gajria, M., Jitendra, A.K., Sood, S., & Sacks, G. (2007). Improving comprehension of expository text in students with LD: A research synthesis. *Journal of Learning Disabilities, 40*(3), 210–225. doi:10.1177/00222194070400030301

Gaskins, I.W. (2005). *Success with struggling readers: The Benchmark School approach.* New York: Guilford.

Gaskins, I.W., Satlow, E., Hyson, D., Ostertag, J., & Six, L. (1994). Classroom talk about text: Learning in science class. *Journal of Reading, 37*(7), 558–565.

Gaskins, R.W. (1999). "Adding legs to a snake": A reanalysis of motivation and the pursuit of happiness from a Zen Buddhist perspective. *Journal of Educational Psychology, 91*(2), 204–215. doi:10.1037/0022-0663.91.2.204

Gaskins, R.W. (2009, February). *Improving struggling readers' understanding of narrative and expository texts.* Paper presented at the 54th annual meeting of the International Reading Association West, Phoenix, AZ.

Gaskins, R.W., & Galloway, E. (2008, December). *Why did they do that?! Making sense of human history through the essential understandings.* Paper presented at the 58th annual meeting of the National Reading Conference, Orlando, FL.

Gaskins, R.W., & Galloway, E.P. (2009, December). *Facilitating students' understanding of expository texts in social studies: Applying an instructional approach centered on the essential understandings and the action cycle.* Paper presented at the 59th annual meeting of the National Reading Conference, Albuquerque, NM.

Geography Education Standards Project. (1994). *Geography for life: National geography standards 1994.* Washington, DC: National Geographic Society Committee on Research and Exploration.

Gersten, R., Fuchs, L.S., Williams, J.P., & Baker, S.K. (2001). Teaching reading comprehension strategies to students with learning disabilities: A review of research. *Review of Educational Research, 71*(2), 279–320. doi:10.3102/00346543071002279

Guthrie, J.T., Wigfield, A., & Perencevich, K.C. (Eds.). (2004). *Motivating reading comprehension: Concept-oriented reading instruction.* Mahwah, NJ: Erlbaum.

Hiebert, E.H., & Martin, L.A. (2009). Opportunity to read: A critical but neglected construct in reading instruction. In E.H. Hiebert (Ed.), *Reading more, reading better* (pp. 3–29). New York: Guilford.

Levstik, L.S., & Barton, K.C. (2005). *Doing history: Investigating with children in elementary and middle schools* (3rd ed.). Mahwah, NJ: Erlbaum.

Mandler, J.M., & Johnson, N.S. (1977). Remembrance of things parsed: Story structure and recall. *Cognitive Psychology, 9*(1), 111–151. doi:10.1016/0010-0285(77)90006-8

Martin, N.M., & Duke, N.K. (2011). Interventions to enhance informational text comprehension. In A. McGill-Franzen & R.L. Allington (Eds.), *Handbook of reading disability research* (pp. 345–361). New York: Routledge.

Maslow, A.H. (1999). *Toward a psychology of being* (3rd ed.). New York: John Wiley & Sons.

McNamara, D.S. (Ed.). (2007). *Reading comprehension strategies: Theories, interventions, and technologies.* Mahwah, NJ: Erlbaum.

Moje, E.B. (2010). Comprehending in the subject areas: The challenges of comprehension, grades 7–12, and what to do about them. In K. Ganske & D. Fisher (Eds.), *Comprehension across the curriculum: Perspectives and practices K–12* (pp. 46–72). New York: Guilford.

Pearson, P.D. (2006, July). *Using reading, writing, and language to support inquiry in subject matter learning: The case of Seeds of Science/Roots of Reading.*

Paper presented at the National Geographic School Publishing and Literacy Achievement Research Center's Literacy Institute, Washington, DC.

Pearson, P.D., & Gallagher, M.C. (1983). The instruction of reading comprehension. *Contemporary Educational Psychology, 8*(3), 317–344. doi:10.1016/0361-476X(83)90019-X

Prawat, R.S. (1991). The value of ideas: The immersion approach to the development of thinking. *Educational Researcher, 20*(2), 3–30. doi:10.3102/0013189X020002003

Pressley, M., Gaskins, I.W., Solic, K., & Collins, S. (2006). A portrait of Benchmark School: How a school produces high achievement in students who previously failed. *Journal of Educational Psychology, 98*(2), 282–306. doi:10.1037/0022-0663.98.2.282

Romance, N.R., & Vitale, M.R. (2001). Implementing an in-depth expanded science model in elementary schools: Multi-year findings, research issues, and policy implications. *International Journal of Science Education, 23*(4), 373–404.

Schunk, D.H., Pintrich, P.R., & Meece, J.L. (2007). *Motivation in education: Theory, research, and applications* (3rd ed.). Upper Saddle River, NJ: Prentice Hall.

Shanahan, C. (2009). Disciplinary comprehension. In S.E. Israel & G.G. Duffy (Eds.), *Handbook of research on reading comprehension* (pp. 240–260). New York: Routledge.

Shanahan, T., & Shanahan, C. (2008). Teaching disciplinary literacy to adolescents: Rethinking content-area literacy. *Harvard Educational Review, 78*(1), 40–59.

Smith, H. (2001). *Why religion matters: The fate of the human spirit in an age of disbelief*. New York: HarperCollins.

Stein, N.L., & Glenn, C.G. (1979). An analysis of story comprehension in elementary school children. In R.O. Freedle (Ed.), *New directions in discourse processing: Vol. 2. Advances in discourse processes* (pp. 53–120). Norwood, NJ: Ablex.

Tierney, R.J., Readence, J.E., & Dishner, E.K. (1995). *Reading strategies and practices: A compendium* (4th ed.). Boston: Allyn & Bacon.

Trigger, B.G. (2003). *Understanding early civilizations: A comparative study*. New York: Cambridge University Press.

Vacca, R.T., & Vacca, J.A.L. (2007). *Content area reading: Literacy and learning across the curriculum* (9th ed.). Boston: Allyn & Bacon.

Walsh, K. (2003). Basal readers: The lost opportunity to build the knowledge that propels comprehension. *American Educator, 27*(1), 24–27.

CHAPTER 9

Understanding and Scaffolding Students' Research Processes: Stories From the Classroom

Joyce E. Many

I am sitting in the back of a classroom of 10- and 11-year-olds in Aberdeen, Scotland, taking notes for an ethnographic study on students' processes as they learn to do research. A student carrying an oversized book catches my eye. His name is Ian (all names are pseudonyms). He has been working for six weeks on a project focusing on leaders during World War II. He pulls out a sheet of paper from his desk and hunches over the pages of his resource. He is beginning a section on a new leader, and I can predict his process, as it is one that this young researcher has used before. First, Ian will laboriously copy paragraph after paragraph onto a sheet of paper. Next, using his copied text, he will begin line-by-line paraphrasing of this information into his report booklet. When he has finished putting all of the information "into my own words," as Ian would say, then he will go on to the next world leader that he planned to study.

This vignette shares a glimpse of what conducting research meant to Ian. To those of us who have taught intermediate-grade students to do research, the processes that he used may include some elements that are familiar and others that seem unusual. Often, what many teachers say when introducing students to research is, "Read information and then put it into your own words"—a dictum that Ian had learned. Teachers stress repeatedly the warning not to copy, and indeed, close scrutiny of Ian's final project report on world leaders absolved him of any suspicion of plagiarism. Ian worked laboriously to change complex sentences into simple sentences. He removed pronominal references and reworded each line one step at a time. Ian also demonstrated other practices that many teachers encourage.

After Early Intervention, Then What? Teaching Struggling Readers in Grades 3 and Beyond (2nd ed.) edited by Jeanne R. Paratore and Rachel L. McCormack. © 2011 by the International Reading Association.

He worked with a clear plan in mind and brainstormed about leaders that he might address, writing their names on a planning web. His final project booklet contained 21 pages of information and drawings related to world leaders, such as Adolf Hitler, Winston Churchill, Franklin Roosevelt, Joseph Stalin, Benito Mussolini, and Chiang Kai-shek. However, Ian's story also raises some questions: Why did he first copy all information verbatim from his resource onto a separate sheet of paper? Did he use multiple sources of information? What did he learn from this activity?

To help teachers think through these issues, I share stories in this chapter of how students approach research and how teachers can support students' processes in ways that can help even less proficient readers experience success. These stories are drawn from data gathered in two ethnographic studies. Both studies examined classroom situations in which students were involved in the process of conducting research over extended periods of time. In the first inquiry, the one in which I met Ian, the self-directed nature of a Scottish classroom provided me with an opportunity to describe processes that students use to work from text and their impressions of what it means to do research (Many, Fyfe, Lewis, & Mitchell, 2004). The second study (Many, 2002) was conducted in a school with a diverse student body in the southern United States. I spent a year in the third/fourth- and fifth/sixth-grade classrooms of this school during interdisciplinary units of instruction over the course of a year. The teachers and I discussed the students' processes, and the teachers worked to scaffold the conceptual understandings and strategy use of their students. The stories I share from these classrooms illustrate what the teachers and I learned as we considered how to help struggling readers be involved in meaningful inquiry.

Meaningful Research: Constructing a Personal Understanding of Information

What does it mean to do research? Actually, it can mean different things to different students and different teachers. When one sits and thinks about what it means to do research, one might find that *research* can be defined in a range of ways, depending on the purposes for that research. For some, research means accumulating information. Take, for instance, the process of Claudia, an 11-year-old in Ian's class:

Claudia sits at a long table near the back of the classroom with two other students. All of the students in her class are involved in a three-month interdisciplinary unit on World War II, and each is also conducting a personal research project on a self-chosen topic related to the war.

Claudia has just completed her project, "Aberdeen at War," which is in the form of a 17-page booklet of writings, drawings, and photocopied information. I have talked with her throughout her research process and compared her project booklet to the source texts that she has used. Her primary focus in putting together her World War II research project is to find "something interesting," something that her teacher would want to share with the class.

Although Claudia follows her teacher's direction to create a planning web for her topic, her method of doing research has involved thumbing through books and finding something interesting to include, or finding out what her classmates are doing and doing something similar in her project booklet. Thus, Claudia often finds information through serendipity rather than as the result of a concentrated search. The strategies of working from texts that she uses are primarily photocopying, verbatim copying, and drawing and labeling. On a number of occasions, including on her initial brainstorming on her planning web, she includes information that she liked, regardless of whether it has a direct connection to her topic.

As I talk with Claudia, however, she is very pleased with her booklet. Assessing her project, she notes, "I think I did quite good. I find it interesting….I don't have as much as other people do [but] I think I did quite good." As we talk, she comments that she would not change anything about her work. She clearly feels that she has been successful in fulfilling her own expectations of what it means to do research.

————————

To Claudia, research meant collecting interesting information. To Ian, research meant something else entirely; research was putting things in your own words, a process of transferring information from an author's source text to your own report. When grading his efforts, many teachers would award his final project with an "A." His work stayed on topic, addressed a vast amount of detailed information about a variety of world leaders, and was carefully laid out with illustrations and pictures to supplement his report. If a teacher turned an eye to Ian's processes, however, a number of questions might arise. He seemed to have problems using the table of contents and index of his text. His procedure of first copying out relevant passages verbatim was a coping strategy that he had learned because of difficulties he had encountered in finding his place in the large book from one day to the next. Ian also showed little interest in working from multiple sources; to him, research was about rewriting information from a source and putting it into his own words. Because his text obviously had plenty of information, he did not see a need to go to other resources. Finally, although his product was impressive, Ian had difficulty talking freely about what he had learned. As I watched him interact with his peers during small-group discussions about world leaders, he seldom shared information unless he was reading directly from his project booklet. He seemed to have transferred the information into his own words without building his own understanding of the content itself.

The perspective to research that I address in this chapter differs from the notion that Claudia demonstrated (i.e., the idea that research is collecting or accumulating information) and from Ian's impression (i.e., that research involves transferring information). Rather, I consider research as a transformative process leading to personal understanding. Such an inquiry perspective involves different research processes and different strategies in working from text. The contrasts between these different task impressions of what it means to do research and ways of working from text are found in Table 9.1.

As illustrated, when students view research as transforming information, they are involved in a complex set of research processes: planning, searching, finding, recording, reviewing, and presenting. These processes do not occur in a linear fashion; rather, they are recursive throughout the research investigation. This recursive nature is illustrated in the following story about Allison, another student in Ian and Claudia's class:

Table 9.1. Students' Task Impressions, Research Processes, and Strategies for Working From Texts

Ways of Working	Task Impressions		
	Accumulating Information	Transferring Information	Transforming Information
Research subtasks	Finding and recording	Searching, finding, and recording	Planning, searching, finding, recording, reviewing, and presenting
Strategies used to work from sources	Photocopying, verbatim copying, and drawing and labeling	Sentence-by-sentence reworking and read-remember-write	Cut-and-paste synthesis and discourse synthesis

I am sitting at the table where I take notes and talk to students during my daily visits to the classroom. Allison walks to my table and says hi. Ms. Lindsey, her teacher, has told me that she is pleased with the work Allison is doing in her research on Anne Frank.

I ask Allison how "Anne Frank" is going. She responds, "I'm not doing just Anne Frank. I'm doing Jewish customs and history, too." I ask her if she will talk with me about her project, and together we look at her planning web. In the center of her web are the words, "Anne Frank." On rays extending out from the center, she has written, "Introduction to Anne Frank," "Jewish symbols," "Jewish customs, religion," "Jewish history, the annex, things I like about Anne Frank's diary," "Life in hiding," "Life under the Nazis," and "Concentration camps."

She explains, "I'm writing about Jews and what they were like and what they went through and all that." "How did you come up with these things?" I ask. She replies, "By reading bits of the book [*The Diary of Anne Frank*], I decided, 'Things I like about Anne Frank's diary.'...I had this book from the library, and it said the stuff that the Nazis did, making rules they had to obey, and I got that idea from that book." Pointing to the section on the concentration camps, she notes, "[I got that] from that big book on Anne Frank [an informational text]. Ms. Lindsey gave me the idea for the Jewish customs and religion. I don't have anything on Jewish history yet."

As Allison continued her search for information, she drew from numerous books on Anne Frank as well as general texts with information about the Jewish religion, the Nazis' treatment of the Jews, and concentration camps. She sent away for and received information from the Anne Frank Foundation. To Allison, doing project work involved finding many books about her topic and writing what she knew after reading them. Her work involved identifying what she wanted to learn and searching for sources that might reveal that information. Her research involved looking at the table of contents to identify specific sections of interest, taking notes, and changing and adapting plans in light of what she learned along the way. Allison viewed research as transforming information. She was involved in a recursive process of planning and then searching for and finding information. She developed ways to record and review her information and to consider if she had addressed her topic sufficiently. She thought through how to present that information effectively to the people whom she considered her audience.

For teachers, the stories of Allison, Ian, and Claudia raise important questions: What can teachers do to help all students be involved in research that leads to personal understanding? How do teachers scaffold students' research processes? What strategies do students need to be able to use to conduct such research? How in particular do teachers help struggling readers? I believe that teachers need to consider specific ways to support students as they engage in research. I had an opportunity in a second ethnographic study to work with two teachers, Joy Ward and Susan Henderson, who continually involved students in ongoing research projects throughout the course of their school year. These teachers used instructional conversations to scaffold their students' perspectives on what it meant to do research and on the processes involved, and to scaffold their students' use of specific strategies to work from text. In the following section, I share stories from these classrooms to illustrate how these teachers helped their third- through sixth-grade students learn both content and processes.

Supporting Students' Efforts to Learn Through Research

The students in the upper elementary classrooms (third/fourth and fifth/sixth grades) have been studying the Caribbean. The teachers have read *The Cay* by Theodore Taylor aloud with students from both classes. Today, the third- and fourth-grade students are spread out around their classroom, working on their individual research.

Joy, their teacher, is sitting at a large table with Curtis, an 11-year-old student from her class. Curtis is doing a research project on reggae and has been talking to Joy about what he has learned. Looking over the packet of work he has turned in, Joy says, "You have information from one source. This is the information gathering phase. If you have only one source, how do you know if this is true?" Joy flips through some pages that Curtis has printed off the Internet and notes a few pictures that would be good to use in the project. She continues, "There is nothing here that belongs to you. The part where you are telling me all this stuff, it is not in this package. There is nothing here that tells me what you know."

She notes that he has talked to her about his project, so she knows that he has learned some things, but what he has handed her does not show what he knows. She explains, "This is stuff that anyone one could have printed off. Your dad could have printed it out while you were asleep. This doesn't show what you know."

Joy elaborates on the difference between printing out information and doing something that shows what he has learned. In essence, Curtis needs to make it his own. Raising the question of how a person can be certain of the accuracy of the information retrieved from the Internet, Joy then explains, "I want you to read an encyclopedia article, or let me know that you have read an article, and show me that you know that this [the information from the Internet] is true. I could put something on the Internet, and I don't know anything about reggae. If you read this and then read something else that matches, then you may find this could be true, but just printing it off the Internet doesn't show me what you know, and just telling me it is true is not enough. Unless you look up the source of who put that information there, or you compare the information with other sources and find that it says the same thing, you cannot be certain that the information is accurate."

In this instructional conversation, Joy provided Curtis with the support and guidance he needed to gather information from multiple sources. Conversations like these are vital aspects of the curriculum in this school, which is grounded in a social-constructivist perspective toward literacy learning. The teachers believe that social interaction is the key to students' knowledge construction (Vygotsky, 1978) and use instructional conversations in one-on-one, small-group, and whole-class settings to scaffold students' progress to new developmental levels.

According to Vygotsky (1978), a student's actual developmental level refers to what a learner can understand or perform independently. What a learner can do with the support of a teacher can be described as being at the learner's level of potential development. The distance between these levels is deemed to be the zone of proximal development and is where instructional scaffolding occurs. Through scaffolding, a teacher provides the assistance that a learner needs (Roehler & Cantlon, 1997). Such scaffolding enables learners to develop understandings or use strategies of which they would not have been capable on their own (Macrine & Sabbatino, 2008; Meyer, 1993). As the learner gains more competence and moves toward independence, the support can be withdrawn gradually (Bruner, 1986, 1990). Through such scaffolding, teachers are able to engage students and support their academic achievement (Raphael, Pressley, & Mohan, 2008).

During the year of observing in these multiage classrooms, I was able to look closely at how Joy and the fifth/sixth-grade teacher, Susan, scaffolded students' research processes, which involved supporting students' growing understanding of what it means to do research, the processes involved, and the use of specific strategies that the students needed to work from texts. The processes that Joy and Susan used moved from those providing substantial teacher support (i.e., modeling, supplying information, clarifying, assisting), to processes inviting more student participation (i.e., questioning, prompting, focusing attention), and finally, to processes requiring the most student involvement (i.e., encouraging self-monitoring, labeling, affirming).

In Joy's conversation with Curtis, she used two scaffolding processes: clarifying and supplying information. Clarifying involves explaining concepts or strategies to which a student has already been introduced. Since the beginning of the year, the class had been involved in conducting various research investigations. The importance of sharing what one knows through research projects had always been implicit in their curriculum. Each unit ended with students presenting their research to the class. For this particular interdisciplinary unit on the Caribbean, though, students had begun to turn to the Internet as a resource to a far greater extent than had been the case for previous research projects. Like Curtis, many students had cut and pasted information from websites or simply printed relevant pages. Joy's explanation that these printed pages did not show what Curtis knew helped clarify the fact that even if a student read and could talk about what was printed off the Internet, handing in such information did not illustrate personal understanding.

The second scaffolding procedure that Joy used with Curtis involved supplying information. Over the last month, Joy, Susan, and I had discussed how use of the Internet was underscoring a need for students to engage in critical literacy (Many, 2000). For example, although the Internet provides virtually a limitless resource of information, readers must systematically consider the authenticity of information drawn from this resource (Kiili, Laurinen, & Marttunen, 2008). Joy's discussion of the importance of verifying the truth of Internet information supplied Curtis with something important to consider. The strategy she suggested of turning to additional sources as a cross-checking mechanism was new to him. After this conversation, she decided to bring these issues up with students in both classes. As shown in the vignette that follows, Joy uses a range of scaffolding procedures to help the students understand the strategies that they need when drawing on resources for their research projects:

The third/fourth- and fifth/sixth-grade classes have come together for a sharing session. Joy explains that something Curtis had done in his research was a problem and that she realized others were having the same problem, too. She asks Curtis to share, and he begins, "I got a bunch of papers off the Internet and tried to turn it in to Joy, and she wouldn't accept it, because my dad could have printed it off. I know a lot of stuff, but the stuff I have been saying is not in there." Joy continues, "It is like he can talk to me about his project, but nothing he has [turned in] has shown me what he knows about it."

Joy walks to the bookshelf and picks up a physics book. She hands the book to Susan and notes, "I can't just hand this book to Susan and say that this book is what I've learned about teaching physics." Joy goes on, leading the students to see how handing Susan this book doesn't show what she, Joy, has learned.

Joy is in the process of preparing a new unit to teach the students about physics. Drawing on her work to prepare the unit, she explains, "I haven't taught this before, so I need to research how to teach physics." She tells them that to research physics, she would not just look at one book. She picks up another text on the shelf and says, "I would look at this other book and the one that Tori and I found." Tori, a fourth-grade student, gets that text and brings it to Joy. "When I think about how I am going to teach physics to you all, I am going to look through all three of these and get ideas. Also, I am going to call up someone I know, who knows about physics, and I will ask, 'If I am teaching students about physics, what things should I consider?' Now, suppose I took this book, and Alexander [a sixth-grade student known for his intelligence] doesn't think much about it, and maybe someone else also thought it might not be a good source. If I just taught right out of this book, would that be a good decision? I don't know if stuff in this book is right. Just because it is a book, it doesn't mean that I know everything in it is right."

Joy reads some reviews off the back cover of the book, and together with the class, they talk about the fact that these reviews are designed to sell the book. They decide that even if these reviews are good, one would need to be cautious, because the publisher would not have put a bad review on the outside cover. She would need another way to judge whether the information in this book is accurate.

Joy goes on to the next book, "Suppose I got out this book, and it says that everything in this other book isn't true? What would I do?" The students volunteer things that she could do to decide which book is correct. Together, they brainstorm that she could talk to a mechanic, read another book, look at the computer, talk to more people, and look at more sources.

Then, Joy goes back to the example with Curtis, "I asked Curtis to talk about this, because there are other people who have had similar experiences. We need to look at both what we know about the things and where we are getting the information we are telling. If you know a lot of information, you need to transmit it and let us hear it and share it." Alexander jumped in, "Remember when I was doing research on jazz? It said a date, and I looked in another book, and the date was completely different in the second book. I still don't know which date was right."

Joy agrees, "That is right. Sometimes we get conflicting information….If I read something about the person who wrote this book [holding up the teaching physics book again] and found out he was a professor at a college, then I might think he knows a lot about it. If I read that he changed tires at a gas station…." She pauses, and the students shake their heads and murmur, "No." Joy finishes her thought, "Then he might still know about it." Her voice stresses the word "might" with an indication that she is not as sure about his knowledge in contrast to the college professor. "What if he lived on a desert island for the last 20 years?"

They discuss how physics is a rapidly changing field and that it would be important to have up-to-date information. Joy stresses, "You have to find out where the person got the information. How do you know they know?" She continues, "It is the same way with sources from the Internet. I could write something about reggae and put it on the Internet." Curtis jumps in, "But you don't know anything about reggae." Joy nods, smiling, "The person who put the pages on the Internet might not either. How would you know?" Remembering their discussions, Curtis volunteers, "You should read something else to make sure it is true." Joy agrees, "Good idea. Read something else and see if it matches."

In this vignette, Joy is building the students' overall impression of research as transforming information. She clarifies that research involves learning and then sharing what one knows. The importance of developing a personal understanding is stressed throughout the instructional conversation. She also uses other scaffolding processes to develop students' abilities to search and find information and review the authenticity of their sources. She uses modeling as she draws on her own experience of researching physics in preparation for the classes' upcoming unit. She uses scaffolding processes, such as questioning and prompting, to have students consider how they might deal with conflicting information between sources. Joy continues to elicit student involvement through questioning and prompting as she has the classes consider ways to verify the credentials of authors and the authenticity of information. Finally, when Curtis responds with what a person should do to verify information from the Internet, she labels and affirms his recommendation.

In addition to developing students' understanding of research processes and what it means to do research, Joy and Susan also worked with readers who needed support in using basic strategies in reading, working from text, and writing. The range of strategies that these teachers scaffolded can be found in Table 9.2.

The scaffolding of the strategies used independently occurred most frequently as teachable moments arose in one-on-one and small-group situations. Research investigations were integral to the social studies and science curriculum, therefore substantial class time was spent with the students engaged in such activities. As the students worked, the teachers held conferences with individuals, discussing their topics and their research processes. As shown in the following vignette, this approach allowed the teachers to understand their students' difficulties and provide the support and guidance that struggling students needed to develop effective strategies:

Table 9.2. Scaffolding Students' Use of Strategies

Reading Strategies	Working From Text	Writing and Composing Strategies
• Using context • Scanning • Map reading • Decoding and pronunciation	• Searching for and locating information • Identifying relevant, authentic, and accurate information • Understanding text formats • Using computers • Note-taking	• Planning • Labeling • Drafting • Revising • Editing • Publishing

Earlier in the day, Susan's class had gone to the local library to look for resources for their investigations into types of shelters. She asks, "Tell me something about the process this morning. What was helpful?" Glenda responds, "The computers because you didn't have to go through the aisles to find something." Susan agrees but then notes, "Sometimes when you find a section, then you can find a lot of books there that can help." "One of the things that was frustrating," comments Rita, "was that sometimes you couldn't find what you wanted when you got to the shelf."

Susan leads the class in considering things that were beneficial or frustrating. They discuss the words that they had brainstormed before they went to the library. The words were examples of things they might look up. Susan notes that some of their words were very specific instead of general and that the very specific words probably would not have a whole book listed for them. She then encourages the students to take some time and begin reading through their books, using sticky notes to mark important passages.

As the students begin, Glenda catches Susan's eye. Glenda is eager to begin writing. Susan encourages Glenda to take the next 15 minutes to read her book. Unsure whether she is supposed to just read, Glenda asks again. Susan explains, "I want you to just take it in, just read and take it in."

Susan notices that June is not reading about her project. Taking a book from the center of the table, Susan sits down with June and says, "Let's see if we can find something in here." She begins to leaf through the resource with June looking on. June's investigation is to find out about the shelters used by an African tribe. Susan asks if June has found out if it is a tribe in Kenya. June does not know. She says that she has been on the computer twice but has not found anything. Susan tells June to look through the book while Susan finds an additional resource. While she is examining another book, Glenda exclaims to Susan, "Ooh, look!" Glenda and Susan hunch over Glenda's book and then call June to come over. Glenda and Susan have found where June's tribe is located. Susan says, "June, you have a job to do. Go find an atlas and look up *Johannesburg*." Susan then asks June to repeat aloud what she should do. When she cannot, Susan repeats that June should get an atlas and clarifies what June should look for. June asks where the atlas is, and Glenda offers to help. Together, Glenda and June go to find the atlas.

When they return, Glenda and June begin thumbing through pages in the atlas. Susan notes, "There is an easier way to do this," and she reminds June of the index at the back. Susan grabs a book and calls attention to the word *Johannesburg*, writing the word down on a sticky note. She places the sticky note in front of June and then tells her to look in the index and find the latitude and longitude for Johannesburg.

Susan circulates through the room and then returns to June. Susan calls June's attention to the guide words at the top of the page in the atlas. Susan reads the guide words and calls attention to the letters. As June begins to look at the proper page, Susan places the sticky note on the page. When June finds the word, Susan explains that the numbers tell the map that it is on, the page number, and the map coordinates, M2. She uses the note to help June focus on the correct number in the index. Then, June looks to find the page. When she gets to the page, Susan prompts her to find M2. She shows June the *M* and they find the 2 together. Then, Susan goes to get the book that Glenda was using, so they can find how far her tribe lived from Johannesburg. They look back and forth from the small map in Glenda's book to the large atlas. Susan calls attention to the curve of the land on the small map and how the page on the large atlas does not show that curve. She explains that they will have to go to the next page to find that curve of land.

Then, Susan notes, "Here is what we could have done. If we are looking for a tribe, then an area might have been named for that tribe. What could we have done?" Susan draws attention to how they looked up Johannesburg and prompts June to consider: "What could we have done to look up the area we are trying to find?" June guesses that they could have looked up the name of the tribe. Susan tells June to use the guide words to look up the name of the tribe. June flips through a large number of pages very quickly. She seems to be using the guide words to some extent, but when she gets close to the pages that she needs, she begins to look down column after column on a number of pages.

Susan comes by again and talks to her about whether she has found anything similar to the name of the tribe. Together, they decide that there is nothing in the index. Susan begins talking about the clues that they have identified at this point. They know that the tribe is located near Johannesburg and Swaziland. She notes that the name of the tribe is probably too specific to find a whole book on it. They will probably have to find a book on South Africa in general. She suggests that June also look at the old *National Geographic* magazines that they have available.

_____

In this vignette from her fifth/sixth-grade classroom, Susan provides the assistance that June needs to be able to work with sources. The support that Susan provides allows the student to pursue her investigation and work with texts that she was unable to use independently at that time. At times, Susan prompts and focuses June's attention, encouraging her involvement. When needed, Susan clarifies the process or assists June directly to ensure her continued progress. Susan also provides opportunities for June to attempt to use strategies on her own but stays closely attuned to her difficulties in order to offer the support that she needs to continue her investigation.

Support Strategies to Assist Struggling Readers

The vignettes from these classrooms provide increased understanding of students' impressions of research and the processes and strategies that students use when they set out to conduct inquiries. The instructional conversations running through these vignettes also illustrate the ways that teachers can support students' efforts to investigate information. Drawing on these stories, I highlight five support strategies that teachers who work with struggling readers might consider when working to scaffold students' abilities to do research.

Support Strategy 1: Give Students Time to Roam

Typically, the first step that our students encounter when teachers assign a research project is the need to decide on a topic. The first support strategy that teachers need to remember, especially when working with struggling readers, is to ensure that the students have an opportunity to explore the subject in general before settling down to a focused investigation. In her work with Curtis, Joy referred to this as the information gathering phase. Susan prompted her students to refrain from taking notes and instead spend time reading and just taking in information. I offer that particularly when working with an unfamiliar topic, students should go through a process similar to Claudia's as she collected interesting information. The research processes at this point focus on simply finding information. Students might photocopy or print information from a wide variety of resources, collect artwork, or check out numerous books. Only after they have begun to develop background knowledge in a topic can students begin to form meaningful questions, review their resources for relevant information, and search purposefully for additional information to answer their questions.

Support Strategy 2: Help Students Find a Range of Sources

One advantage that students had in both of the contexts discussed in this chapter is that their teachers encouraged use of a wide range of sources and supported their students' development of strategies to gather information from these sources. In most classrooms, typical sources for research reports include encyclopedias and expository texts. Although texts of this nature may be available on a range of readability levels, struggling readers often have difficulty reading such texts. In looking at the strategies that the Scottish students used to work from text, it was clear that when readers tried to use complex resources, they chose less demanding strategies for working from the text, such as line-by-line paraphrasing or verbatim copying. Even students who typically worked to synthesize information from across multiple texts would fall back on these strategies when they encountered texts that were difficult for them. However, teachers in these schools also encouraged use of interviews, works of art and music, and historical fiction. Such resources enabled less proficient readers to learn information from a variety of means, and students proved capable of drawing across such sources effectively when giving research presentations or creating products based on what they had learned.

In addition to encouraging students to use both typical and novel sources of information, the teachers' use of class time for personal research investigations ensured that students had the support they needed when working from text. Ms. Lindsey, the Scottish teacher, continually recommended specific texts for her individual students to consider. Joy conferred with students regularly, guiding their planning and replanning, their ability to search for new texts, and their consideration of the importance of cross-checking the accuracy of information as well as of verifying the credibility of the authors. Susan circulated throughout her classroom, identifying teachable moments by watching her students' attempts to use the indexes of books, conduct searches on the Internet, use guide words, and highlight relevant information in text. By staying aware of their students' needs, conceptions of research, research processes, and strategy use, the teachers were able to support their struggling readers' abilities to find and effectively use relevant sources of information for their investigations.

Support Strategy 3: Make Note-Taking a Read–Understand–Write Strategy

If students are going to use their research investigations to develop personal understanding, one key strategy that needs to be taught explicitly is the ability to take notes through a read–understand–write approach. Although students may photocopy or verbatim copy during the information gathering phase, or even do line-by-line paraphrasing of information as they rework specific sentences, such strategies do not ensure that they construct meaning from their research. As Joy remarked to Curtis, someone else could print information off the Internet for students. Even if they are directly involved, activities such as cutting and pasting from Internet sources does not mean that individuals have learned any information. Both Susan and Joy used whole-class minilessons to model how to read and glean key points from resources. Teachers can also provide students with scaffolding by first having students listen to information and write down key points and then have them work in similar ways from written texts. Although many teachers have students create note cards as they conduct research investigations, the key emphasis of ensuring that students are developing an understanding of what they are learning is crucial to research as a meaningful inquiry process.

Support Strategy 4: Have Students Consider the Source

A fourth support strategy that is vital in today's society is the practice of having students carefully consider the source of their information. This need is explored in the vignettes from Joy's class as she discussed the issue of author credibility with Curtis, and later as she discussed with the students her own process of conducting research on physics. As she stressed, critical consideration of the author's credentials is vital. Teachers themselves may not have encountered such an emphasis until they were students in college, and many may not have encountered an emphasis on how to teach students to do research as part of their teacher preparation programs (Ruiz & Many, 2009). Often, teachers in the early years, particularly those who have attempted to have elementary and middle school students conduct their first research project, have been content simply to encourage students to have resources besides an encyclopedia. If students found multiple published sources on their topics, then these teachers felt that the students were successful.

However, in the world today, students and adults have access to a limitless supply of resources on any topic. Many of the documents that they encounter, though, have not gone through any type of review process for quality or accuracy of content. Consequently, for the students of today, the ability to critically evaluate the credibility and authenticity of information should be considered a basic literacy skill (Many, 2000). As Joy explained and then modeled, such critical literacy skills involve strategies such as cross-checking information by comparing sources and considering the background and credibility of the author or the website. Teachers can also consider providing a guide or script to scaffold students' ability to evaluate sources on the Internet (Macrine & Sabbatino, 2008). For instance, a list of questions could be used to direct students' attention to the credibility and relevance of sources (see Table 9.3). Such questions can prompt students' thought processes as they consider whether a source can be trusted and if it will provide good information that can be used to inform their understanding of a specific topic.

Support Strategy 5: Consider What You Value

Finally, the vignettes from these classrooms remind teachers that if they are going to support students' research processes, then they need to begin by looking closely at what the teachers value. Is the production of grammatically correct, polished final products high on a particular teacher's list? Is the teacher interested in having students turn in a set of note cards and a formal report? Does it matter if they can talk about their work and answer questions about what they learned? Is the teacher concerned about whether students have been willing to take risks with

Table 9.3. Prompts for Students to Use to Evaluate Credibility and Relevance of Sources

Credibility	Relevance
• Is this a good source to use? • Is the person who wrote this an expert? • Who published this source? • Does the source have a date that helps me know that the information is recent? • Is the information written in a way that I can understand what is being said? • Does the author tell where his or her information came from?	• Will this source give me good information for my topic? • Are there a number of paragraphs that relate to my topic? • Does this source teach me something new about my topic? • Does this source do a good job of explaining something that was confusing to me? • How does the information in this source compare to what I have learned from other sources?

new strategies in working from texts? Does the teacher wonder what his or her students think research is all about?

What teachers value shapes what they expect from students, what they reward with praise and high grades, and ultimately what students learn from the research activities that they carry out. To illustrate, consider the excerpts in Table 9.4 from the research products produced by three of the Scottish students, Jean, Ian, and Allison. If teachers primarily value products, then they might praise Ian's work to the highest extent. Careful checking would indicate that Ian had not plagiarized from his source; rather, he had carefully written the information in his own words. His

Table 9.4. Comparisons of Excerpts From Students' Final Products

Jean's Project	Ian's Project	Allison's Project
In world war 2 women had to do men's work when they wear fighing a war men work on farm's and factories they had hard Jobs to do. So when men went to war the women had to there work for them. The women had to feed little baby's if they had baby's they would have to do the men's work at the same time. They had to tidy up the house as well as doing the other things as well as doing the house work. The women have hard work when the mean area at war. And if the men come home they are very happy to see them. The women had baby's gass mask's.	Benito Mussolini was the son of a outspokenly socialist blacksmith from central Italy. He use to be a socialist journalist. When he joined the army he rose to the rank of the corporal. In 1919 Benito Mussolini founded the Fascist party, so named from its fasci di combattimentor ("combat groups"). Mussolini spoke from the benches of the extreme right. Nobody dared to sit there. At the same time was Mussolini was in the parliament blackshirted supporters had created a reign of terror on the streets. The post war Italy was suffering from the acute economic social and political unrest.	Nazis first set up Concentration Campus they were some kind of prisons in 1939 there were three kinds of camps in Astora and Germany and in other Countries Some Concentration Camps became Exterminations camps people were murdered or worked to death most people were killed in the gas chambers Eight million people were murdered in concentration Campus six million of them were Jews Jews were taken to concentration Camps by Germas. Children were taken away from there familys and put to separate Concentration Camps Anne and her sister died in a Concentration Camp with a dises called Typho Margot died with it and then a couple of days later Anne died with it to.

report is carefully edited and polished. When teachers look at Jean's and Allison's work, they might note the less complex sentence structure, the frequency of misspelled words, and a less impressive range of content.

However, if teachers have been closely attuned to the processes that their students have been using, then teachers would appreciate struggling reader Jean's ability to draw on multiple oral sources of information to develop her understanding of children's experiences during the war. Her dedication in taping her grandparents' discussions of their memories of war-time events and then listening to tapes and constructing a written report was considerable. Despite her difficulties with reading and writing, she had been capable of drawing from both her grandparents' conversations and the information presented in class to create a written document illustrating what she had learned.

Turning to Allison, teachers' examination of her processes would have helped them appreciate her efforts to synthesize information from three different texts to create this section of her report. Looking at her report in comparison to Ian's, however, one sees a less polished product. If teachers focus primarily on the final product, and perhaps reward Ian with the higher grade, then teachers are in danger of limiting their students' development of more complex strategies in working from texts. To truly synthesize across multiple sources, students must move away from sentence-by-sentence reworking to a strategy such as read–understand–write. However, at least initially, students' resulting products are more likely to contain grammatical inconsistencies and spelling errors, simply because the structure of the text no longer matches that of the original source text. Consequently, if teachers value research as a means for developing personal understanding through inquiry, then teachers will have to be cognizant of, reward, and praise developments in process as well as products.

Summary

The vignettes from these classrooms offer us an opportunity to explore how students come to know what it means to do research. Teachers must begin with an understanding of students' task impressions and the processes and strategies needed to carry out meaningful investigations. Second, teachers need to create classroom opportunities to frame instructional conversations around their students' research projects. Through such conversations, teachers can provide the scaffolding necessary to support struggling readers' attempts to become involved in meaningful inquiries.

TRY IT!

1. In this chapter, I emphasized the importance of guiding students to use a range of resources as they research and write about a topic. Consider the topics that students in your classroom will study next. Make a list of the resources that would offer students useful information. How will you make each of these resources accessible to your students? What additional support will you provide to students who find reading and writing difficult?

2. To help students learn to attend to and evaluate the trustworthiness of the sources that they discover as they conduct research on a topic, locate three or four resources on the topic of study from an array of sources. Work with students to examine the authors' credentials, modeling for them the types of questions that they should ask and the information that they should seek to determine the author's credibility.

REFERENCES

Bruner, J. (1986). *Actual minds, possible worlds.* Cambridge, MA: Harvard University Press.

Bruner, J. (1990). *Acts of meaning.* Cambridge, MA: Harvard University Press.

Kiili, C., Laurinen, L., & Marttunen, M. (2008). Students evaluating Internet sources: From versatile evaluators to uncritical readers. *Journal of Educational Computing Research, 39*(1), 75–95. doi:10.2190/EC.39.1.e

Macrine, S.L., & Sabbatino, E.D. (2008). Dynamic assessment and remediation approach: Using the DARA approach to assist struggling readers. *Reading & Writing Quarterly, 24*(1), 52–76. doi:10.1080/10573560701753112

Many, J.E. (2000). How will literacy be defined in the new millennium? *Reading Research Quarterly, 35*(1), 65–67.

Many, J.E. (2002). An exhibition and analysis of verbal tapestries: Understanding how scaffolding is woven into the fabric of instructional conversations. *Reading Research Quarterly, 37*(4), 376–407. doi:10.1598/RRQ.37.4.3

Many, J.E., Fyfe, R., Lewis, G., & Mitchell, E. (2004). Traversing the topical landscape: Exploring students' self-directed reading–writing–research processes. In R.B. Ruddell & N.J. Unrau (Eds.), *Theoretical models and processes of reading* (5th ed., pp. 684–719). Newark, DE: International Reading Association.

Meyer, D.K. (1993). What is scaffolded instruction? Definitions, distinguishing features, and misnomers. In D.J. Leu & C.K. Kinzer (Eds.), *Examining central issues in literacy research, theory, and practice: Forty-second yearbook of the National Reading Conference* (pp. 41–53). Chicago: National Reading Conference.

Raphael, L.M., Pressley, M., & Mohan, L. (2008). Engaging instruction in middle school classrooms: An observational study of nine teachers. *The Elementary School Journal, 109*(1), 61–81.

Roehler, L.R., & Cantlon, D.J. (1997). Scaffolding: A powerful tool in social constructivist classrooms. In K. Hogan & M. Pressley (Eds.), *Scaffolding student learning: Instructional approaches and issues* (pp. 6–42). Cambridge, MA: Brookline.

Ruiz, A.M., & Many, J.E. (2009). Are they ready to teach students how to do research? An examination of secondary teacher education programs. In K.M. Leander, D.W. Rowe, D.K. Dickinson, M.K. Hundley, R.T. Jimenez, & V.J. Risko (Eds.), *58th yearbook of the National Reading Conference* (pp. 144–155). Oak Creek, WI: National Reading Conference.

Vygotsky, L.S. (1978). *Mind in society: The development of higher psychological processes* (M. Cole, V. John-Steiner, S., Scribner, & E. Souberman, Eds.) Cambridge, MA: Harvard University Press.

CHAPTER 10

Using Reading Guides With Struggling Readers in Grades 3 and Above

Michael C. McKenna, Susan Franks, and Gail E. Lovette

Ms. Williams's (pseudonym) fifth-grade class is made up of a diverse group of readers. Some are English learners, and a handful are reading below grade level. Many of her students find their science text difficult to understand. Its vocabulary is challenging, its organization (including innumerable figures and sidebars) is confusing, and its factual content can be overwhelming to students at times. Ms. Williams has used a number of approaches to help her students contend with these issues. She has tried various questioning strategies during postreading discussions, conducted chapter previews to acquaint the students with the organizational patterns, and provided extensive background knowledge prior to asking her students to read the text. However, such strategies have proved only partially effective. They fail to target the crux of her students' problem, which involves acquiring factual information from their science text.

Ms. Williams is at her wit's end. She is tempted to sidestep the text entirely and simply present its contents through lecture, demonstration, and discussion. She is concerned, however, about her students' limited ability to learn through text. Avoiding the text would help them achieve mandated science objectives, but it would shortchange their development as readers. What should she try next? We believe that all of the students in Ms. Williams's class would benefit from reading guides, an evidence-based instructional strategy that encourages students to comprehend challenging nonfiction.

A reading guide, also called a study guide or strategy guide, is a list of questions and other tasks to which students respond while reading. The purposes of such guides are to focus students' attention, help

After Early Intervention, Then What? Teaching Struggling Readers in Grades 3 and Beyond (2nd ed.) edited by Jeanne R. Paratore and Rachel L. McCormack. © 2011 by the International Reading Association.

them process content, and model strategic reading. Unlike worksheets completed at the end of a text, reading guides are especially effective, because they provide instructional supports to students through questions and activities as they are reading (McKenna & Robinson, 2011). Guides can be used with any type of reading selection, but we are concerned in this chapter with the most challenging material that students face: expository prose. Our intent is to make a case for the use of reading guides by teachers in the intermediate grades. To do so, we describe reading guides in detail, offer suggestions for the construction and use of guides, briefly examine their research base, and attempt to anticipate and address possible teacher objections.

One type of reading guide, the anticipation guide, consists of a list of statements to which the reader must respond prior to reading a selection. Figure 10.1 presents a brief anticipation guide for this chapter. Before you read the remainder of this chapter, we invite you to place a check mark in the "Before Reading" column next to each of the statements with which you tend to agree.

Anticipation guides are useful whenever the content of a reading selection targets possible misconceptions that students may bring with them as they begin to read (Duffelmeyer, 1994). Anticipation guides can also serve as motivational devices that engage students in the material they will read (Kozen, Murray, & Windell, 2006). Such guides represent one of several types that Wood, Lapp, Flood, and Taylor (2008) have cataloged and discussed in detail. It has been our experience, however, that fitting guides into discrete categories may be too limiting. Later in this chapter, we describe an approach to creating reading guides that is flexible and invites teachers to be creative.

Figure 10.1. Anticipation Guide for This Chapter

Before Reading	Statement	After Reading
	Publishers of most commercial textbooks supply reading guides that can be used by teachers.	
	The effectiveness of reading guides has been supported by virtually every research study on record.	
	Reading guides are more appropriate for use in the middle grades than in upper elementary grades.	
	Reading guides are intended to support independent reading and usually work best when students complete them outside of class.	
	Creating a reading guide would probably require too much time on my part.	

How Well Do Reading Guides Work?

Researchers have investigated the effectiveness of guides in numerous studies. Alvermann and her colleagues (Alvermann & Moore, 1991; Alvermann & Swafford, 1989) have found that reading guides were one of the few content-literacy strategies supported by every investigation that had been conducted. Most of these studies, however, involved students in the middle grades and higher and focused on the comprehension of particular selections. Consequently, the results were fairly predictable: Middle school (i.e., grades 6–8) students' comprehension of a particular reading selection tends to be better with a guide than without one, especially when the measure of comprehension is based on information targeted by the guide.

Although encouraging, these studies did not do enough to persuade us that guides should become a mainstay of instruction, so we designed a study (Franks, McKenna, & Franks, 2001) to find out whether guides could be used prior to the middle school grades and also whether their use leads to improved comprehension of text that is read when guides are unavailable. According to Chall's (1996) stage model of reading development, most students have attained sufficient fluency by the time they enter third grade to support the reading of nonfiction, which means that reading guides may be an appropriate instructional strategy for students of this age. However, we know of few third-grade teachers who use them. Guides may, in fact, be an ideal approach because of the support they provide to students who are just beginning to learn through text.

In our study, third-grade teachers developed four reading guides based on selections from their science textbooks. They used the guides with their students at various points during the school year, carefully coaching students in how to complete the guides. Following the use of the fourth guide, the students were asked to read an unfamiliar science passage that was unrelated to any of the concepts that they had studied during the year. This time, they were given no guide, yet they significantly outperformed comparable students who had not been instructed with reading guides during the year.

Our study provides evidence that students as young as grade 3 can benefit from reading guides and that the effects are not limited to the selections covered by the guides. Rather, they appear to result in better comprehension ability, not just improved comprehension of the selections themselves. This is an important distinction, one that argues strongly for the regular use of reading guides as a means of building better comprehension.

We believe that guides influence comprehension ability by modeling the strategic processes that proficient readers use as they tackle challenging new material. Good readers pose questions as they read, make notes to themselves, and may reorganize key concepts to understand them better. When teachers assist students as they complete reading guides, the teachers help sharpen these processes and confirm their importance.

Constructing a Reading Guide

Few commercial publishers provide ready-to-use reading guides to accompany their textbooks. The few we have seen have a standardized look and exhibit little creativity. Therefore, in nearly all cases, if you wish to use a reading guide, then you must first construct it. This may be a somber prospect for busy teachers, but there is a bright side. Creating your own reading guide will allow you to tailor it to the specific needs of the students in your classroom. If, for example, you are teaching several English learners, then you can design your guide to include activities with key vocabulary terms found within the reading. Reading guides can also be modified to address the unique learning needs of students with exceptionalities in your classroom. As reading guides are best used as in-class activities, the time you spend creating them can be thought of as instructional planning time. That is, instead of planning a customary lesson, you can construct a guide in roughly the same amount of time.

What is the best way to create an effective guide? Because guides vary with the selection and with a teacher's purposes, there is no blueprint to follow. A one-size-fits-all approach will simply not work. Depending on the makeup of learners, it may be necessary to modify a reading guide for individuals or groups of students, especially in today's diverse classrooms that include English learners, struggling readers, and gifted students. Reading guides provide an excellent opportunity to differentiate instructional materials based on the particular reading abilities and language needs of students. Although you will have the same content objectives for all students, the reading guides will vary by the level of support they provide. We offer the following general suggestions for constructing an effective reading guide.

Analyze the Material

Read the selection carefully to decide what to emphasize. Think about the thought processes that the students must use to fully understand the material. For example, if a science textbook chapter presents the three major classifications of rocks, then you might want to include a three-column chart or other graphic organizer in the guide.

Identify the Information to Support Assessment Items

Look ahead to a formative or summative assessment that will measure the extent to which your students have mastered the content of the selection. Make sure that the guide is aligned with this assessment and does an adequate job of preparing students for it.

Make the Guide Interesting and Interactive

A simple list of questions will not do. Look for ways of varying the tasks that you present to students and look for tasks that require them to translate material from the printed selection into some other form. For example, completing charts, building diagrams, answering questions in their own words, illustrating key vocabulary terms, and writing brief responses to prompts are a few of the ways that students' real interaction can be encouraged.

Monitor the Length and Difficulty of the Guide

It is important that a reading guide not be an intimidating document. It should be easier to read than the selection itself, of course, and should contain plenty of blank space for students to complete tasks. The guide should also be fairly brief and might cover only a section or so of an entire chapter or text, as there is not enough time for students to complete reading guides for all of the nonfiction reading that they will do.

Include Page Numbers and Subheadings Where Answers Can Be Found

Page numbers and subheadings provide signposts that are useful to students as they work through a reading guide. Students will need to go back and forth between the book and the guide, and they will need to keep their bearings as they do so.

Include Comprehension Aids

Try to anticipate possible difficulties that your students will face as they read. A good reading guide should do more than focus attention and set purposes for reading. The guide should also assist students as they encounter possible pitfalls. For example, the guide might provide quick definitions or synonyms for key terms, include bridging comments that link new content with previously covered material, or provide clarifying statements that paraphrase or summarize a difficult passage. The guide might also give indications that some of the material is either extremely important or might be skipped or skimmed over. This is precisely the kind of advice that will encourage independent strategic reading on the part of your students in the future.

Maintain a Text File

By creating the guide as a Microsoft Word document, you will be able to modify your guide for future use. Having a Word file can also help you enliven the guide to make it visually appealing to students. You can accomplish this goal by choosing a variety of fonts and point sizes, adding clip art, and using Word functions to create and embed tables and graphic organizers.

Review Your Own Purposes

When you have completed a draft of your guide, reexamine it critically to judge whether it will accomplish your instructional purposes. Ask yourself whether a student who successfully completes the guide will possess the level of content mastery that you expect. After constructing the guide, it is a good idea to complete it yourself. Doing so not only provides you and your classroom support personnel with a key as you assist students but also alerts you to trouble spots that you may have overlooked previously. Now, the guide is ready to present in class.

Figure 10.2 presents a possible reading guide that covers this chapter. (We have tried to follow our own advice to be creative.) Use it as an example of how a reading guide might look. We encourage you to complete it as well. If you do so, introspect and ask yourself whether the guide improved your comprehension and resulted in greater interaction with the material.

Teaching With a Reading Guide

Reading guides are likely to be unfamiliar to your students, so do not assume that they will be able to complete a guide without assistance. Younger developing readers and older struggling readers will need considerable support if they are to succeed, which means initially

Figure 10.2. Sample Reading Guide for This Chapter

- In your own words, define reading guide (pp. 207–208): _____

  _____

- List three purposes of reading guides:

  1. _____

  2. _____

  3. _____

- Define anticipation guide: _____

How Well Do Reading Guides Work? (p. 209)

Check all statements that are true. Correct all statements that are false.

	Reading guides tend to improve comprehension of a reading selection.
	Reading guides tend to improve comprehension ability.
	Reading guides have been successfully used in grade 1.
	Reading guides have been successfully used in nonfiction.

Constructing a Reading Guide (pp. 210–212)

- Why is there no blueprint to follow in constructing a reading guide?

  _____

- Fill in the blank: _____ size does not fit _____.
- Under each step in writing a guide, jot down key ideas that you think are important to remember when constructing a reading guide:

  1. Analyze the material. _____

  _____

  2. Identify information to support assessment items. _____

  _____

  3. Make the guide interesting and interactive. _____

  _____

  4. Monitor the length and difficulty of the guide. _____

  _____

  (continued)

Figure 10.2. Sample Reading Guide for This Chapter (Continued)

5. Include page numbers and subheadings where answers can be found. _____

_____

6. Include comprehension aids. _____

_____

7. Maintain a Microsoft Word file for the guide. _____

_____

8. Review your own purposes. _____

_____

• Why is it a good idea to complete a guide that you have written yourself? _____

_____

Teaching With a Reading Guide (p. 215)

• Why do you need to model the use of guides for the whole class? _____

_____

• Why not use guides with every nonfiction selection? _____

_____

• Complete the chart below by listing possible teacher objections to guides in the left-hand column. In the right-hand column, provide arguments that address these concerns. We have discussed some of each in this chapter, but you may be able to think of more.

Possible Teacher Objections to Reading Guides	Counterarguments

completing one or more guides together as a class. Project the guide onto a screen or board and complete it with student input as you make your way through a reading selection in class. Think aloud as you complete the guide. Make visible the thought processes that you use to respond to questions and other tasks required by the guide. If you are fortunate to have a classroom equipped with interactive technology, then completing a reading guide together can be a very engaging and collaborative activity for students.

Provide students with their own copies of the guide and monitor their performance, even though they may simply be copying your projected guide at first. You may need to meet with small groups of students or confer with them individually to further support them. As students understand how guides operate, begin to assign them without demonstration and guided practice. Students will still complete each guide in class, but you can transfer more of the responsibility to them. Even as students become increasingly competent in using the guides, you will need to continually monitor students' efforts.

Completing guides also affords an opportunity for collaboration. Students might work with partners or in small groups, but we advise you not to attempt to group students until the nature of reading guides is well understood. When and if you do move to partnering and group work, do so experimentally. It is important that roles are defined clearly, that all students participate, and that the mix of students allows for productive group work. In our experiences, reading guides are especially effective when paired with structured, cooperative activities. Once students have mastered completing reading guides, you can take it to the next level by having students create and share their own guides for other expository texts. This activity provides students the opportunity to utilize several comprehension strategies, including generating questions before, during, and after reading.

Remember that guides cannot be used with every nonfiction selection that your students read, as there is simply not enough time. Fortunately, even the occasional use of reading guides can have a profound influence on the way students approach reading to learn. It is difficult to imagine a better investment of class time. Reading guides should be intended to support students as they encounter challenging text. We also strongly recommend providing ample opportunities for students to engage with nonfiction texts at a level that they can read independently.

A Final Word

Take a moment to reconsider the five statements in the anticipation guide in Figure 10.1. Use the second column to record your postreading responses. Have your opinions changed? We suspect that one or more of them probably have. Anticipation guides of this sort can be effective whenever new content may be at odds with prior notions. We believe that a brief anticipation guide works well at the beginning of a full reading guide. Had we actually provided a stand-alone version of the reading guide displayed in Figure 10.2, we would have placed these five statements at the beginning of it. After you had completed the rest of the guide, you would have been instructed to return to the statements to consider them anew.

TRY IT!

1. Start small. For the first subsection of a textbook or nonfiction trade book, prepare a reading guide based on the suggestions that we offered in this chapter. Next, explain to your students how the guide works, introduce the selection, and give them the opportunity to complete the guide in class. Then, see for yourself how well the use of a guide improves comprehension. Compare the quality of postreading discussion after the use of a guide with the discussion of the next segment, which students will read without a guide. Explore the difference still further by asking students to reflect on their comprehension with and without a guide.

2. The jigsaw technique (Aronson, Stephan, Sikes, Blaney, & Snapp, 1978) allows teachers to differentiate materials based on reading level and affords students the opportunity to act as "experts" in the content that they have just read. In jigsaw, begin by forming "home teams" of four or five students. Each team member is responsible for a trade book or article written near their instructional level. These texts are all on the same topic, and you must select them in advance to represent several readability levels. You will need to prepare a guide for each home team. One home team member meets with a member of each of the other teams that are responsible for the same text. These "expert teams" work together to complete the guide. The members then return to their home teams and present the information contained in their text, using the completed guide as a prompt.

3. Combine reading guides with reciprocal teaching (Palincsar & Brown, 1984). As with jigsaw, students work in teams but do not regroup. In

reciprocal teaching, members of a cooperative team move together through a nonfiction text, page by page or section by section. For each segment, they first predict the content and then read it to test their predictions. After the students finish reading, they seek clarifications about confusing content, pose questions to one another, and summarize the segment before moving on. The cycle repeats until the students reach the end of the assigned text. We believe that guides can be easily coupled with reciprocal teaching. As students independently read each segment, they complete the corresponding section of the guide. Afterward, their clarifications will focus on any difficulties that they may have experienced in completing the guide, and their summarizing will likewise be anchored in the guide.

REFERENCES

Alvermann, D.E., & Moore, D.W. (1991). Secondary school reading. In R. Barr, M.L. Kamil, P.B. Mosenthal, & P.D. Pearson (Eds.), *Handbook of reading research* (Vol. 2, pp. 951–983). White Plains, NY: Longman.

Alvermann, D.E., & Swafford, J. (1989). Do content area strategies have a research base? *Journal of Reading, 32*(5), 388–394.

Aronson, E., Stephan, C., Sikes, J., Blaney, N., & Snapp, M. (1978). *The jigsaw classroom*. Beverly Hills, CA: Sage.

Chall, J.S. (1996). *Stages of reading development* (2nd ed.). Fort Worth, TX: Harcourt Brace.

Duffelmeyer, F.A. (1994). Effective anticipation guide statements for learning from expository prose. *Journal of Reading, 37*(6), 452–457.

Franks, S.T., McKenna, M.C., & Franks, G. (2001, April). *Using action research to increase elementary students' reading comprehension in science.* Paper presented at the annual meeting of the American Educational Research Association, Seattle, WA.

Kozen, A.A., Murray, R.K., & Windell, I. (2006). Increasing all students' chance to achieve: Using and adapting anticipation guides with middle school learners. *Intervention in School and Clinic, 41*(4), 195–200. doi:10.1177/10534512060410040101

McKenna, M.C., & Robinson, R.D. (1997). *Teaching through text: A content literacy approach to content area reading* (2nd ed.). New York: Longman.

Palincsar, A.S., & Brown, A.L. (1984). Reciprocal teaching of comprehension-fostering and comprehension-monitoring activities. *Cognition and Instruction, 1*(2), 117–175. doi:10.1207/s1532690xci0102_1

Wood, K.D., Lapp, D., Flood, J., & Taylor, D.B. (2008). *Guiding readers through text: Strategy guides for new times* (2nd ed.). Newark, DE: International Reading Association.

Widening the Lens: School and District Policies, Initiatives, and Interventions for Struggling Readers

CHAPTER 11

Under the Radar, Struggling to Be Noticed: Older At-Risk Students

Anne McGill-Franzen and Jennifer Lubke

What happens to struggling, or potentially struggling, readers when the reading goes mostly silent? Our measures of their progress run the risk of becoming exceedingly superficial: answers to worksheet questions, numbers of books or pages read, occasional oral fluency measures, Accelerated Reader test scores. How do we track and appropriately document the complexities of reading development beyond the early grades when the reading mostly goes silent?

Meet Jason and Lauren

In our graduate-level course and practicum on the diagnosis and correction of classroom reading problems, we occasionally encounter referrals of "struggling" older students who possess a puzzling array of surface-level skills but are failing to demonstrate appropriate gains in the traditional classroom. These students may be described as exceptionally average, in the sense that it is their seeming "averageness" that merits close inspection but which often causes them to escape our attention in the classroom.

Jason (all names are pseudonyms) is an 11-year-old fifth grader referred for tutoring by his parents when his teachers expressed concern over his oral reading proficiency, which was not developing at the same pace as his comprehension. His case is not atypical (e.g., Valencia & Buly, 2004) and presents a bit of a quandary. If he can comprehend what he reads, what difference does it make if he reads fast or sounds good? Our task was to decide if a fluency intervention was, in fact, needed and, if so, to identify methods to improve Jason's fluency while continually supporting his comprehension skills.

After Early Intervention, Then What? Teaching Struggling Readers in Grades 3 and Beyond (2nd ed.) edited by Jeanne R. Paratore and Rachel L. McCormack. © 2011 by the International Reading Association.

Lauren is a 13-year-old seventh grader who might be viewed as just another typical adolescent, trying to fit in at a large, suburban middle school. Her reading teacher identified her as reading at or just below grade level. That, in itself, did not suggest a particularly desperate situation, yet she was referred by her parents because of a variety of academic struggles that they had tried to mediate through parent–teacher conferences, behavior modification strategies, and private tutors. Again, Lauren's case poses a quandary for someone charged with designing a reading intervention. Is this just another instance of an unmotivated teenager in need of an attitude adjustment? Or, did perceptions of her reading level merit a closer look?

As might be expected, the more time we spend with students like Jason and Lauren, the more we perceive them as less and less typical but, rather, as individuals with interests, beliefs, and motivations all their own. On many of the individual reading assessments that Jason and Lauren completed, they demonstrated reading competencies at or above their designated grade levels. Additionally, they proved that they could self-select appropriate books for independent reading, and when invested in a text, they read confidently and with motivation, demonstrating the three dimensions of fluency: speed, accuracy, and expressiveness (Allington, 2009; Rasinski, 2003; Rasinski & Padak, 2001; Topping, 2006). Through formal interviews and impromptu conversations, we learned that Jason and Lauren read independently and enjoyed purchasing novels at school book fairs, used book stores, and large retailers. They had access to reading materials at home and occasionally recommended and shared books with friends and family members.

In light of discouraging reports about Jason's and Lauren's inconsistent academic performance, we found these results puzzling. Even Lauren, when probed about her schoolwork, shrugged and said, "I'm just average." We concluded that Jason and Lauren were, indeed, "struggling" readers, but not in the traditional, academic sense. They seemed to be getting by, yet theirs is a struggle to be noticed. Adolescents, more so than young children, link their beliefs about the role of effort in achievement to their interactions with teachers, and the control that students feel over their own academic performance tends to decline as they grow older (Van Ryzin, 2011). By offering students like Jason and Lauren more choice in the classroom environment, more opportunity for collaboration, and more instructional support, teachers can influence motivation and effort. Unless such a paradigm shift occurs, the strengths and needs of preadolescent and adolescent readers like Jason and Lauren will continue to escape our attention.

Using Qualitative Assessment Data

In this section, we describe the types of assessments that we used to better understand the circumstances and conditions that seemed to interfere with successful reading for Jason and Lauren and provide teachers the insight to work with these students in ways that enable them to achieve higher levels of success.

Jason

Using a variety of qualitative assessments, we determined that Jason is a transitional reader and writer (Bear, Invernizzi, Templeton, & Johnston, 2008). He no longer looks at just letters in print but is beginning to tackle chunks of letters and entire phrases, and he has developed an expansive at-a-glance vocabulary (i.e., sight words) to help him do this (Bear et al., 2008). He is now at a point where he should begin to read with more speed, expression, and comprehension, which is called the "increasing fluency phase" (Brown, 2003, p. 729).

Fluency is significant because of its influence on comprehension and motivation. Although often associated with reading aloud and simply sounding good, fluency is, in fact, complex. A fluent reader is one who can read quickly and accurately with expression and comprehension (Allington, 2009), frequently described in terms of raw numerical scores for reading rate (i.e., number of words per minute [WPM]) and reading accuracy (i.e., number of words correct per minute [WCPM]). Fluency is all of that, but it is also more. Brown (2003) describes the cognitive benefits of fluency:

> Increased fluency, in turn, makes reading even more successful and enjoyable and provides increased motivation to read. This reciprocal relationship between cognition and motivation—mediated by fluency—is what fuels the transition from "learning to read" to "reading to learn." (p. 730)

Jason's Qualitative Reading Inventory–4 (QRI–4) results and oral reading records confirmed the complexity of this "reciprocal relationship." His comprehension scores on the QRI–4 indicated grade-level performance when he was permitted to look back at the text. He read the fifth-grade word list with 90% accuracy. Based on this information, we gave him a fifth-grade narrative passage. His initial comprehension score without look-backs was 63% and with look-backs 100%.

We asked Jason to read aloud a variety of 100-word passages from a collection of trade paperbacks and high-interest novels of increasing difficulty (grade-level equivalent 4 and up). He read each passage with near-perfect accuracy (98–100% total acceptability). Jason rarely looked to his tutor to supply unknown words as he read orally. He had confidence and took risks when confronting unknown words. When faced with an unfamiliar word, he slowed down, looked back, and sounded it out. He self-corrected mispronunciations about a third of the time.

However, Jason proved to be a "clunky, word-by-word reader" (Allington, 2009, p. 92). He worked admirably at conveying expression during oral reading, but these efforts were hampered by a halting pace punctuated with long pauses. When probed about his slow rate, Jason said he believed that reading fast would cause him to "miss a part and not understand." This, combined with his consistent use of finger tracking while reading, led us to suspect an overreliance on strategies learned in the early grades, strategies that would become less and less suitable as demands on comprehension and volume of reading increased in middle school and beyond.

Allington (2009) recommends that teachers and tutors should know what factors are adversely affecting a student's fluency before enacting a fluency intervention. After several sessions with Jason, we knew that his reading rate was in the bottom percentile for his grade-level norm. Yet, he possessed a large sight-word vocabulary, demonstrated good decoding skills, and self-monitored while he read. Why did he seem to struggle when reading aloud? To dig deeper, we performed additional fluency trials and a miscue analysis based on data collected during paired reading sessions with his tutor.

One possibility is the stress that oral reading places on the student. Allington (2009) suggests collecting data on passages read cold (i.e., without practice) and passages read silently and then aloud. Does the student demonstrate dramatic differences in reading rate and accuracy when allowed to preread silently? If so, the teacher or tutor should consider the oral reading task as being at odds with the student's normal reading behavior. In other words, reading aloud impairs fluency for some developing readers. To explore this concept, we asked Jason to read a grade 5 (level U) adaptation of a Sherlock Holmes mystery story, alternating between cold read-alouds and silent prereading of selected passages. On both the cold and preread passages, he averaged 99% accuracy. Yet, on the passages that he rehearsed silently, his average rates of 92 WPM and 92 WCPM outpaced those of the unrehearsed passages, which were 83 WPM and 82 WCPM.

Miscue analysis is an informal, qualitative assessment that reveals "general patterns of reader behavior" (Leslie & Caldwell, 2006, p. 80).

According to Rasinski (2003), teachers and tutors can perform a miscue analysis to pinpoint the needs of students performing below grade level and not developing as expected. We wrote down all of Jason's miscues during his oral reading of passages from the first three chapters of *The Lightning Thief* by Rick Riordan (2005), then we categorized the miscues and calculated percentages. The results indicated that Jason was not a wild guesser. When faced with an unknown word, his miscues were often grammatically and phonetically similar, which is typical of a transitional reader. Jason was still learning to consolidate his knowledge of letters, sounds, and text structure with his growing awareness of more sophisticated words and their meanings.

When we used the word recognition prompts and fix-up strategies with Jason, his face would sometimes brighten, and he would say, "Oh, I know that!" This happened with words like *nauseous* and *tortilla*. Other times, it was clear that he had no prior exposure to the word—at least that he could remember. On these occasions, we prompted him to read all around the word, above and below it, looking for context clues that would help unlock the meaning of the new word.

Readers with deep fluency (Topping, 2006) can control their reading rate for maximum comprehension. The more they comprehend, the more they can reflect on and learn from their reading. For example, slowing down is a valid fix-up strategy for Jason, but he needs to understand that reading faster and more smoothly will expose him to a higher volume of words and ideas, ultimately increasing his learning.

Lauren

Lauren fits the strategic fluency profile (Topping, 2006). She is a good comprehender who can manage a mental juggling act between meaning extraction and speed regulation. Although her comprehension scores on the Burns/Roe Informal Reading Inventory and the QRI–4 were satisfactory, we began to suspect that Lauren, like many self-professed "average" students, was accustomed, and possibly even trained, to read only for surface-level comprehension. Her answers were suitable for standardized tests and the all too frequently used initiate-respond-evaluate mode (Mehan, 1979), but she did not seem to be engaging in deep thinking or meaning making. For example, when asked a concept question on the QRI–4 about biography, Lauren supplied an almost verbatim dictionary definition of the word that she said her reading teacher had drummed into her. On comprehension questions about author's purpose, Lauren repeatedly framed her answers as "to inform," "to entertain," and "to persuade," which is highly suggestive of standardized test answer stems.

To confirm, or disconfirm, our hunches, we performed two additional informal assessments. First, following the advice of Applegate, Quinn, and Applegate (2002), we gave Lauren two open-ended questions to provide additional evidence about her inferential comprehension abilities. Second, we undertook an analysis of her responses to the comprehension questions on the QRI–4 and the Burns/Roe Informal Reading Inventory.

Lauren's constructed responses to open-ended questions gave us several insights into her abilities and needs as a reader. After she responded to a prompt about courage, we asked her to read her writing aloud and discuss it. In so doing, she drew on prior knowledge to make thematic connections across texts. She also revealed important predisposing factors toward intrinsic motivation, such as curiosity and text involvement (Guthrie & Wigfield, 2000). Lauren's less detailed response to a second open-ended question was revealing for what it lacked. This was a postreading question, designed to prompt her to evaluate the central character's actions and support her claims (Applegate et al., 2002). Her one-sentence reply suggested that she needs help forming and supporting opinions related to ideas in the text, one of Caldwell's (2008) "good reader behaviors" (p. 4)

Finally, using an adaptation of the comprehension response form (Dewitz & Dewitz, 2003), we analyzed Lauren's comprehension errors on the two major informal reading inventories, and the instructional pathways became clearer. The results for explicit questions, with more than half the errors arising from faulty elaboration, go hand in hand with Lauren's reliance on prior knowledge and possibly a "desire to please" (Dewitz & Dewitz, p. 426). Of the 15 implicit questions missed, more than a quarter depended on her ability to make relational inferences, as opposed to causal inferences. The analysis form also made it clear that understanding vocabulary in context is an area to strengthen with Lauren.

How Can We Support the Literacy of Students Like Jason and Lauren?

According to Spear-Swerling's (2004) road map for understanding reading development, Lauren and Jason demonstrate automatic word recognition, increasing fluency, and, we believe, the potential to perform as strategic readers if supported by teacher modeling and direct instruction. Without targeted instruction, however, Jason and Lauren are likely to continue to perform at a basic level, recalling information but not considering and connecting it in ways that help them reach deep and sustained levels of understanding. Like the striving readers described by Dennis (2009), students like this possess distinct abilities and needs that must be targeted with appropriate instructional strategies. Otherwise, they run the risk of continuing to perform just under the radar, escaping our notice and never realizing their full potential.

As busy classroom teachers, we may not have the luxury of administering all the qualitative assessments that a clinical setting allows. In the next section, we ask what we can do as classroom teachers to notice and respond to learners like Jason and Lauren. A first step is to look beyond the labels we assign, or as Hagood, Alvermann, and Heron-Hruby (2010) suggest, "contest the deficit assumptions that can hold back both teachers and students in their efforts to learn" (p. 75). Invoking what has been called "turn-around pedagogies" by Comber and Kamler (as cited in Hagood et al., p. 7), Hagood and colleagues propose "connecting and reconnecting students with literacy" (p. 75) through analysis and use of students' everyday culture as well as attending to normative performance standards for reading. If we hold that literacy is embedded in cultural practice, then unpacking cultural practice, or identifying "what's in your backpack" (p. 7), may provide insight into ways to reconnect students with literacy. In other words, if we want to know what students are reading or thinking, we need to observe, listen, and talk with them. Two examples of talking with students on the run follow. The first concerns the books in students' backpacks (or not), and the second relates to the confusions that students experience while reading content area texts.

Unpack Students' Backpacks: Is There a Cultural Text Here?

As part of a recent evaluation of the K–12 reading program in a rural southeastern United States school district with declining state test scores, we not only took notes during classroom lessons but also asked students what they were reading and why they selected that particular book. Of the 20 or so preadolescent and adolescent students who were randomly tapped to tell us about their reading, the majority cited one or more popular series books: Maximum Ride, a series of seven science fiction and fantasy books by James Patterson; *Cirque du Freak* by Darren Shan, part of the Vampire Blood Trilogy and the 12-book The Saga of Darren Shan; Percy Jackson and the Olympians, a five-book series about demigods by Rick Riordan; the Twilight Saga by Stephenie Meyer; the Diary of a Wimpy Kid series by Jeff Kinney; and of course, the Harry Potter series by J.K. Rowling. Although many of these books would be considered challenging for struggling readers, the content of many, if not most, is accessible via video, television, movies, manga, and graphic novels—all interpretable texts with interchangeable content in multiple media formats. The books the students carry, whether or not they can read every word, represent who they are to their peers: "Like you, I am a reader of manga!"

Many students read magazines that are typically available only at home: "When I can get *Field & Stream*, I read it"; "I read my mother's magazines, like *Woman's Day* and *Cosmopolitan*." This phenomenon is consistent with the results of a recent study of adolescent magazine selections, with girls typically choosing lifestyle or celebrity magazines, such as *Seventeen* and *Tiger Beat*, and boys choosing magazines such as *GamePro* and *North American Whitetail* (Allington & Gabriel, 2010). With the exception of the Harry Potter series, students did not obtain their books and magazines from the classroom or school library. To a student, these middle-grade and adolescent readers cited their peers and movies as the impetus for selecting books and, to a lesser extent, the attraction of themes such as saving the earth (e.g., the Maximum Ride series); genre, such as horror and science fiction; or "funny writing." Sadly, we also learned that some students did not read at all during the school year, only during summers and only those books listed on the summer reading list.

Go Backstage: Talk to Students

Nicholson (1982) and his New Zealand colleagues were early proponents of talking with students to find out what they are thinking and recommended that teachers use interview techniques to probe students' understandings as a supplement to the usual written assessments. In an exploratory study conducted several decades ago that presaged current issues of academic language, Nicholson had middle-grade students read content area texts and talked with them about their confusions and understandings. He called these side-by-side conversations with students "'riding mind waves'" (p. 2) to get at the strategies they used to try to understand complex text and circumvent difficulties. Similar to the confusions and strategies used by Lauren and Jason, the students in Nicholson's study were confused by subject-specific vocabulary and relied on prior knowledge to construct elaborations that were not actually related to the meaning of the text. One example taken from a social studies text is that of the word *Peking*, the city in China, that a student read as "pecking." This student, echoing the sentiments of other struggling readers, said that he gets "lost when you gotta blimmin' watch the damn words" (p. 5). Nicholson argues that teachers need to help students "arbitrate better between the knowledge which they bring to the text, and the text information on the page" (p. 7), particularly the difference between their everyday meanings of words and the subject-specific meanings of those same words in reading content area text.

In addition, Nicholson (1982) notes the vast disparity in reading volume between high and low achievers, referred to as "reading 'mileage'" (p. 7). Academic engagement in literacy, defined by Reed and Vaughn (2010) as "students' interest in learning, their internal motivation to work hard and do their best, and their ability to effortlessly enact strategies to support their learning" (p. 170) is the most challenging aspect of teaching older struggling readers. In fact, Reed and Vaughn argue that the self-perceptions of students as readers and their feelings about reading mediate the effectiveness of experimental interventions to improve achievement.

A Turn-Around Pedagogy of Engagement

A number of researchers and teachers have embraced the notion of a turn-around pedagogy (Comber & Kamler, 2006), one that has as its goal the improvement of achievement among those students who are marginalized in different ways from the beat of classroom life. Central to a redesigned or turn-around pedagogy is finding out "what makes kids tick" (p. 26), what they are thinking and doing, and especially what they are doing well. By getting to know the interests of students and what they have invested in these interests, teachers may come to see students as resourceful rather than deficit. It is the teacher's job to connect students with literacy in ways that support their development, build on what they know, and sustain their engagement with learning.

Engaged Reading: A Means to Achievement

Recently, reading researchers have begun to dig a bit deeper into the widely held observation that students who read more achieve at higher levels than those who do not. On national and international assessments, such as the National Assessment of Educational Progress and the Programme for International Student Assessment, engaged readers, that is, those from low-income and low-education homes who reported reading books for their own interest, significantly outperformed unengaged readers from advantaged backgrounds (Guthrie, Schafer, & Huang, 2001). Achievement and engagement are reciprocal; reading a lot increases achievement, and increased competence and expertise sustains motivation to read. Likewise, a downward spiral takes hold when students lack reading competence and the motivation to persevere. Commonly referred to as the Matthew effect (Stanovich, 1986), the less students read, the less exposure and experience they have with words and content. Fewer reading-to-learn experiences translate into less competence, not only in skilled reading but also in knowledge of subject areas. For a fourth or fifth grader two years behind peers, Guthrie and his colleagues (2003) estimate that the student would have to read for three hours per day or more to raise his or her achievement to grade level. This point underscores what is needed in the turn-around literacy pedagogy: a radical rethinking of language arts curricula, particularly the time allocated to reading instruction and the promotion of engaged reading, if students who lag substantially behind their peers are to close in on grade-level progress.

Engaged reading in classrooms is defined as active, focused reading in a range of topics and genres under the guidance of teachers, not simply recreational reading (Guthrie, 2004). Engaged reading is strategic; that is, it requires the use of skills and strategies to gain conceptual understandings. Engaged reading is also social and collaborative, typically involving the sharing of knowledge and information seeking strategies. Moreover, recent meta-analyses have demonstrated which classroom practices are highly likely to develop reading engagement and significantly influence achievement: providing interesting and varied texts and student choice, emphasizing content, and providing opportunities for peer discussion and collaboration (Guthrie & Humenick, 2004).

The Multitext Curriculum: A Way Into Ideas for All Students

In most classrooms, the middle-grades curriculum is based on a single textbook or trade book that everyone in the class reads at the same time. In contrast, text sets enable a multibook, multilevel curriculum in content area classes. An expanded definition of *literacy* includes the reading of nontraditional texts, such as Internet sources and the reading of cultures, so a multilevel, multitext curriculum should include these resources as well. Thus, text sets are collections of materials that can include digital texts, Internet-based resources, books, video, artwork, music, maps, and artifacts that support the reading, writing, and concept development of a range of learners at varying levels of achievement and with varying interests and background experiences.

Typically unified by a topic, genre, or format, students with widely different language abilities may be able to access important concepts when the curriculum is layered in this way. Likewise, a multitext curriculum makes possible the exploration of divergent perspectives on an important topic or concept by providing voice to those not always represented in traditional or canonical reading lists. Text sets also enable students to experience the variety of forms that authors use to express their ideas. In designing a text set on a particular topic, it is important to identify texts that represent a range of genres (e.g., magazines, newspapers, reference resources, biographies) and the interests of students and reflect students' first language and culture. In designing a text set that focuses specifically on genre, it is imperative to select exemplars of the genre that can accommodate a range of reading levels as well as students' interests and language abilities.

As an example, we provide a text set of biographies about prominent African Americans—historical figures, pop culture icons, and sports stars (see Table 11.1). In an intervention study (McGill-Franzen & Zeig, 2008), these texts were selected to enhance low-achieving fifth graders'

Table 11.1. Text Set of African American Biographies

Title	Author(s)	Topic	Lexile Level	Guided Reading Level
Martin Luther King, Jr. and the March on Washington	Frances E. Ruffin	Historical figures	480	B
Martin Luther King Jr.	Pam Walker	Historical figures	450	F
Tiger Woods	Pam Walker	Sports	200	F
Grant Hill: Smooth as Silk	Mark Stewart	Sports		F–L
Will Smith	Kristin McCracken	Pop culture	1230	F–L
Let's Read About...Martin Luther King, Jr.	Courtney Baker	Historical figures	380	H
Harriet Tubman	Catherine Nichols	Historical figures	280	J
Happy Birthday, Martin Luther King	Jean Marzollo	Historical figures	460	L
Salt in His Shoes: Michael Jordan in Pursuit of a Dream	Deloris Jordan with Roslyn M. Jordan	Sports	460	L
Home Run Heroes: Big Mac, Sammy and Junior	James Buckley, Jr.	Sports		M

(continued)

Table 11.1. Text Set of African American Biographies (Continued)

Title	Author(s)	Topic	Lexile Level	Guided Reading Level
NBA All-Star Kevin Garnett	Steve Aschburner	Sports	710	N
NBA Superstar Shaquille O'Neal	Lyle Spencer	Sports	670	N
We'll Never Forget You, Roberto Clemente	Trudie Engel	Sports	480	O
Stealing Home: The Story of Jackie Robinson	Barry Denenberg	Sports	930	O–P
Michael Jordan: Basketball's Best	Chip Lovitt	Sports	1010	Q
Usher	Morgan Talmadge	Pop culture	760	Q
Aunt Harriet's Underground Railroad in the Sky	Faith Ringgold	Historical figures	680L	R
A Picture Book of Martin Luther King, Jr.	David A. Adler	Historical figures	760	S
Martin Luther King, Jr.: A Man With a Dream	Jayne Pettit	Historical figures	760	S
Shaquille O'Neal: Big Man, Big Dreams	Mark Stewart	Sports	760	S
Brandy	Cynthia Laslo	Pop culture	970	T
Rosa Parks: My Story	Rosa Parks with Jim Haskins	Historical figures	800	U
Duke Ellington: The Piano Prince and His Orchestra	Andrea Davis Pinkney	Historical figures	790	

Note. Lexile levels and guided reading levels were not available for all books.

understanding of the biography genre and extend information provided in the core reading program. Students selected a subject, read several biographies, and developed a timeline of important events and turning points in the life of their subject. To construct the timelines, students had to

> reread and revisit texts, determine important information, synthesize information, and make judgments about which events to incorporate. Not only did students learn the content, but the need to select important

information created an authentic context for rereading, thus developing fluency and strategic comprehension. (p. 404)

By engaging in sustained reading of text set materials and discussion around text set topics, genres, or formats, students of every level of achievement and learning style can develop expertise and experience particular perspectives from which to question, debate, and inform their peers.

Purposeful and Interesting Fluency Development: An Alternative to Unrehearsed Oral Reading of Textbooks

Although struggling middle-grade students are often given the task of reading aloud, round-robin style, part of a text or book, they are rarely given the opportunity to read orally as a performance (Worthy & Broaddus, 2001). Yet, as noted by Kuhn, Groff, and Morrow (Chapter 1 of this volume), the opportunity to practice reading is related to fluent reading, and fluent reading is inextricably tied to comprehension. Students who struggle to decode individual words, even those who are able to decode accurately, spend so much of their cognitive energy on word identification that there is often little left to access the meaning of the text. Through repeated experiences with words, students are able to automatically, and seemingly effortlessly, remember the words. Authentic ways to engage middle-grade students and adolescents in practicing their oral reading include rehearsing a text or part of a text to perform for an audience: tell a joke, enact a script, give a speech, inform peers about a topic, or share a funny, interesting, or sad part of a story. In preparing for a particular performance, students practice with appropriate prosody, pitch, and rate. (See Kuhn, Groff, & Morrow, Chapter 1 of this volume, for additional ideas related to fluency development of older readers.)

Conclusion

Middle school readers, like Lauren and Jason, who can identify words and answer low-level comprehension questions typically fall below the teacher's radar and fail to receive the kind of instruction that will permit them to read in ways that lead to academic engagement, deep levels of comprehension, and knowledge building. By taking the initiative to notice these students—the cultural values and preferences in their backpacks and the confusions they experience in using their everyday language to understand content-specific academic texts—teachers can learn to negotiate a turnaround with the potential to bring all students into full participation.

By engaging with a number of books on a particular theme, for example, students performing below the radar experience repeated exposures to topic-specific vocabulary, which provides them with opportunities to develop fluency and word meanings. Likewise, texts organized with particular formats, repeated literary devices, or characters and plots provide comprehension scaffolds for students who may lack confidence or grade-level reading achievement. By providing students with opportunities for collaboration and discussion, choice, multiple interesting and multimodal texts, and time to develop deep understandings of topics, authors, characters, perspectives, and genres, teachers can engage and motivate all students. As Langer (2011) notes, all students, including those who struggle to be noticed, build academic literacy through academic engagement:

> Through this process of focusing, narrowing, searching, considering, questioning, judging, tuning, and rejecting, they learn not merely to receive knowledge, but to own it. They make sense. And if they probe deeply enough and connect wisely enough, they create knowledge. That knowledge is theirs, available to them for whatever purposes they wish in whatever experiences they encounter. (p. 2)

If current attitudes toward reading achievement persist—as described by Applegate and colleagues (2002), attitudes that largely regard achievement as a simple measure of literal comprehension and recall—then it is highly possible that Jason and Lauren will achieve just enough to pass through middle and high school. If, however, reading achievement is reconceptualized as a complex blend of deep thinking about texts combined with a desire to converse and write critically about those texts, then these students demand our attention.

TRY IT!

1. *MP3 players*—Studies have shown that audiobooks, or talking books, have positive effects on students' vocabulary development and fluency (Topping, 2006). MP3 players enable teachers to easily and cheaply download, transfer, and share digital texts with students, as opposed to expensive single-user resources like books on tape and compact disks. Work with your librarian or textbook publisher to acquire digitally recorded titles that can be transferred into a database such as iTunes

and then downloaded to individual MP3 players for students to check out (Bomar, 2006). Students may listen to text selections before, during, or after instruction, or they may choose and listen to digital texts as a silent reading alternative. Pairing conventional print texts with their digital versions boosts students' confidence and motivation by helping them independently access difficult material, such as those selections commonly found in literature anthologies or content-specific trade books.

2. *Book acting service project*—Book acting is a blend of teacher-initiated story retelling and drama, in which adults initially model interactive read-alouds with carefully selected children's literature and information books. Eventually, the adult role recedes as students, usually working in small groups facilitated by the adult, engage in dramatizations and reenactments of the stories (McGee, 2003). As a twist on this early literacy strategy, intermediate-level or adolescent-age students can work in small groups to select appropriate stories and reenact them for younger audiences. By collaborating with peers and rehearsing multiple interactive read-alouds prior to performance, students develop fluency and take ownership of high-quality texts. New literacies may be integrated into the project by encouraging students to storyboard, videotape, edit, and publish their dramatizations.

3. *Blogs*—Reluctant readers need opportunities to engage and collaborate with fellow readers and writers through book clubs, idea circles, author studies, and writing workshops (Guthrie & Wigfield, 2000). A classroom blog can serve as a powerful new literacies platform for student engagement in these kinds of response activities. Blogs can also help mediate the 21st-century challenge of bridging "discontinuity between home, community, and school interests and competences, rather than only promote only 'schooled' literacy experiences" (Topping, 2006, p. 108). Start your own classroom blog using instructional frameworks such as HOT blogging (Zawilinski, 2009), which includes four recursive steps that lead to multiplicity and synthesis across students' posts. The ultimate realization of discussion mediated through the blog tool is when students can synthesize their reading of the text along with the posts and comments of their classmates. When done well, it brings a whole new level of transparency and accountability to discussion and meaning making never before seen in classrooms.

REFERENCES
Allington, R.L. (2009). *What really matters in fluency: Research-based practices across the curriculum.* Boston: Allyn & Bacon.

Allington, R.L., & Gabriel, R. (2010, December). *Leveling magazines: Considerations for selecting and using magazines in middle school classroom and school libraries.* Paper presented at the 60th annual meeting of the National Reading Conference, Fort Worth, TX.

Applegate, M.D., Quinn, K.B., & Applegate, A.J. (2002). Levels of thinking required by comprehension questions in informal reading inventories. *The Reading Teacher, 56*(2), 174–180.

Bear, D.R., Invernizzi, M., Templeton, S., & Johnston, F. (2008). *Words their way: Word study for phonics, vocabulary, and spelling instruction* (4th ed.). Boston: Allyn & Bacon.

Bomar, L. (2006). iPods as reading tools. *Principal, 85*(5), 52–53.

Brown, K.J. (2003). What do I say when they get stuck on a word? Aligning teachers' prompts with students' development. *The Reading Teacher, 56*(8), 720–733.

Caldwell, J.S. (2008). *Reading assessment: A primer for teachers and coaches* (2nd ed.). New York: Guilford.

Comber, B., & Kamler, B. (2006). Redesigning literacy pedagogies: The complexities of producing sustainable change. In W.D. Bokhorst-Heng, M.D. Osborne, & K. Lee (Eds.), *Redesigning pedagogy: Reflections on theory and praxis* (pp. 19–32). Rotterdam, The Netherlands: Sense.

Dennis, D.V. (2009). "I'm not stupid": How assessment drives (in) appropriate reading instruction. *Journal of Adolescent & Adult Literacy, 53*(4), 283–290. doi:10.1598/JAAL.53.4.2

Dewitz, P., & Dewitz, P.K. (2003). They can read the words, but they can't understand: Refining comprehension assessment. *The Reading Teacher, 56*(5), 422–435.

Guthrie, J.T. (2004). Teaching for literacy engagement. *Journal of Literacy Research, 36*(1), 1–29. doi:10.1207/s15548430jlr3601_2

Guthrie, J.T., & Humenick, N.M. (2004). Motivating students to read: Evidence for classroom practices that increase reading motivation and achievement. In P. McCardle & V. Chhabra (Eds.), *The voice of evidence in reading research* (pp. 329–354). Baltimore: Paul H. Brookes.

Guthrie, J.T., Schafer, W.D., & Huang, C. (2001). Benefits of opportunity to read and balanced instruction on the NAEP. *The Journal of Educational Research, 94*(3), 145–162. doi:10.1080/00220670109599912

Guthrie, J.T., & Wigfield, A. (2000). Engagement and motivation in reading. In M.L. Kamil, P.B. Mosenthal, P.D. Pearson, & R. Barr (Eds.), *Handbook of reading research* (Vol. 3, pp. 403–422). Mahwah, NJ: Erlbaum.

Guthrie, J.T., Wigfield, A., Barbosa, P., Perencevich, K.C., Taboada, A., Davis, M.H., et al. (2003, April). *Increasing reading comprehension and engagement through concept-oriented reading instruction.* Paper presented at the annual meeting of the American Educational Research Association, Chicago.

Hagood, M.C., Alvermann, D.E., & Heron-Hruby, A. (2010). *Bring it to class: Unpacking pop culture in literacy learning.* New York: Teachers College Press.

Langer, J.A. (2011). *Envisioning knowledge: Building literacy in the academic disciplines.* New York: Teachers College Press.

Leslie, L., & Caldwell, J. (2006). *Qualitative reading inventory–4* (4th ed.). Boston: Allyn & Bacon.

McGee, L.M. (2003). Book acting: Storytelling and drama in the early childhood classroom. In D.M. Barone & L.M. Morrow (Eds.), *Literacy and young children: Research-based practices* (pp. 157–172). New York: Guilford.

McGill-Franzen, A., & Zeig, J.L. (2008). Drawing to learn: Visual support for developing reading, writing, and concepts for children at-risk. In J. Flood, S.B. Heath, & D. Lapp (Eds.), *Handbook of research on teaching literacy through the communicative and visual arts, A project of the International Reading Association* (Vol. 2, pp. 399–411). New York: Routledge.

Mehan, H. (1979). *Learning lessons: Social organization in the classroom.* Cambridge, MA: Harvard University Press.

Nicholson, T. (1982). *"You get lost when you gotta blimmin watch the damn words": Another look at reading in the junior secondary school.* Unpublished manuscript, University of Waikato, Hamilton, New Zealand. (ERIC Document Reproduction Service No. ED223980)

Rasinski, T.V. (2003). *The fluent reader: Oral reading strategies for building word recognition, fluency, and comprehension.* New York: Scholastic.

Rasinski, T., & Padak, N. (2001). *From phonics to fluency: Effective teaching of decoding and reading fluency in the elementary school.* New York: Longman.

Reed, D., & Vaughn, S. (2010). Reading interventions for older students. In T.A. Glover & S. Vaughn (Eds.), *The promise of Response to Intervention: Evaluating current science and practice* (pp. 143–186). New York: Guilford.

Spear-Swerling, L. (2004). A road map for understanding reading disability and other reading problems: Origins, prevention, and intervention. In R.B. Ruddell & N.J. Unrau (Eds.), *Theoretical models and processes of reading* (5th ed., pp. 517–573). Newark, DE: International Reading Association.

Stanovich, K.E. (1986). Matthew effects in reading: Some consequences of individual differences in the acquisition of literacy. *Reading Research Quarterly, 21*(4), 360–407. doi:10.1598/RRQ.21.4.1

Topping, K.J. (2006). Building reading fluency: Cognitive, behavioral, and socioemotional factors and the role of peer-mediated learning. In S.J. Samuels & A.E. Farstrup (Eds.), *What research has to say about fluency instruction* (pp. 106–129). Newark, DE: International Reading Association.

Valencia, S.W., & Buly, M.R. (2004). Behind test scores: What struggling readers really need. *The Reading Teacher, 57*(6), 520–531.

Van Ryzin, M.J. (2011). Motivation and reading disabilities. In A. McGill-Franzen & R.L. Allington (Eds.), *Handbook of reading disability research* (pp. 242–252). New York: Routledge.

Worthy, J., & Broaddus, K. (2001). Fluency beyond the primary grades: From group performance to silent, independent reading. *The Reading Teacher, 55*(4), 334–343.

Zawilinski, L. (2009). HOT blogging: A framework for blogging to promote higher order thinking. *The Reading Teacher, 62*(8), 650–661. doi:10.1598/RT.62.8.3

LITERATURE CITED

Riordan, R. (2005). *The lightning thief.* New York: Miramax.

CHAPTER 12

It's Never Too Late to Learn: Implementing RTI² With Older Students

Douglas Fisher, Nancy Frey, and Diane Lapp

Jack (all names are pseudonyms) arrived on the first day of ninth grade with nothing: no backpack, no folders, no pencils, no lunch money, and no friends. He did, however, arrive with funds of knowledge and experience that he had gained from participating in his numerous Discourse communities (Gee, 1996; Moll, Amanti, Neff, & Gonzalez, 1992), and fortunately for Jack, he had arrived at a school that valued the unique experiences and characteristics of each of its students. Being new to the school and district, nobody yet knew him. Jack was enrolled in classes and introduced to a number of peers who served as ambassadors for new students. The first few days of school were devoted to team building, antibullying conversations, and identifying expectations. These experiences were planned in response to evidence that in many places, adolescents are bullied and regularly miss school because of their fears (Frey & Fisher, 2008). These experiences were also intended to ensure that students understood the culture of the school and how they were expected to treat one another and could expect to be treated by the adults in the school.

By the end of the first week of school, Jack and his peers had completed a number of screening assessments. In Jack's case, the screenings suggested that he read well below grade level and had gaps in his prior knowledge in both history and science. His mathematical knowledge was on par with other students his age. The findings from the screening tools suggested to the school staff that Jack would benefit from additional assessments and probably from supplemental interventions designed to increase his background knowledge and literacy skills.

We share more about Jack throughout this chapter. Fortunately for his learning success, the school he attends uses a Response to Instruction and Intervention (RTI²) model to examine students' progress and determine

After Early Intervention, Then What? Teaching Struggling Readers in Grades 3 and Beyond (2nd ed.) edited by Jeanne R. Paratore and Rachel L. McCormack. © 2011 by the International Reading Association.

which students continue to require new levels of intervention. The implementation of the RTI^2 model allows the faculty to implement their motto, "It's never too late to learn."

What Is RTI^2?

RTI^2 is an organizational system for allocating support and services for students at risk of school failure. RTI^2 has its roots in the Response to Intervention (RTI) systems designed to replace the discrepancy model used in special education for identifying learning disabilities (Ardoin, Witt, Connell, & Koenig, 2005). In the past, students who were identified using a discrepancy formula (i.e., achievement in comparison to IQ) had to wait to fail before receiving specialized instruction as required by federal law (i.e., the Individuals with Disabilities Education Improvement Act of 2004). In an RTI system, students are monitored as interventions are implemented and their progress, or lack of progress, is assessed and used to make decisions about subsequent supports, including referral for special education services (Barnett, Daly, Jones, & Lentz, 2004).

Unlike RTI, in which the focus is on an individual student, RTI^2 is a whole-school initiative in which resources are matched with need. This initiative includes a number of components, including screening tools, progress monitoring, and three tiers of instruction and intervention. In this chapter, we explore each of these components and how they can be used in middle and high schools to ensure that students learn.

Screening Tools

Screening is a type of assessment that provides a snapshot of appropriate grade-level skills. These tools are quick, easy, and affordable. In schools with sophisticated RTI systems, screening tools are used at the start of every year for every student as well as for any student who transfers into the school during the school year. Students who do not perform well on screening tools participate in additional assessments and/or supplemental interventions. Screening tools allow school systems to determine needs early rather than wait for students to fail and teachers to ask for help. For a screening tool to be useful, it should meet three criteria (Jenkins, 2003):

1. Identify students who require further assessment
2. Be practical
3. Generate positive outcomes by accurately identifying students without consuming resources that could be put to better use

There are a number of screening tools available for younger students, but fewer for middle and high school students. Some schools use norm-referenced assessments as screening tools, such as the Gates-MacGinitie Reading Tests, which provide scores in comprehension and vocabulary. Others use checklists developed by the school's district office. At Jack's school, teachers administer a graded spelling assessment. In addition, they collect a writing sample and score it using an analytic writing inventory. They also administer locally developed background knowledge assessments for each subject area. For example, the life science background knowledge assessment asks students to indicate how they would know something is alive. If students miss several of the questions on the same topic, teachers are alerted to the lack of background knowledge on the topic. A checklist for screening tools can be found in Figure 12.1.

Figure 12.1. Checklist for Schoolwide Screening Tools

	Status	
Standard	**In place (✓)[a]**	**Priority (1-2-3)[b]**
Screening is schoolwide, meets accepted psychometric standards, and has evidence of documented reliability, and concurrent and predictive validity within the particular school setting.		
Individuals involved in the screening measures' administration, scoring, and interpretation are appropriately trained.		
The site obtains reading screening data or information about reading skills following a designated fixed schedule.		
At least 95% of the students participate in the schoolwide screening. Reasons for excluding students from the screening are reasonable and appropriate (e.g., severe, profound disabilities).		
Alternative methods to obtain information about reading skills for students excluded from reading assessments have individual curricular relevance and allow students' achievement to be measured and evaluated.		

Note. From *Responsiveness to Intervention (RTI): How to Do It* (p. 1.9), by E. Johnson, D.F. Mellard, D. Fuchs, & M.A. McKnight, 2006, Lawrence, KS: National Research Center on Learning Disabilities. Used with permission.
[a]If the practice has been implemented, indicate that with a check mark (✓). [b]If the practice is being developed, rank its priority: 1 = highest priority through 3 = lowest priority.

Progress Monitoring

Simply determining a student's current performance level is insufficient; assessment must be followed by appropriate instruction. As teachers, we monitor all students' progress as a matter of routine. In the case of students participating in an RTI[2] process, progress is monitored more frequently and more precisely. The purpose of progress monitoring is not simply to add an additional layer of measurement for the purpose of determining achievement but rather to examine progress over time. Presenting data in the form of graphs is especially effective, because it provides a visual representation of the trends in the student's learning and the student's responsiveness to a particular intervention. When the trend data show little or no progress, the intervention should be adjusted. Sound practices for progress monitoring include systems that are in place to administer, analyze, and share information, as well as to make adjustments to the intervention when the student is not progressing. Within progress monitoring, determining exactly what should constitute success is somewhat ill defined, especially for students who are significantly behind their grade-level peers. In RTI[2], our short-term, ongoing assessments are intended to monitor students' acquisition of the requisite knowledge and ideas rather than gains in overall achievement levels.

Each student's funds of knowledge are assessed, and the results provide teachers with a place to begin instruction. Within the general education setting (i.e., Tier 1 instruction), classroom teachers incorporate interventions aimed at developing the background knowledge necessary for successful learning. Follow-up assessments (i.e., progress monitoring instruments) then reassess the same information to determine if students have acquired the requisite knowledge. A checklist for progress monitoring can be found in Figure 12.2.

Assessments. In early reading intervention, it is common for students to be assessed on knowledge of constrained skills, that is, skills that comprise a finite body of knowledge (e.g., phonemic awareness, phonics). In part, this is because these skills are relatively easy to measure (Paris, 2005), but constrained skills are early developmental reading skills that older struggling readers have very often mastered. What they typically have difficulty with, however, is vocabulary and reading comprehension, which are characterized as unconstrained reading skills (Paris, 2005) that continue to improve across one's lifetime. As such, they are both harder to teach and harder to measure, but relative ease of measurement should not dictate what is monitored. An example of a sound measure of overall reading comprehension is the informal reading inventory. Although more

Figure 12.2. Checklist for Progress Monitoring

Standard	Status	
	In place (✓)[a]	Priority (1-2-3)[b]
Scientific, research-based instruction includes the continuous progress monitoring of student performance across all tiers.		
Teachers follow a designated procedure and schedule for progress monitoring and for regrouping students as needed.		
Measures are administered frequently to inform instruction and curricular placement decisions (i.e., in Tier 1, at least every three weeks; in Tier 2 and beyond, one to three times per week; in special education, three to five times per week).		
Progress monitoring occurs in all tiers, including general education.		
Progress monitoring measures are appropriate to the curriculum, grade level, and tier level.		
Data resulting from progress monitoring are documented and analyzed.		
Progress monitoring uses a standardized benchmark by which progress is measured and determined to be either sufficient or insufficient.		
Teachers use progress monitoring data to evaluate instructional effectiveness and be informed about the potential necessity for changing the instruction.		
An established data management system allows ready access to students' progress monitoring data.		
After progress monitoring, a graph is completed to display data for analysis and decision making and to indicate percentages of students at risk, at some risk, and at low risk.		
Staff members receive training in the administration and interpretation of progress monitoring measures.		
The school designates reasonable cut scores and decision rules for the level, slope, or percentage of mastery to help determine responsiveness and distinguish adequate from inadequate responsiveness.		
Cut scores are reviewed frequently and adjusted as necessary.		
The school provides a rationale for the cut scores and decision rules (e.g., normative or specific criterion reference).		

Note. From *Responsiveness to Intervention (RTI): How to Do It* (pp. 2.18–2.19), by E. Johnson, D.F. Mellard, D. Fuchs, & M.A. McKnight, 2006, Lawrence, KS: National Research Center on Learning Disabilities. Used with permission.
[a]If the practice has been implemented, indicate that with a check mark (✓). [b]If the practice is being developed, rank its priority: 1 = highest priority through 3 = lowest priority.

time-consuming to administer because of the one-to-one nature of the test, informal reading inventories offer a means for assessing student progress over a period of time. We typically administer these once a month using different forms of the passages to gauge whether the intervention approach is working. We prefer the Qualitative Reading Inventory–5, because it provides narrative and informational text passages, and its norms allow comparative analyses.

Curriculum-Based Measurements. Curriculum-based measurements frequently are used to assess progress during an intervention. We use one for writing that is based on the work of several researchers (McMaster & Espin, 2007). This analytic writing tool assesses a student's progress based on a sample composed during a short writing period (6–10 minutes). Examined features include the following:

- Total words written
- Average number of words written per minute
- Total words spelled correctly
- Total number of complete sentences
- Average length of complete sentences
- Correct punctuation marks
- Correct word sequences
- Incorrect word sequences

The writing prompt can be administered to a group of students. Although the individual scoring can be labor-intensive, we often ask students to count the total number of words written and calculate the average number of words written per minute. The other elements require a more skilled eye, especially the correct and incorrect word sequences. This feature is the number of times two adjacent words are used correctly in terms of spelling, grammar, capitalization, and context. Word sequences include the last word in one sentence and the first word in the next. Because of the qualitative nature of the results, it is easy to gauge the relative progress of a student participating in an intervention. We find this measure more useful than holistic measures, such as writing rubrics, which are not strongly correlated with standardized writing measures at the secondary level (Diercks-Gransee, Weissenburger, Johnson, & Christensen, 2009).

A third type of curriculum-based measure that we use is in vocabulary knowledge of the discipline. This approach, described by Espin, Shin, and

Busch (2005), involves identifying vocabulary specific to the content being studied (in this case, social studies) and providing students with a list of words and definitions for them to match. This simple paper-and-pencil task takes only a few minutes to administer and has been shown to be a valid measure of progress across time and when compared with standardized test results. The tested vocabulary is typically extracted from the textbook and classroom instruction and provides a solid indication of whether a content-based intervention is having a desired effect on the student's knowledge of the content.

Course Competencies. Another way to monitor students' progress in middle and high school classrooms is through the use of course competencies, that is, assessments of expected learning outcomes for the course. For example, in our ninth-grade English class, we have six competencies focused on essay and letter writing, two competencies on vocabulary, and one competency on each of the following: oral language, poetry, persuasive techniques, letter writing, and summarizing. Important, the competencies allow students to demonstrate their understanding in a number of ways, including multiple-choice assessments, projects, performances, and presentations.

In addition to contributing to students' grades, competencies indicate, on an ongoing basis, which students need supplemental or intensive interventions. Any student who scores below 70% on a competency receives an "incomplete" and is automatically included in Tier 2 supplemental interventions, which means that the student will receive additional small-group guided instruction designed to close the understanding gap. As students master the content, they retake the competencies, and their grades are replaced. This policy clearly communicates to students, "It's never too late to learn." It also serves as a motivator for students to participate fully in supplemental and intensive interventions, because they know that improvements in their understanding will translate to grade changes and recognition of effort.

An essay by one of our students, Rocio, provides a useful example. Rocio did not receive a passing score on her first essay. The opening paragraph of her essay, in response to the essential question that we had been studying, Does race matter?, demonstrates her need for supplemental intervention:

> Race is a strong word for people who even pay attention at the word that's why race has become so strong because we make it strong. It really doesn't have to mean nothing. Race is another simple word that we think is a big

deal. Race doesn't matter to me so why does it has to matter to all the other people.

Interesting, Rocio said that this was the first essay that she had ever submitted. In middle school, she had failed all of her content area classes as a result of not having completed her work, and she had been labeled a "behavior problem" rather than a student who desperately needed additional instruction. Knowing this, we viewed this essay attempt as major growth toward her continuing skill development and ownership of her learning. After receiving significant core instruction as well as intensive (small-group) and supplemental (individual) intervention, Rocio's next essay, a response to the essential question, Can you buy your way to happiness?, began as follows:

Priceless

Can you buy your way to happiness? I know that I can't because happiness can't be bought. But what about you? Do you think you can buy your way to happiness? Do you think you can spend wisely so that you are happy? I doubt it. Happiness comes through your life when you least expect it. Not when you're putting cash on the table. Happiness is priceless. You can only get happiness from your family, friends, and health, which I will explain in this essay.

Her response demonstrates her progress as well as her need for continued support. As with other students who participate in RTI[2] efforts, Rocio left the school year changed for the better. Without progress monitoring through competencies, she likely would have continued to be behaviorally marginalized and unlikely to have received the types of supplemental interventions that resulted in tangible growth rewards.

Rocio, like Jack, attends a school that uses RTI[2] approach to organize support. We next explore each of the three tiers commonly used in RTI[2] at their school.

Tier 1: Quality Core Instruction

Students' access to quality core instruction is critical. Every student deserves an excellent teacher who can scaffold learning. In an effective RTI model, 70–80% of students should respond to Tier 1 (Fisher & Frey, 2010); when that is not the case, the school system's first priority should be to improve the quality of core instruction rather than focus on supplemental interventions. In other words, Tier 2 (supplemental) and Tier 3 (intensive) interventions cannot compensate for a lack of high-quality core instruction. High-quality core instruction must be based on appropriate grade-level standards and expectations and should include five components:

1. *Established purpose*—When teachers clearly communicate their purpose to students, learning occurs (Marzano, 2009). Important, the purpose of the lesson should focus on what students should learn rather than what they will do. In other words, an established purpose of "today we will watch a video about the French Revolution" will not sufficiently alert students like Jack so that his learning is focused. Instead, the purpose of "determining the order of events occurring during the French Revolution" provides students with information about what they should know and what they are accountable for.

2. *Teacher modeling*—This component allows students to get inside the head of an expert and understand that person's thinking. When teachers model, they provide students with both the what and how of thinking. It is not enough for teachers simply to provide an example of their thinking to students. Students need to develop an understanding of the cognitive and metacognitive processes used by proficient readers and thinkers in each subject area. Important, teacher modeling must occur every day in every class. Influencing cognitive strategies takes time and must occur across the curriculum. Consider the effects on our student, Jack, of two different ways to model making predictions. In the first example, a teacher might model predicting while reading *Island of the Blue Dolphins* by Scott O'Dell (1960) by saying, "I predict that Karana will survive through the night." Although this might help Jack understand the events in the text, it probably will not help him transfer the habit of predicting to books that he is reading on his own. In the second example, his teacher modeled predicting by saying, "I think Karana's brother Ramo is dead, because the author is telling me that the dogs are moving around a circle. It doesn't sound like they are fighting anymore, and the author tells me that Ramo is laying still. If they were still fighting, he wouldn't be still, and the dogs wouldn't be walking in a circle. I'll read on to see what happens." In this case, Jack was provided with evidence from the text that his teacher used to make predictions. Over time and with lots of examples, Jack, Rocio, and their peers used the same procedures to understand the texts they read.

3. *Productive group work*—To really understand the content, students have to interact with one another and the topic. They have to

wrestle with ideas, share their understandings, ask and answer questions, and agree and disagree. This group interaction is critical to understanding and should be part of every lesson, but simply inviting students to interact is insufficient for ensuring learning. Instead, students have to be taught how to interact and should be held accountable for their interactions. We think of this component of the lesson as productive group work, as the group members interact along the way, yet each member is accountable for his or her part or task.

In Jack's case, he had previously been a member of a number of groups, but he did not talk or contribute, and thus he did not learn much. Unfortunately, his teachers did not notice, and he received good grades on the projects, mostly because of the skill levels of his peers. In productive group work, Jack is accountable for his part of the product. For example, while working on their iMovie project, his group re-created a scene from the book that they were reading, *Shattering Glass* by Gail Giles (2002). Each member of the group had to perform on and off camera. Jack assumed the role of an adult from the school and was the sound monitor for the recording. As he interacted with the other members of his group, his understanding of the text increased, as did his social skills, motivation, literary analysis skills, and sense of his intellectual strength.

4. *Guided instruction*—As students work in productive groups, their teacher meets with small groups to check for understanding through questioning, then prompts or cues students to address misconceptions. Guided instruction is especially helpful, because as students get older, they will generally not ask questions in front of the whole class. As part of high-quality core instruction, all students spend some time with their teacher in guided instruction. The amount of time and the frequency of guided instruction depend on which students are developing understanding and which are not; those with weak understanding spend more time in guided instruction.

5. *Independent learning tasks*—Eventually, students complete tasks on their own that demonstrate their understanding of the content. Unfortunately, independent learning tasks are often assigned prematurely in the instructional cycle. Before completing independent tasks, students deserve to understand what is expected of them and how a proficient thinker completes the task. They also deserve time to consolidate their understanding with peers through productive group work and scaffolded instruction that is based on

their misconceptions and mistakes, which are identified and clarified through guided instruction. Once again, Jack's experiences provide a useful example of the effectiveness of aligning independent learning tasks with this instructional cycle. When he was assigned a writing task in the past, he failed to complete the work, because he was unsure what to do. In contrast, in his present setting, when he is assigned a writing task for which he has received high-quality core instruction, he happily tries his best and knows that his teacher will meet with him to talk about additional changes that he can make to improve his writing.

Tier 2: Supplemental Instruction and Intervention

Some students need additional small-group instruction that is designed to supplement the quality core instruction they receive. Of course, as we described in the previous section, all students have access to small-group, needs-based instruction as part of high-quality core instruction. Tier 2's additional guided instruction is typically delivered to groups of three to five students three times per week for 30 minutes. Often, this guided instruction can be integrated within regular classroom instruction while other students are engaged in productive group work. Sometimes, this additional guided instruction is provided before or after school. Regardless of when and where guided instruction is provided, it includes four recursive processes:

1. *Questions to check for understanding*—During guided instruction, the teacher poses a question for students to consider. The question should be designed to assess both students' understanding of the topic and their ability to synthesize and evaluate information. Two points merit teachers' consideration. First, poorly constructed questions will negatively impact the rest of the process, and second, teachers can only resolve errors and misconceptions at the level of question they ask. Resolving a misconception by asking a knowledge-level question might result in increasing students' basic levels of knowledge but will not result in supporting their ability to synthesize or evaluate content.

2. *Prompts for cognitive and metacognitive processes*—When errors or misconceptions arise in response to checking for understanding, the next step in guided instruction provides the teacher with an opportunity to prompt the learner. We reserve the word *prompt* for cognitive and metacognitive work. For example, a teacher might prompt a student by saying, "Consider what you would do in

this situation," or "When you think about the character's actions, does your answer still hold?" You might also ask a metacognitive question, such as, "How do you know you're right?" Essentially, prompts are designed to facilitate students' cognitive and metacognitive processes such that they develop habits of thinking about the texts they read.

3. *Cues to shift attention*—When prompts for cognitive or metacognitive work fail to resolve the error or misconception, the next step is to cue the learner in a more direct way. This involves directing attention to something missed or not noticed. Of course, there are a number of cues that teachers can use, such as physical, verbal, visual, gestural, environmental, and positional. For example, a prompt such as "Look at the chart at the bottom of the page to help with your answer" shifts the reader's attention to a salient feature. Essentially, cues are designed to help students become expert noticers such that they use resources in their responses.

4. *Direct explanations and modeling*—When prompts and cues fail to resolve the error or misconception, the teacher can provide the students with a direct explanation while modeling his or her thinking. By doing so, the teacher reassumes the primary responsibility of increasing students' understanding. At the end of a direct explanation, the teacher again checks for understanding.

So, what might supplemental, guided instruction and intervention look like in the secondary classroom? During a recent classroom visit, a quick look around the room suggested that students were working. Several were typing away on computers, others were reading in comfortable chairs, and still others were working together and talking at tables. The teacher was seated with a group of four students. There was a purpose statement on the board, which read, "We can analyze persuasive techniques that public speakers use by identifying key terminology that is convincing or sways our thinking." On closer examination, we saw that the students working on computers were searching public speech records and writing analyses of these speeches. One of the groups working together at the tables was creating a poster that identified specific techniques used by Martin Luther King, Jr. Each student was adding to the collaborative poster in a different color marker. Another group was creating a similar poster based on speeches by President John F. Kennedy. There was also a group of students meeting with the teacher. Each member of this last group was selected based on progress monitoring assessments that indicated a need for Tier 2 supplemental interventions. Each of the students in the group had a copy of the "Ain't I a Woman?" speech by Sojourner Truth. The teacher invited one of the students to begin the conversation by summarizing the text:

Amanda: So, I think it's about her wanting rights.

Jasmine: She's saying that she is equal and should have the same rights.

Jack: Yeah, and she says that blacks and women should have equal rights.

Nick: She's kinda hard to understand. I know she wants rights, but I don't get her point. Saying you want rights isn't gonna make people change.

Teacher: Nick, she does say she wants rights, but how is she trying to convince her audience? Remember, she's trying to persuade them.

Nick: She uses repetition, I get that. But, saying it over ain't gonna make it so.

Jasmine: The repetition is kinda cool, though. It makes her speech kinda like a poem.

Teacher: What else does she do to persuade her audience? Jack?

Jack: Well, I see repetition like Nick. I don't know.

Teacher: Think about the time, historical time. It's 1851.

Nick: Yeah, only men had full rights.

Amanda: Oh, and women were trying to get rights back then at that time.

Jack: So, is she saying that she should get the same rights if women get rights?

Jasmine: Yeah, I think that's it. She's saying "Hey, I'm a woman, too, and I should get rights when other women get rights."

Amanda: It's hard to think about this. There really was a time when everyone didn't have rights.

Teacher: There sure was, but what other technique is she using here to make her point? [All of the students look at her and stare. No one answers.]

Teacher: Look right here. [points to a line of text]

Jasmine: Yeah, that's the question she keeps repeating.

Nick:	I got it. It's not just repeating it. The question is rhetorical. There really isn't an answer to be provided. She provides the answer and proof herself.
Teacher:	Interesting. And what about here? [points to a line of text]
Jack:	No way. I missed it before. It's emotional, and it's an analogy. I guess I got too much focused on the repetition to notice that.

The conversation continues with the teacher prompting and cueing her students. In doing so, she guides their understanding such that they can apply what they have learned with their peers in productive group work and in their independent learning tasks. She did not simply quiz the whole class and then move into individual helping, nor did she jump to direct explanation by telling her students what to think. Instead, she scaffolded their understanding, saying just the right thing to get the learners to do the work. She used instructional moves and language that provided explicitly intended differentiated feedback (Gainer & Lapp, 2010). She encouraged, supported, extended, and assessed accountable student learning that was occurring as part of the supplemental interventions provided to students.

Tier 3: Intensive Intervention

If students fail to respond to quality core instruction and supplemental interventions, then intensive interventions are warranted. In general, these are individualized, one-on-one lessons that last between 20 and 30 minutes and occur at least three times per week. In addition to increasing the frequency of instruction, the frequency of assessment increases as well. Over the course of about 18 weeks, data are collected and analyzed to determine if the student is making progress.

An Example of the Power of Intensive Intervention

Fifteen-year-old Mario was unable to complete an essential essay being addressed by students schoolwide on the topic of "who am I?" until he received intensive intervention from his teacher. Because Mario was a very shy boy, his grandmother allowed him to miss school and stay at home with her, where she gave him individual attention that was not always school related. After many conversations with Mario and Grandma, they realized that he needed to learn to function in a larger environment in order to prepare himself to participate in the world of work after high school.

Prior to Mario receiving intensive intervention from his teacher, he had been participating in core instruction in his 10th-grade English classroom. His teacher, Heather Anderson, had designed instruction that included classroom discussions about topically related texts that were being shared as read-alouds. Ms. Anderson and the students also shared and analyzed a "who am I?" poem that she had written about herself. As part of the core instruction, students participated in purposeful lessons, related group and partner activities and sharing, and in-class writing activities designed to support them for individually writing their essays.

An example of a read-aloud that the class returned to often was J.M. Barrie's (1950) classic *Peter Pan*. When they were younger, most of the students had seen Disney's movie version but had never read or heard the original text. They were intrigued that Peter, Wendy, and the Lost Boys seemed so different to them when viewed through their teenage eyes. The students discussed whose identity had changed, their own or the characters'. In addition, the students read autobiographies and biographical descriptions and essays about persons of interest to them (e.g., Lady Gaga, Muhammad Ali, Malcolm X, Sharon Draper, President Barack Obama, Jay-Z) to analyze how each author's personal story was shared.

The students each made a collage that shared their identity. If they were unable to complete this alone, they were encouraged to talk with friends to get ideas about their perceived characteristics. The students later used their collages to help write their essays. They also completed a characteristics chart (see Figure 12.3), which they discussed with partners and then revised and used as a basis to create papier-mâché masks (see Figure 12.4). On the outside of the mask, the students put images and words about what they show people on the outside. Then, on the inside of the mask, they put images and words of what they keep hidden on the inside. This very powerful project was presented among a small group of peers.

Ms. Anderson also provided supplemental small-group instruction that was designed to scaffold each student's understanding. Some groups needed to have their writing supported by completing paragraph and sentence frames (see Figure 12.5), and some needed more detailed conversation about the teacher-created story map (see Figure 12.6). Others needed help writing the introductory hook, and still others needed help with editing.

Through all of this instruction, Mario was unable to write a complete draft of his work. He was, however, attending regularly and had amassed phrases that identified who he was, but he was unable to craft it into an

Figure 12.3. Student Characteristics Chart

Name:	
Who am I?	Why do I matter?
What do I show others on the outside?	Why do I matter right now, in this moment, in the here and now?
Who am I on the inside? What do I hide from others and keep locked inside?	Why do I matter in the future? In the long run, how do my decisions affect the future? What are my goals?

Figure 12.4. A Student's Papier-Mâché Mask

Figure 12.5. Who Am I? Sentence and Paragraph Frames

- The characteristics of _____, _____, and _____ are ones that I think show who I am, because…
- If I were to overhear my classmates describing me, I think they would say…
- _____ is one of my favorite activities, because…
- Some of my biggest accomplishments have been…
- My biggest fears prevent me from…
- I know that I can accomplish….
- My three most important characteristics are….
- These characteristics are important, because….
- I make a difference, because…
- Others have made a difference in my life, because….
- Their interactions have inspired me to…

Figure 12.6. Teacher-Created Story Map

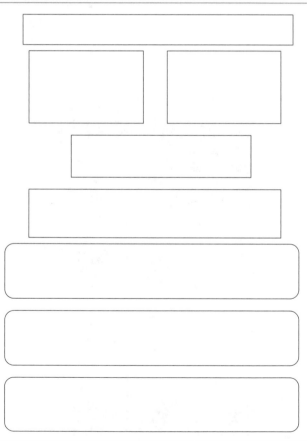

essay. This alerted his teacher to his need for more intensive individualized instruction. As the other students worked on segments of their projects and essay, Mario met one on one with Ms. Anderson for 20 minutes daily for one week. She worked with him to share his thoughts orally about who he was. She recorded their conversations and typed a draft of what he had shared. She shared with Mario a blank story map (see Figure 12.6) to help him organize his thinking. As they listened and read the draft, Mario redesigned the story map in his own way to better organize what he had said (see Figure 12.7). He used a completed version of this strategy guide as support for writing his essay. Once the first complete draft was written, he was able to have it edited by a peer, another teacher, and himself. The checklist for the assignment, used by Mario and all of the other students in the class, can be found in Figure 12.8. As seen in his final essay (see Figure 12.9), Mario shared his developing identity through a story format. Once his essay was completed, he used it to finish his mask, which Ms. Anderson encouraged him to share with one of his friends.

Like all students, growth for Mario is not complete, but 11th grade has begun. He has been at school every day and is much more participatory

Figure 12.7. Mario's Story Map: Who Am I?

| Let's Catch Their Attention |
| Describe Him |
| Share an Internal Conflict or Problem |
| Reflection and Move to Action |
| Transition |
| Insights, Introspection, and Solution |
| New Beginnings: Leave Them Wondering |

Figure 12.8. Checklist for Essay

Name: _____ English Period: _____

Essential Essay Question Check-Off List and Scoring Sheet: Who Am I?

___ My essay addresses the essential question: Who am I? (5 points)

___ My essay has a *minimum* of six paragraphs. (15 points)

   ___ Introduction/hook paragraph

   ___ *Minimum* of four body paragraphs

   ___ Closing statement/summary paragraph

___ My essay is properly formatted. (16 points)

   ___ My essay is typed using size 12 Times New Roman and double spaced.

   ___ The top left corner has my name, date, and English period (single spaced).

   ___ The title is centered at the beginning of the essay.

   ___ Each paragraph is indented.

___ My essay uses correct spelling and avoids common errors. It makes sense and addresses the question at all times. (23 points)

___ A minimum of three different people, including myself, proofread and edited my rough draft. (Think about whether it makes sense, answers the essential question, and uses correct spelling and punctuation!) (6 points)

   Signatures

   _____ Myself (2 points)

   _____ A Peer (2 points)

   _____ An Adult (2 points)

___ My edited rough drafts were turned in with my final draft. (You *must* show that they were all edited by being written on.) (5 points)

___ My final draft and rough drafts were turned in by 3:30 on Friday, June 4. (5 points)

___ *5 bonus points* for turning in your final essay and creative component by 3:30 on Wednesday, June 2.

during core instruction. Because each teacher at his school implements RTI², his performance will continually be assessed as a way to ensure that the instruction he receives supports his learning and social development.

Referral for Special Education Testing and Services

If after the best efforts, students fail to make progress and do not respond to the quality instruction and intervention they have received, it is likely time for a referral for special education testing. This does not mean that

Figure 12.9. Mario's Final Essay

Mario Milton
English, Per. 4
June 2, 2010

Who Am I?: The Emergence of Aries

There once was a boy named airy. He felt unconfident, shy, and vulnerable as he entered middle school. He was so unsure of himself; he didn't know how he should style his hair, what to wear, and who to hang out with. After months went by he began to interact with a certain unique group that stood out to him because of their looks and the way they carried themselves. Their style was one of arrogant confidence. He thought if he could only get himself into this group he would become one of the elite populars at school.

After not much effort he was amazed that he was welcomed into the group with open arms. Soon the new molding of another person began taking place. It started with the new style of his hair, black with blond chunks all around. He was now sporting a razor cut. Then came the different clothes, accompanied by piercings. A new airy was emerging. Now part of the elite group he began to feel like he was on top of the world. All of it seemed like such a rush. As a result of being in this group he was becoming well known by others at his middle school.

By eighth grade everything was going great so airy continued doing what he had been doing the past two years-being a part of the group. Toward the end of the year, he noticed something that jarred him; his new group of friends didn't seem so great anymore. He was getting tired of doing the same old things and instead started to notice things that should have been obvious to him all along. All of the drama this group was causing and the destruction they were creating for others began to seem so negative to him. They were all failing middle school.

Why hadn't he seen all of this before? Why hadn't he heard his Grandma's suggestions that he was on the wrong track? Was it because he was caught up in all of the thrills? Was it because he needed to belong, even to a group that was so unlike him inside? Was it because he was afraid if he lost this group he would be an out-cast again? He decided he had to put an end to all of this because this just wasn't who he was. He decided he must stand up to them. He wasn't afraid of not belonging anymore. He wasn't afraid of what they were going to think about him. All he knew was that it felt right to separate himself from them. He knew he was doing the right thing separating from all of the unnecessary drama. He realized he was a lone wolf and that he could stand-alone until he could find others he felt right with. He knew this could take a day, months, or even years, but he was not afraid. He had to be true to himself.

Entering high school airy felt like he was again entering sixth grade, except this time he knew how to better interact with his peers and his surroundings. He started to try to hang out with peers he normally wouldn't have chosen but that didn't feel right. So during his first year of high school life was calm but boring. He was pretty much a loner. airy realized he didn't want calm and boring, he still wanted fun and adventure, but not in ways that were destructive to himself or

(continued)

Figure 12.9. Mario's Final Essay (Continued)

others. During this long time of not having a small group of friends airy got to do a lot of learning and self-reflection. Would he make the same mistakes again or would he still search for those he could call true friends?

As airy got older and started experiencing new things, he discovered that you can't just sit and wait for things to fall in your lap; you have to go and look for it. He then started to find /people who had the same interests as he. The more he did this the more his group of friends started to expand. He was learning about all different types of people and things he had never experienced in his younger years. He was maturing and the chip on his shoulder was beginning to fade away. Now he didn't worry about if someone didn't like him for what he looked like or how he acted, because he was ok with himself. He stopped thinking about suicide. He had become that person he had always wanted to be. He was finally happy.

Standing in the mirror one morning he noticed how much he had changed inside and out. He realized that interactions with himself and others had caused him to grow in so many positive ways. He turned around, stopped at the door, and looking back at himself in the mirror said, "no longer will you be airy, you will now be know as Aries." Aries is sustained by people, experiences, learning and all that I know I have yet to become. Aries/I will stay alive for the journey.

the student has a disability, but rather that the system has yet to meet that student's needs, and he or she might need a more formalized system of support. Students who meet the criteria for special education services receive some additional supports.

Accommodations and Modifications

Accommodations and modifications allow the teaching team to make changes to the curriculum that benefit the student. Accommodations change how the student accesses the curriculum, but they do not change the curriculum itself. Common accommodations include large print, Braille, and changes to input and output routes. For example, if the class were writing essays, a student modification may be a graphic organizer with a bulleted list of main points. The student would compose the same essay but with the support of the graphic organizer.

Funding

The additional supports and services that students with disabilities need to be successful are funded, in part, by additional money that the school or district receives for qualified students. This money only flows when students have been assessed and have been determined to have a disability. Important, federal law in the United States provides for a percentage of these funds to be used in a prereferral system, so special educators can participate in RTI initiatives.

Related Services

In addition to the support of a special education teacher, qualified students with disabilities may also access the services of physical therapists, speech and language therapists, occupational therapists, and counselors and psychologists. In addition, in some states, a reading specialist can be written into the students' individualized educational plan, such that the student receives reading instruction from a qualified provider. These related services are mobilized only when the student qualifies for special education services, and the amount of service is determined during the annual Individualized Educational Program meeting.

Due Process

Although all students have rights, there are specific procedural guarantees in special education. Parents have a right to due process and can challenge any recommendation made by the school staff. In doing so, there are guidelines for addressing the dispute. Students without disabilities, even students receiving Tier 2 and Tier 3 interventions, do not have specific rights to due process.

Conclusion

RTI^2 provides a framework for teachers to engage in continued quality improvement. By focusing on the three tiers of RTI^2, needs can be more easily identified. For example, a focus on Tier 1 ensures that all students have access to quality instruction, which also allows teachers to focus on students who continue to struggle with school through supplemental and intensive interventions. It is important to remember that the majority of students who require intervention support in middle and high school already received intervention in elementary school. At the secondary school level, the interventions have to relate to the curriculum that students are expected to learn as well as the skills that students need to be successful. When RTI^2 is implemented well, students like Jack soar.

TRY IT!

Implementing RTI^2 involves knowing your students well and continually assessing if they need supplemental and intensive instruction in addition to their core class instruction.

1. Consider the students in your high school or classroom and choose one you have observed having difficulty with a particular instructional task or assignment. Using the examples in this chapter and your own background knowledge, what assessments will help you identify the student's particular instructional needs? Plan a Tier 1 intervention (i.e., a classroom-based lesson) to provide the student with extra help in successfully completing the task. As you prepare your lesson, also consider the ways that you will monitor the student's progress. What evidence or documentation will you use to determine if the Tier 1 intervention was sufficient?

2. If the student continues to struggle, step back again and consider what you will do next. Reread the sections in the chapter that detail Tier 2 interventions. Use the guidelines to help you plan a Tier 2 intervention for your focal student. Upon completion of the instructional sequence, step back yet again and consider the process. In your instructional setting, what are the ways in which you could incorporate the ideas within this chapter to improve struggling students' opportunities to learn?

REFERENCES

Ardoin, S.P., Witt, J.C., Connell, J.E., & Koenig, J.L. (2005). Application of a three-tiered Response to Intervention model for instructional planning, decision making, and the identification of children in need of services. *Journal of Psychoeducational Assessment, 23*(4), 362–380. doi:10.1177/073428290502300405

Barnett, D.W., Daly, E.J., III, Jones, K.M., & Lentz, F.E., Jr. (2004). Response to Intervention: Empirically based special service decisions from single-case designs of increasing and decreasing intensity. *The Journal of Special Education, 38*(2), 66–79. doi:10.1177/00224669040380020101

Diercks-Gransee, B., Weissenburger, J.W., Johnson, C.L., & Christensen, P. (2009). Curriculum-based measures of writing for high school students. *Remedial and Special Education, 30*(6), 360–371. doi:10.1177/0741932508324398

Espin, C.A., Shin, J., & Busch, T.W. (2005). Curriculum-based measurement in the content areas: Vocabulary matching as an indicator of progress in social studies learning. *Journal of Learning Disabilities, 38*(4), 353–363. doi:10.1177/00222194050380041301

Fisher, D., & Frey, N. (2010). *Enhancing RTI: How to ensure success with effective classroom instruction and intervention.* Alexandria, VA: ASCD.

Frey, N., & Fisher, D. (2008). The underappreciated role of humiliation in middle school. *Middle School Journal, 39*(5), 4–13.

Gainer, J., & Lapp, D. (2010). *Literacy remix: Bridging adolescents' in and out of school literacies*. Newark, DE: International Reading Association.

Gee, J.P. (1996). *Social linguistics and literacies: Ideology in Discourses* (2nd ed.). Bristol, PA: Taylor & Francis.

Jenkins, J.R. (2003, December). *Candidate measures for screening at-risk students*. Paper presented at the National Research Center on Learning Disabilities's Responsiveness-to-Intervention Symposium, Kansas City, MO. Retrieved April 3, 2006, from www.nrcld.org/symposium2003/jenkins/index.html

Johnson, E., Mellard, D.F., Fuchs, D., & McKnight, M.A. (2006). *Responsiveness to intervention (RTI): How to do it*. Lawrence, KS: National Research Center on Learning Disabilities.

Marzano, R.J. (2009). *Designing and teaching learning goals and objectives*. Bloomington, IN: Marzano Research Laboratory.

McMaster, K., & Espin, C.A. (2007). Technical features of curriculum-based measurement in writing: A literature review. *The Journal of Special Education, 41*(2), 68–84. doi:10.1177/00224669070410020301

Moll, L.C., Amanti, C., Neff, D., & Gonzalez, N. (1992). Funds of knowledge for teaching: Using a qualitative approach to connect homes and classrooms. *Theory Into Practice, 31*(2), 132–141. doi:10.1080/00405849209543534

Paris, S.G. (2005). Reinterpreting the development of reading skills. *Reading Research Quarterly, 40*(2), 184–202. doi:10.1598/RRQ.40.2.3

LITERATURE CITED

Barrie, J.M. (1950). *Peter Pan*. New York: Charles Scribner's Sons.

Giles, G. (2002). *Shattering glass*. Brookfield, CT: Roaring Brook.

O'Dell, S. (1960). *Island of the blue dolphins*. New York: Houghton Mifflin.

AUTHOR INDEX

Note. Page numbers followed by *f* or *t* indicate figures or tables, respectively.

Burns, M.S., 139
Busch, T.W., 243–244
Byrne, B., 58

C

Caldwell, J., 226
Calkins, L., 119
Cammack, D.W., 84
Cannon, J., 16
Cantlon, D.J., 192
Carlisle, J.F., 45, 46
Carlo, M., 47
Carr, E.M., 67, 68, 84
Carr, S.C., 146
Celano, D., 70
Certo, J.L., 25
Chall, J.S., 3, 66, 67, 68, 84, 209, 217
Chard, D., 13, 59
Charest, E.M., 41
Cheng, A., 31
Child Trends DataBank, 42
Chinn, C., 93
Chomsky C., 12
Christensen, P., 243
Christie, R.G., 32
Ciardiello, A.V., 23
Ciborowski, J., 67
Cielocha, K.M., 83
Clark, K., 142
Clarke, P., 46
Clay, M.M., 94
Cocking, R.R., 163
Coiro, J.L., 84
Collins, R., 107
Collins, S., 164
Comber, B., 227, 229
Connell, J.E., 239
Council of Chief State School Officers, 116, 140, 147
Creech, S., 21
Crew, G., 40
Csikszentmihalyi, M., 165
Cullinan, B.E., 40
Cunningham, A.E., 6, 69
Cunningham, P.M., 96
Cushman, D., 10
Cziko, C., 70

D

Dakos, K., 40

Dalton, B., 42, 45, 48, 50
Daly, E.J., III, 239
David, A.D., 80
Davis, M.H., 72
Dawkins, M.P., 107
de Maupassant, G., 76
Dean, T.R., 83
Deci, E.L., 165
Delta Air Lines, 141
Denenberg, B., 232t
Denman, G.A., 23, 25
Dennis, D.V., 227
Dewey, J., 164
Dewitz, P., 226
Dewitz, P.K., 226
Diamond, J., 165
Diercks-Gransee, B., 243
Dishner, E.K., 163
Dole, J.A., 163
Donahue, P.L., 138
Donald, J.G., 163
Donovan, C.A., 143
Donovan, M.S., 163, 164, 165
Dorn, L.J., 139, 142, 147
Dowhower, S.L., 5, 93
Doyle, K., 83
Dreeben, R., 107
Dreyer, L.G., 91
Duffelmeyer, F.A., 208, 217
Duffy, G.G., 117, 163
Duke, N.K., 78, 93, 143, 144, 162, 163
Dunston, P.J., 72
Durand, M., 46
Durgunoglu, A., 47
Durkin, D., 119
Duthie, C., 24, 33

E

Edmonds, M., 3
Edwards, E.C., 73
Ehri, L.C., 91, 93
Elley, W.B., 69
Elster, C.A., 23
Engel, T., 232t
Erekson, J., 5
Erickson, H.L., 164
Esbensen, B., 40
Espin, C.A., 243–244

Williams, J.P., 144, 145, 162
Williams, W.C., 21
Wilson, P., 24
Wilson, P.T., 69
Windell, I., 208, 217
Winne, P.H., 165
Witt, J.C., 239
Wixson, K.K., 24, 119, 142
Wolf, S.A., 23, 37
Wolfe, P., 144
Wolter, B., 46
Wood, K.D., 67, 70, 208, 217
Wooldridge, S.G., 32
Wooten, D., 40
Worthy, J., 24, 233

Worthy, M.J., 121
Wysocki, K., 75

Y

Youngs, S., 144

Z

Zawilinski, L., 235
Zeig, J.L., 231
Zimet, E.K., 24, 33
Zimmermann, S., 143
Zoch, M.P., 80

SUBJECT INDEX

Note. Page numbers followed by *f* or *t* indicate figures or tables, respectively.

After Early Intervention, Then What? Teaching Struggling Readers in Grades 3 and Beyond (2nd ed.) edited by Jeanne R. Paratore and Rachel L. McCormack. © 2011 by the International Reading Association.

CIM. *See* Comprehensive Intervention Model
clarifying, 193
classroom blogs, 235
collaborative charts, 29
Common Core State Standards, 140, 147
community of language, 73–74, 84
comparisons. *See* paired comparisons
compound morphology, 45
comprehension, 98, 100; comprehensive curriculum, 117–119; Improving Comprehension Online (ICON), 43, 48–53; instructional components, 117, 117f; literature discussion groups for, 137–161; through question-answer relationships (QARs), 115–136; research-based principles for supporting, 143–146; strategies for, 118; for struggling readers, 137–161; of text, 137–161
comprehension aids, 211–212
Comprehensive Intervention Model (CIM), 142, 147
conceptual learners, 67
conferences, 152
Connect It! activity, 49t, 50
context clues, 78–79, 225
core instruction, 245–248
course competencies, 244–245
Creapalabras (Word Creation) game, 58–59
credibility of sources, 202, 202t
cross-age reading, 13–14
cues: miscue analysis, 224–225; to shift attention, 249. *See also* prompts
cultural texts, 227–228
culturally relevant poetry, 29–30
culture: aspects of, 166–167, 168f; core issues of, 167, 169f
curriculum: "balanced," 119; comprehensive comprehension curriculum, 117–119; multitext, 230–233; "staircase curriculum," 120
curriculum-based measurements, 243–244

D

derivational morphology, 45
"Different Kinds of Poetry" chart, 29
differentiating instruction, 105; approaches for individuals, 12–14

difficult texts: accessible, 3–20; grouping routines and instructional practices that mediate, 90–112; instructional interventions for, 92–93
digital photography, 37
digital storytelling, 82
direct explanations, 249
Discourse communities, 238
discussion groups, 137–161
discussions: of books, 152–153; of texts, 145–146
district policies, initiatives, and interventions, 219–261
Dive In activities, 49t, 50, 51–52
diverse learners, 21–41
"Don't Miss This One" chart, 29
Drop Everything and Read, 14–15
due process, 259

E

echo reading, 8
Edublogs (website), 85
ELs. *See* English learners
embedded strategy instruction for skillful reading, 145
engaged reading, 229–230
engagement: active, 68–74; turn-around pedagogy of, 229–233
English learners (ELs), 42, 45–46, 67; biliteracy pilot intervention, 53–62; instructional supports for, 104
essays, 252; checklist for, 255, 256f; example, 257f–258f
explanations, direct, 249
explicit instruction: of specific words, 75–77; teaching genre explicitly, 144–145
expository text about history, 162–185
external sources, 123, 124f
Eyejot (website), 14

F

fifth graders: biliteracy pilot intervention with, 53–62, 54t, 57t, 61f; example at-risk student, 221, 223–225, 226–227; ICON intervention with, 48; topics for interviews with, 54t; Web It! activity for, 51f, 51–52
fluency, 223; automatic word recognition and, 4–5; cognitive benefits of,

223; deep, 225; increasing, 223; instructional approaches for flexible groups, 9–12; instructional approaches to increase, 6–14; prosody and, 5; purposeful and interesting development of, 233; reading fluency beyond primary grades, 3–20; in reading process, 3–5; suggestions for assisting with, 16–17

fluency-oriented oral reading (FOOR), 9–11

follow-up assessments, 241

FOOR (fluency-oriented oral reading), 9–11

found poetry, 30

fourth graders: inquiry activities, 124–125, 125f; literature discussion groups, 137–138; Think & Search with, 127f, 128

funding, 258–259

G

Gates-MacGinitie reading tests, 240

genre studies: 10-step format for, 148f; introduction of units, 147–149; preparation guide for, 157; previewing and selecting books for, 150; teaching explicitly, 144–145; text mapping across texts, 154–155

Gettysburg, Battle of (sample instructional plan), 179, 180f–181f

grades 3-6: literature discussion groups, 137–161; reading guides for struggling readers in, 207–217. See also fifth graders; fourth graders; third graders

Great Plains (sample instructional plan), 175, 175f–176f

group work: expert teams, 216; flexible groupings, 9–12, 101–102, 102f; fluency approaches for, 9–12; literature discussion groups (LDGs), 137–161; poster presentations, 60, 61f, 61–62; productive, 246–247; project work, 60–62; routines that mediate difficult text, 90–112; small groups, 102–103, 103f; text discussions, 145–146

guided instruction, 247, 248–249

guided practice, 79

guided reading, 102, 103f. See also literature discussion groups (LDGs)

H

haiku, 30

Hayes, Jody, 83–84

Hear It! activity, 49t, 50

Hispanic/Latino students, 91, 98–99

history: American Civil War (sample unit), 179–181, 180f–181f; expository text about, 162–185; Jamestown (sample unit), 177f, 177–178, 178f–179f

HOT blogging, 235

human features of places, 166–167, 168f

I

ICON. See Improving Comprehension Online

iMovie projects, 247

Improving Comprehension Online (ICON), 43, 48–53; prereading activities, 48–52; within-reading word work, 53

"In My Head" QARs, 128f, 128–131

"In the Book" QARs, 126–128, 127f

independent learning tasks, 247–248

independent practice, 79

independent reading: benefits of, 69; time for, 14–15

independent word learning strategies: instruction of, 77–80

individuals: approaches for, 12–14

Individuals with Disabilities Education Improvement Act, 139

inflectionally morphology, 45

information: personal understanding of, 187–191; supplying, 193–194

information gathering: support for, 199–200

inquiry activities, 124–125, 125f

Institute of Education Sciences, 48

instruction: action cycle approach, 171–174, 174–181; biliteracy pilot intervention, 53–62; comprehension instruction, 117, 117f; differentiating, 105; embedded strategy instruction for skillful reading, 145; explicit, of specific words, 75–77; factors to consider, 6–7; guided, 247, 248–249; Improving Comprehension Online (ICON) approach, 48–53; to increase fluency, 6–14; of independent word learning strategies, 77–80; for individuals, 12–14; intervention in action, 93–98, 98–100, 100–105; that mediates difficult text, 90–112; monitoring, 102–104; morphological awareness instruction, 45–46; planning and implementing, 94–97, 99, 102; planning and monitoring, 102–104; through question-answer relationships (QARs), 115–136; research-based vocabulary instruction, 66–89; Response to Instruction and Intervention (RTI²), 238–261; scaffolded approaches for teaching vocabulary, 74–80; for special education learners, 108; of specific words, 75–77; strategy instruction minilessons, 149–150; supports for English learners, 104; Tier 1, 239, 241, 245–248; Tier 2 (supplemental), 244, 245, 248–251; Tier 3 (intensive), 244, 251–256; vocabulary instruction, 55–56, 66–89; for word analysis, 79–80

integrating ideas, 173–174, 176f, 178f–179f, 181f

intensive intervention (Tier 3), 244, 251–256

intermediate grades: Think & Search in, 127f, 128. See also specific grades

Internet-based instruction. See Improving Comprehension Online (ICON)

intervention programs, 139–140; intensive (Tier 3), 244, 251–256; packaged programs, 139–140; Response to Instruction and Intervention (RTI²), 238–261; for struggling readers, 155–156; students likely to benefit from, 94; supplemental (Tier 2), 244, 245, 248–251; Tier 1 instruction, 139

Iowa Test of Basic Skills (ITBS), 98

ITBS. See Iowa Test of Basic Skills

J

Jamestown (sample unit), 177–178; guiding questions for, 177f; instructional plan for sample lesson, 177, 178f–179f

jigsaw technique, 216

journals, 151, 151f

K

knowledge: activation of background knowledge, 143–144; developing, 173, 176f, 178f, 181f; organized, 163–164, 164–165; providing prior knowledge, 143–144

knowledge handicaps, 92

Kuzior, J.T., 83

L

Lakota Sioux culture (example unit), 174–175, 175f–176f

language: community of, 73–74, 84

Language Alert activity, 49t

Latino students, 42, 91, 98–99

laughter, 25–27

LDGs. See literature discussion groups

learners. See students

learning, independent, 247–248

linguistic context, 46–48

listening: reading-while-listening, 12–13

literacy: building foundations for struggling readers, 1–112; definition of, 230

literary stances, 118

literature discussion groups (LDGs), 137–161; components of, 147–149, 149–150, 151, 152–153, 154–155; discussing books in, 152–153; for struggling readers, 147–155

M

manufactured crisis, 116

mapping: narrative maps, 148, 149f; text mapping, 154–155, 155f; vocabulary maps, 56, 58t

masks, 252, 253f

Massachusetts, 47, 53, 91

Matthew effects, 4, 80, 230

mentor texts: narrative text maps for, 148, 149f

metacognitive processes: prompts for, 248–249

Microsoft Word (software), 212

middle grades: poetry for novices (and some for nudges), 40–41; Think & Search in, 127f, 128. See also specific grades

minilessons, 149–150

miscue analysis, 224–225

Q

QARs. *See* question-answer relationships

qualitative assessment data, 223–227

Qualitative Reading Inventory–5, 243

Qualitative Reading Inventory–II, 98

quality core instruction, 245–248

question-answer relationships (QARs), 120–121; Author & Me, 128f, 128–131, 132; collaborative list of external sources for, 123, 124f; comprehension instruction through, 115–136; core QARs, 126–131; extension and application of, 133; first paired comparison, 123–126; focus areas, 122; "In My Head" QARs, 128f, 128–131; "In the Book" QARs, 126–128, 127f; inquiry activity, 124–125, 125f; On My Own, 128f, 128–129, 131; paired comparisons for, 121, 122f; and reading cycle, 131–132; Right There, 126, 127f, 132; teaching, 121–122; Think & Search, 126, 127f, 127–128, 132

questions, 133; to check for understanding, 248; example guiding questions, 177f; generating, 172, 175f–176f, 178f, 179f, 180f, 181f

R

read-alouds, 59

readers: emerging to sophisticated readers, 127f, 127–128; struggling readers, 1–112, 113–217. *See also* students

reading: choral reading, 9; cross-age, 13–14; echo reading, 8; embedded strategy instruction for skillful reading, 145; engaged, 229–230; fluency in, 3–5; fluency-oriented oral reading (FOOR), 9–11; "good reader behaviors," 226; guided, 102, 103f; independent, 14–15, 69; partner reading, 7–8; prereading activities, 48–52; providing opportunities for, 68–72; purpose for, 144, 151; self-selected poetry reading, 29; silent, 14–15, 102, 103f, 152; strategies for, 196t; with support, 11–12; sustained, 14–15, 233; within-reading word work, 53; word-by-word, 224; writing about, 146, 153, 154f

reading accuracy, 223

reading aloud, 105

reading comprehension, 143–146

reading cycle, 131–132

reading fluency: beyond primary grades, 3–20. *See also* fluency

reading guides: combined with reciprocal teaching, 216–217; constructing, 210–212, 216; effectiveness of, 209–210; interesting and interactive, 211; jigsaw technique for, 216; length and difficulty of, 211; page numbers, 211; purposes for, 212; sample, 213f–214f; for struggling readers in grades 3 and above, 207–217; subheadings, 211; teaching with, 212–215

reading interventions: students likely to benefit from, 94. *See also* intervention programs

reading mileage, 229

reading response logs, 151; sample entry, 151f; sections, 153

reading-while-listening, 12–13

reciprocal teaching, 216–217

referral for special education testing and services, 256–259

relevance of sources: prompts for evaluating, 202, 202t

research: example student processes, 187–188, 190, 194–195, 197–199; excerpts from final products, 203t, 203–204; meaningful, 187–191; scaffolding, 186–206; student task impressions, processes, and strategies, 189, 189t; supporting student efforts to learn through, 191–199; as transforming information, 195–196

research-based vocabulary instruction, 66–89

response logs, 151; sample entry, 151f; sections, 153

Response to Instruction and Intervention (RTI²), 239–251; with older students, 238–261

Response to Intervention (RTI), 139, 147, 239

Right There QARs, 126, 127f, 132

RTI. *See* Response to Intervention

RTI². *See* Response to Instruction and Intervention

S

Say It! activity, 49t, 50

scaffolded instructional approaches:

prompts for writing about reading, 153, 154f; for teaching vocabulary, 74–80

scaffolding research, 186–206; processes for, 193; for readers who need support, 196, 196t

school and district policies, initiatives, and interventions, 219–261

screening tools, 239–240; checklist for, 240t; criteria for, 239; schoolwide, 240, 240t

selecting books, 150

self-monitoring, 113–217

semantics, 43–45; activities that promote, 49t, 49–50; scoring inventory for depth of word knowledge, 52, 52t

sentence and paragraph frames, 252, 254f

sentence completions, 76

serial retellings, 70, 71–72

service projects, 235

seventh graders: example at-risk student, 222, 225–226, 226–227

sijo, 30

silent reading, 102, 103f, 152; uninterrupted sustained silent reading, 14–15

small groups, 102–103, 103f. See also literature discussion groups (LDGs)

social factors, 166–167, 168f, 169f

social networking, 83–84

social studies, 165–169

sources: collaborative lists of external sources, 123, 124f; considerations for, 201–202; finding, 200; prompts for evaluating credibility and relevance of, 202, 202t

Spanish: biliteracy pilot intervention, 53–62; poetry in two languages, 37–38

special education services: instruction for special education students, 108; referral for, 256–259; related services, 259

special education students, 98, 108

"staircase curriculum," 120

story maps, 252–255, 254f, 255f

storytelling: digital storytelling, 82; serial retellings, 70, 71–72

strategy guides, 207–208

strategy instruction: embedded, for skillful reading, 145; minilessons, 149–150

struggling readers, 67; building foundations in literacy for, 1–112; comprehension for, 113–217;

interventions for, 155–156; LDGs for, 147–155; literature discussion groups for, 137–161; older at-risk students, 221–237; reading guides for, 207–217, recommendations for, 66–89; school and district policies, initiatives, and interventions for, 219–261; self-monitoring, 113–217; support for, 142, 199–204

student observations, 27–29

student outcomes, 98, 100, 104–105

student research: example processes, 187–188, 190, 194–195, 197–199; excerpts from final products, 203t, 203–204; processes, 189, 189t; scaffolding, 186–206

students: emerging to sophisticated readers, 127f, 127–128; as experts, 216; identifying students in need of extra help, 93–94, 99, 100–102; levels in intermediate- and middle-level classrooms, 66–67; monitoring, 97, 99–100, 104; older at-risk students, 221–237; struggling readers, 1–112, 113–217; talking with, 228–229. See also English learners (ELs)

study guides, 207–208

subheadings, 211

supplemental intervention (Tier 2), 244

supplying information, 193–194

support strategies, 199–204

survival, 166–167, 168f, 169f

sustained reading, 233

syntax, 46; activities that promote, 49t, 49–50

T

talking books, 234–235

teacher conferences, 152

teacher modeling, 246

teacher outcomes, 104–105

teaching: with reading guides, 212–215; reciprocal, 216–217; for vocabulary depth, 42–65

teaching genre explicitly, 144–145

teaching QARs, 121–122

teaching vocabulary, 74–80

technology, 80–84

tenth graders: example intensive intervention for, 251–256

testing: referral for, 256–259

text discussions: group discussions, 145–146; literature discussion groups, 137–161

text files, 212

text mapping: across texts, 154–155; narrative maps, 148, 149f; sample maps, 155f

text set of African American biographies, 231t–232t, 231–233

text summaries, 250–251

texts: accessible difficult texts, 3–20; analysis for constructing reading guides for, 210–211; for biliteracy pilot intervention, 55–56, 57t; cultural, 227–228; difficult texts, 3–20, 90–112; expository text about history, 162–185; multitext curriculum, 230–233; narrative text maps for mentor texts, 148, 149f; selection of, 143; student strategies for working from, 189, 189t; summarizing, 250–251; text mapping across, 154–155; transition texts, 97; working from, 196t

Think & Search QARs, 126, 127f, 127–128, 132

ThinkQuest (website), 83

third graders: poetry flood of, 25–27, 26f; Poetry Performance Day, 34, 35f

Tier 1 instruction, 139, 241, 245–248

Tier 2 instruction and intervention (supplemental), 244, 245, 248–251

Tier 3 instruction (intensive intervention), 244, 251; example, 251–256

timelines, 232–233

transition texts, 97

turn-around pedagogy of engagement, 229–233

U

Universal Design for Learning, 48, 50

V

value, 202–204

verbal explanation, 78

visual elements, 77

vocabulary: for biliteracy pilot intervention, 55–56, 57t; depth of, 43–48, 44f; power words, 49; semantic scoring inventory for depth, 52, 52t

vocabulary development: independent word learning strategies, 77–80; pick-a-word strategy for, 72–73; promoting active engagement and interest in, 68–74; by providing multiple exposures in multiple contexts, 73–74; by providing opportunities for choice, 72–73; by providing opportunities for reading, 68–72; questions for, 76–77; sample questions and prompts for, 76; understanding word meanings, 76–77; within-reading word work, 53

vocabulary instruction, 55–56; integrating technology with, 80–84; by providing explicit instruction of specific words, 75–77; recommendations for, 68; research-based, 66–89; scaffolded approaches for, 74–80; suggestions for, 67–68; teaching for depth, 42–65

vocabulary maps, 56, 58t

W

Wade In activities, 49t, 50–51

WCPM. *See* words correct per minute

Web It! activity, 49t, 51f, 51–52

Weebly (website), 85

"What Is Poetry?" chart, 27–29, 28f

Wide FOOR (fluency-oriented oral reading), 9–11

word analysis, 79–80

word associations, 76

word-by-word reading, 224

word knowledge: independent word learning strategies, 77–80; remembering word meanings, 77; semantic scoring inventory, 52, 52t; understanding word meanings, 76–77; visual elements that aid in remembering meanings, 77; within-reading word work, 53. *See also* vocabulary development

word reading accuracy, 98, 100

word recognition, automatic, 4–5

word walls, 77

words correct per minute (WCPM), 223

words per minute (WPM), 223

"Words We Like" chart, 29

WPM. *See* words per minute

writing: about reading, 146, 153, 154f; rubrics for, 52, 52t; strategies for, 196t; supports for, 252, 254f

writing poetry, 32–35